Be Bigger Than You Think You Are!™

Be Bigger Than You Think You Are!™

Overcoming Our Self-Imposed Limits
To Have The Life We Want

Peter Alessandria

ISBN-13: 978-0-578-57678-7

Library of Congress Control Number: 2019913952

Peter Alessandria
Be Bigger Today LLC
Dover New Jersey

Printed in the United States of America
First Edition, October 2019

TO MY FATHER

I will always love you.

TO MY FAMILY

Thanks for all your love and support

I wouldn't be who I am today without you

Table of Contents

Preface vii

Introduction 1

"Who Do You Think You Are?" 11

Taking Responsibility 41

True Power & True Happiness 73

From F.E.A.R. to L.O.V.E. 99

Decision-Making & The Desire To Feel Better 139

Would You Rather Be Right Or Happy? 183

Forgiveness 221

EPILOGUE 285

APPENDIX 295

RECOMMENDED READING 301

Preface

I suggest you take a few minutes – right now – to set your intention for this book. You're urged to decide – in advance – what you want to get out of reading it. Choose – before you even start – how your life will be different when you're done.

You can do this even if you have no idea what this book is about. You can still choose – this minute – what your experience of reading it will be. This book could contain all blank pages and it could still change your life if that's what you decide. You're that powerful.

Write your intentions on your phone or on a blank page so you won't be surprised when you actually achieve what you want. You also won't credit me for your experience (positive or negative) since you'll see it was all your own doing.

I also urge you to do the written exercises at the end of each chapter. They will help you assimilate the concepts and move your experience from passive to active. The more active you are in learning the material the deeper and longer lasting the change will be.

And either way, make sure you enjoy the ride!

Introduction

"Be Bigger Than You Think You Are!"™

This book has the potential to change your life.

How do I know? Everything in it has changed mine! As you'll read in each chapter, applying these principles to my own life has transformed me in ways I could never have imagined. I know this book can do the same for you. You'll have to do your part. But if you do, you won't be the same person when you're done reading it.

The purpose of this book is, quite simply, to wake you up. It's here to open your eyes to new possibilities for yourself and for the people you love. It will help you stretch beyond your self-imposed limits and move towards an extraordinary life. In short, it will help you to "Be Bigger Than You Think You Are!"™

In fact, I believe this book has the potential to change the world!

That's a bold claim, I know. Yet I'm certain that if everyone applied these concepts to their own lives, the world would be a very different place. That's how powerful these ideas are.

As you'll see, I didn't make any of this stuff up. Rather, this book is based on my experience using these principles in my own life for the past 30+ years. Over that time I've spent thousands of hours informally studying various subjects in the areas of spirituality, psychology and personal growth. I've worked multiple 12 Step Programs, read dozens of self-improvement books, attended workshops, seminars and lectures, and then – most importantly – I did my best to apply everything I learned to change my life for the better. I've devoted myself daily for more than a quarter century to expanding my heart and mind so as to better understand the way life works. This book is the culmination of all that learning.

My journey began in 1988, when I moved from New York to California. I was fresh out of law school and bought a one-way plane ticket for Los Angeles. I didn't have any friends or family on the West Coast, yet I was on my way to pursuing my dream of becoming an Entertainment Attorney.

As a kid from the East Coast, California was new and exciting, and in many ways very different from what I was used to. One way it was different was the ubiquitous personal growth movement that was happening there at the time. All manner of workshops, trainings and seminars were being offered. From EST to Esalen and everything in between, California was the focal point of the New Age/Human Potential/Spiritual Growth movement. Most of those trainings promised to show me how to be a better person and lead a happier life. Now more than 30 years later, I know that those things – and much more – are possible for you and I as a result of reading this book.

After living in California for 20+ years, I returned to the East Coast in 2009. As I'll describe in a minute, I also left the law behind to pursue my passion for art and photography full-time.

A big part of the impetus for writing this book is that I faced some pretty large challenges when I transitioned from lawyer to photographer. But those challenges didn't come from the economy, the marketplace or anything else outside of me. Rather, I had to face some long-standing and deep-seated blocks in my own thinking about who I was and what I was capable of achieving. It took a lot of work, but eventually I was able to overcome many of those blocks. That, in turn, enabled me to accomplish a multitude of things I never would have thought were possible. For instance, as of the writing of this book, I've won 73 awards for my photography. My photos have been published online, and in newspapers and magazines around the world. They have been shown on television, in a feature film and on major websites like National Geographic, The Huffington Post, The New York Post, The Times of London, NBC-TV New York, FOX TV NY, and others. Literally millions of people have seen my work, both online and in print.

I also have two published photography books and have shown my work in dozens of shows, exhibitions and art galleries. I have a business devoted to selling professionally framed signed, Limited Edition Fine Art Prints, and have sold pictures to Collectors as far away as Australia. I have licensed my images for a line of New York City-based souvenirs (I am the NYC-refrigerator magnet magnate[1]). Finally, I also licensed several abstract designs I created to a large international home décor company.

And I did all this without any formal education or training in art or photography. I am completely self-taught!

Now of course, as anyone would expect, there have been some bumps along the way. The transition from lawyer to photographer was definitely not as smooth as I had hoped. Yet even the challenges have contributed to my journey. As you'll read in the pages of this book, those challenges have been a way for me to deepen my understanding and grow as a person.

Today, I try to see life's difficulties as learning opportunities. When I do, they can help move me to the next level. This book is my way to share the knowledge I've gained over the past 30 years from all my experiences. I believe the concepts that I mention are applicable to anyone's life. They can be used to improve your work or business, as well as to enhance your personal life and relationships. Most importantly, they can help improve your relationship with yourself.

As you'll see, a big theme is that we have the ability to choose what we think and how we feel. It occurred to me recently that people who are truly happy are probably happy *despite* the events

---

[1] https://www.peteralessandriaphotography.com/blog/2018/6/refrigerator-magnets-magnate

and circumstances of their lives rather than *because* of them. Thus, it's my belief we can create happy lives or sad lives and everything in-between. Of course, it's easy to be happy when things are going our way. But I believe we can also choose happiness when they're not. It's possible to be joyful even when faced with challenges, disappointments or problems.

As an example, I'm currently back on the West Coast sitting in a hotel room in Yosemite, California. This is the first time I've been back to California since I left ten years ago. Since becoming a fine art photographer, it's been a dream of mine to visit Yosemite and photograph this iconic landscape.

However, to my shock and surprise, in the last 24 hours that dream has all but vanished.

When I arrived yesterday, in what can only be described as a freak accident, I caught my right foot on a curb and tore my calf-muscle. The pain is excruciating and I'm pretty much unable to walk or drive. Not only is there no way I can get out and take photos, but now I'm not even sure I'll be able to make the return flight to New Jersey in six days.

Bummer? Yes. Devastating? Maybe. Painful? Definitely.

As I contemplate my plight, lots of different thoughts and feelings come up. In addition to being anxious about getting back to the East Coast, I'm angry and want to blame the owners of the premises where I tripped (it was a poorly designed walkway that created the tripping hazard.) I'm surprised and confused about what happened: one minute everything was fine and the next – boom – I can't walk or drive. I'm physically in pain and since I'm here on my own, I feel pretty helpless in terms of being able to take care of myself. I feel sad that I'm less than 10 miles from Yosemite National Park and probably won't make it there for even one photo. I'm concerned about what this means for me work-wise – the recovery period for this type of injury is 12 to 16 weeks and as a free-lancer, if I don't work, I don't eat. And I'm really disappointed – I was looking forward to this trip for months and there may not be an opportunity to get back here again, at least not any time soon.

The one thing I know is that I get to decide how I feel about all this. Most of my life I've let people, events and circumstances determine my feelings for me. That was fine when those things were good – but not so fine when they weren't. While the reactions I described above may be "normal" for someone in my situation, I realize I don't have to let the situation itself dictate how I feel. And this isn't the first time I've had to deal with a difficult – even devastating – blow in my life. As I'll describe in a moment, my law career came to an abrupt and unexpected end some ten years ago in 2009.

When I first moved from New York to Los Angeles in 1988, I didn't know anything about the entertainment industry. Yet I eventually realized my dream of becoming an entertainment attorney through a lot of hard work and perseverance. I had to first educate myself about the film and television business. I did this mostly by befriending other entertainment lawyers and asking to read their contracts. While I learned, I supported myself by doing non-entertainment legal work. Once I got enough knowledge, I made the transition and eventually worked for two different independent production companies. In one of those jobs, I got promoted to Vice President of Business and Legal Affairs and travelled as far as Europe and South Africa negotiating production and distribution deals for them.

Several years later, I went out on my own and setup a law practice doing entertainment and intellectual property legal work. I represented writers, producers and directors, as well as a couple of small independent film distributors. Later, I took on a very large out-of-state client and I was their connection to Hollywood. While it had some ups and downs, my relationship with this company, as well as my career as a lawyer in general, were both relatively stable and uneventful.

That is until 2008, when the Global Financial Crisis hit.

For those who don't remember, late 2008 and most of 2009, really sucked. This time brought the scary, almost apocalyptic near-collapse of the global financial system. Major banks around the world teetered on the brink of insolvency. When two big investment banks actually tipped, the world's entire structure of money and finance was thrown into disarray. Governmental intervention staved off complete disaster, but confidence was badly shaken and in the weeks and months that followed, chaos and loss ensued. Companies and individuals alike were hit hard. For some, it was all just too much and they shut down.

At the time of the crisis, I had a nearly 12 year relationship with the out-of-state company. I was an independent contractor and while they didn't go under, the Global Financial Crisis resulted in a regime change as well as a restructuring of the company's internal operations. As a result, many of their outside vendors – including myself – were let go. In a matter of months, I went from a nice six figure income to almost nothing.

While a time of great uncertainty and even stress, I was determined to make something positive out of it. Several years earlier, I had fallen in love with photography and had spent most of my spare time honing my photographic skills. By the time the Global Financial Crisis rolled around, I had gotten pretty good with a camera. Truth is, I had been thinking about switching careers and doing something more fun and creative before the Crisis hit. While I appreciated the lifestyle being a lawyer afforded me, it was never really my passion in life. But like many people who are settled and somewhat prosperous in their work, the risk associated with a change of careers kept me from doing anything more than daydreaming about my desires.

That was until now.

By the Spring of 2009, it was clear that my law business wasn't going to come back any time soon. I had tried many things to get it going again, including looking for new clients, applying for jobs at law firms and production companies – I even sent out resumes for paralegal jobs to get some work on the side. But with the entire business climate in disarray, nothing came.

Eventually I arrived at a cross-roads: what was I going to do with the rest of my life? I kept asking myself, "*If I could do anything that I wanted, what would it be?*" The answer was always the same: *photography*. Yet I had no idea what it meant to have a photography business. I also pondered whether someone could make a living doing something they loved. I agonized over these and related questions for weeks. Finally, after much deliberation, I decided I was going to pursue my passion for photography full-time.

It was at this point that I also made the decision to move back to the East Coast. While I visited New York fairly often, I had been living in California for more than two decades. In recent years, my sisters started having kids and I was constantly flying back and forth for holidays, birthdays, etc. I'm not married and don't have any children of my own so I really enjoyed spending time with my nieces and nephews (I currently have eight!) I also missed the rest of my family and felt like it was time to come home.

At first the transition didn't go so well. I really wrestled with getting my new business going. I couldn't understand what was holding me back. I struggled with things like marketing and sales, and more than once thought maybe I had made the wrong decision.

What I eventually discovered was that it wasn't the recession and poor economy of 2009, that was the problem. It wasn't the absence of a formal education in art or photography, or the competition from all the other photographers out there. It wasn't that I lacked the latest and greatest camera and lighting equipment, or even that I had picked a small town in New Jersey nearly 40 miles away from Manhattan to set up shop. What was getting in my way was a really, really negative self-image. I saw myself as lacking talent, skill and artistic ability. I also had a lot of fear of criticism and rejection. I was certain people weren't going to like my work and I would feel ashamed and embarrassed when they rebuffed me. In fact, as you'll read in this book, my self-image was so negative and my fear was so great, that for most of the first two or three years I couldn't do much more than just sit on the couch watching TV and playing video games. It was my own negative thoughts and beliefs about myself that made moving forward impossible. It was only after realizing what the true problem was and then taking steps to overcome those thoughts and beliefs that my life began to change. How I did that is what this book is about.

Introduction

One of the main ideas is that, like in my own life, what holds many people back is their negative self-image. It's not the outside events and circumstances that are the problem. Rather, we need to change "who we think we are" in every situation that challenges us. We need to overcome our negative beliefs and shift how we see ourselves in a new, more empowered way.

An example of this can be found in Chapter Three where I discuss how I overcame my fear of public speaking. For most of my life I was terrified to speak in front of an audience. I did everything to avoid it and my personal life and business suffered as a result. Today, I love speaking in public. I routinely give talks to groups of adults and students. I've travelled as far as South America to share my knowledge and experience of both photography as well as pursuing our passions in life.

In this regard, when I speak I usually tell the audience that in order for many of us to realize our goals and dreams, we have to be *"bigger than we think we are."* We have to overcome our limiting thoughts and beliefs to have the life we want. This is my message to you as well – Be Bigger Than You Think You Are™ in everything you do. Apply all that you read in this book and watch how your world unfolds in new and exciting ways.

My photography business currently consists of commercial product photography, architectural/interior design photography, and portraits and headshots. That said, my real passion is my fine art photography. I love to create beautiful cityscape and landscape images. In particular, my photos of New York City's iconic skyline have been shown on television, and published in newspapers and magazines around the world. I also really enjoy teaching and lecturing on photography and related subjects.

bebiggertoday.com

Going forward, I plan to use the material in this book for my own classes, seminars and workshops on how to expand our lives. Some of these classes will be available online while others may be attended in person. Please visit my website www.bebiggertoday.com for more information.

Be Bigger Than You Think You Are!™

And if you're curious about my photography, it can be seen at www.peteralessandriaphotography.com.

Thank you for investing your time and money in this book! I hope to see you online or at a live event real soon!

Peter Alessandria
Yosemite, California
February 2019

Chapter One
"Who Do You Think You Are?"

"How you see yourself determines everything."
-Peter Alessandria

I'm told all good books start with a story, so here's mine:

*Once upon a time I was kind of having an argument with someone. (I say "kind of" because I'm not really a confrontational person. In fact, I hate conflict. And I became a lawyer - go figure!) Anyway, at one point during our exchange, the other person stopped, put her hands on her hips and quite dramatically said: "**Who do you think you are?!?**" While the question was meant as an insult, it stopped me in my tracks. I thought: "Wow - what a great question. Who **do** I think I am?!?" (I may have actually said those words out loud because my opponent suddenly had a very perplexed look on her face.) After a few moments had passed and I still hadn't responded, she shook her head in disgust and stormed off never to be seen nor heard from again. Yet her question has remained with me.*

The End.

So... *who do you think **you** are?* Even after all these years, I'm still convinced this is the most important question we can ask ourselves. Why? For this simple reason:

Whoever we think we are is exactly who we will end up being in life.

This is because "who we think we are" informs every choice and decision we make (usually unconsciously), and it's those choices and decisions that determine how our life goes. In the pages of this book, we'll look at how we arrived at our current ideas about ourselves as well as how we can change them for the better.

How do you see yourself

In his groundbreaking 1960 self-help book *"Pyscho-Cybernetics"*,[2] plastic surgeon Maxwell Maltz talked about how a large percentage of his patients, after undergoing cosmetic surgery, essentially became different people. Not only were their physical appearances changed, but over time, their personalities changed as well. In some cases the link between the surgery and the new personality was obvious. For example, many patients who had surgery to correct deformities or other stigmatizing conditions overcame their shyness. But there were also many not so obvious transformations, such as athletes or business people who started performing better after receiving surgery.

Of even greater interest were the cases where a change in the patient's physical appearance had no effect at all on their lives. Even though these patients looked different after their surgery, they didn't feel or act differently. As a result, Maltz concluded that when a patient's personality changed, they were actually responding to a shift in their *internal mental image of themselves*, rather than to a shift in their external appearance. While a new physical appearance could often change their mental appearance,

---

[2] https://www.amazon.com/Psycho-Cybernetics-Updated-Expanded-Maxwell-Maltz/dp/0399176136

this wasn't always the case. Unless the patient actually saw themselves differently in their own minds, nothing would change.

The reason I mention Dr. Maltz and his patients is that another way of saying "who do you think you are" is "*how do you see yourself.*" What thoughts, beliefs and perceptions do you hold about you? This is important because it's impossible to act in a way that is inconsistent with our internal self-image. Everything we think, feel, say and do is grounded in how we see ourselves. This is also why it can be so difficult to change – we strive to be different in one or more areas of our lives. Yet like Maltz's unchanged patients, because we haven't shifted our internal self-image, we remain the same. Or if we do change, that change is short-lived – the pull of our habitual manner of seeing ourselves eventually causes a return to our old ways of being.

For this reason, I will be suggesting that if we want our lives to be different, we must 1) become more conscious of how we see ourselves, and 2) deliberately choose a manner of seeing ourselves that serves us. We have to perceive ourselves differently within our own minds before our lives can change. Thus, the purpose of this book is to help you get a new mental self-image – without the surgery! You're welcome!

The two big problems many of us face when undertaking this work are, first, we're unaware that it's our internal self-image that runs our lives. We almost always think it's the external circumstances and conditions (including other people) that dictate how things go. Second, we're usually completely unconscious of how we see ourselves. The "who we think we are" that runs our lives is often buried deep within our subconscious minds.

In terms of the first problem – understanding and more importantly, *accepting* – that our mental self-image is responsible for everything we experience in life, I'm going to slowly build a case for that. It turns out many of us have great resistance to the idea that we're the cause of our own misery. Moreover, the idea that "who we think we are" determines everything, can, at times, be highly counter-intuitive.

With regard to the second problem – becoming more aware of our subconscious thoughts and beliefs about ourselves – we can jump in with the following example:

Suppose you're confronted with what many people would consider a challenging situation – the unexpected loss of a job. To begin to understand how you see yourself in that situation, notice how you're characterizing the event. Do you label it as *"a disaster"*, *"awful"*, *"scary"* and so on? Or do you use more positive terms, such as, *"I'm free!"* or *"Now I can do what I really want with my life!"* etc. The way you describe the event – either to yourself or others – is the first major clue as to how you see yourself in that situation.

The next clue, which is closely related to the first, can be found in the internal thoughts and feelings you experience. Negative thoughts and feelings probably mean you see yourself in a not-so-positive way. Thoughts like, *"I'm screwed,"* *"There will never be another job like my last one,"* or *"I'm too old to compete in today's market,"* all reflect a "who you think you are" that isn't very confident or secure. On the other hand, if you're thinking and/or feeling positively about no longer having the job, you are probably seeing yourself as someone who can take care of themselves in that situation. You must have some measure of confidence that you're up to the challenge. Optimism and positive feelings are always a reflection of a positive self-image. Thus, the way we describe a situation, and/or how we think or feel about that event internally, give us clues as to who "we think we are."

Now the reason it's so important to identify how we see ourselves is, as we said earlier, it's impossible to act in a way that's inconsistent with our primary thoughts and beliefs about ourselves. Our self-image in any situation will determine how we handle it. In the lost job example, if "who we think we are" is negative, chances are pretty good it will be tough to find a new job. Of course, the opposite would also be true: having a positive self-image may make finding a new job that much easier.

But there's another reason why it's so important to identify how we see ourselves:

It's often much easier to change "who we think we are" than it is to change the situation itself.

For instance, in the above example of losing our job, by the time we're confronted with the company's choice to let us go, it will likely be far too late to do anything about it. In fact, other than being the best employee we could while we had the job, we probably had little-to-no control over the company's decision-making process. (And of course, even the best employees sometimes get let go during times of restructuring, etc.)

Likewise, our personal circumstances at the moment we become unemployed may also be difficult to change. For instance, our monthly expenses will likely be fixed in the short term. This means there's probably not much we can do to change them, at least not right away. In contrast, we can change "who we think we are" at any time.

Yet many of us don't know we can do this. Rather, we're certain who we are is fixed by our past experiences. We say things like, "*This is just the way I am*," or "*I'll never change*," or "*You can't teach an old dog new tricks.*" Not only are such statements untrue, but they can keep us stuck in unhappy circumstances for many years – and maybe even our whole lives.

But it gets worse. Not only do most of us deny that we have the ability to decide how we see ourselves in any given situation; we're unaware that we're *already* doing it. We're deciding in every moment "who we think we are" in relation to every event and circumstance we encounter in life. The fact that we may be unaware that we're doing it doesn't mean we aren't doing it.

Stress!

We feel stress when we focus on things we don't have any control over. In the above example, the decision to fire us – who made it, how they made it and why – is beyond our control. Likewise, our personal financial situation at the moment we lose the job may also be beyond our immediate ability to change. Thus, giving our attention to any of those things will create stress. Focusing on something we can't change reinforces a sense of powerlessness, and it's this sense of powerlessness that lies at the basis of all stress.

On the other hand, focusing on things we can change has the potential to reduce our anxiety. If, as we just said, we always have the ability to change how we see ourselves, then in the job loss example this means we can consciously cultivate more positive thoughts. *"I got this,"* or *"Something good will come from this,"* or *"I can figure this out,"* are examples of more constructive thinking that can begin to shift how we see ourselves in the situation.

Likewise, we want to avoid making ourselves wrong for our mistakes. Many people blame themselves for things like losing a job. We naturally think it's our fault – if only we were better workers we'd still be employed. The truth is, we don't always know why what happens, happens. We could have been stellar performers and still get let go. And even if we did contribute to the problem, what we want to do is learn from our mistakes – not beat ourselves up for them. Self-recrimination can add even more stress to what may already be a difficult situation. I've noticed in my own life that just being nicer to myself can sometimes make a huge difference in how things turn out.

Some people may object to using positive affirmations like those I mentioned a moment ago. They say, we're just making them up; they have no basis in reality. We'll address those and related concerns later. For now, while I agree it may take some effort to shift our internal self-image, it should be obvious that focusing on more positive thoughts and beliefs about ourselves will help reduce stress. Having less stress will, in turn, make us more effective at dealing with whatever problems we have.

The problem lies within
Now if it's true that our self-image determines everything, this would indicate that the source of a problem lies in how we see ourselves and not in the events and circumstances of our lives. This is because how we react is determined by "who we think we are" *relative* to that situation. Our response is always dictated by our internal self-image, not the outside event or circumstance. Accordingly, we can say:

The situation is never the problem; the problem is always – and only – how we see ourselves in that situation.

This may be hard for some of us to accept. We've spent a lifetime looking outside ourselves for the source of our problems. We'll talk about why this is so shortly, but for now notice this is actually good news. If we can almost never change the situation, but we can always change how we see ourselves, then it's possible to transform a negative event into a positive one. By deliberately choosing to see ourselves in a more positive way, we take our power back. Taking our power back alleviates the sense of powerlessness many of us experience in challenging situations. At a minimum, this can lead to better results in whatever problems we're facing today; at a maximum, it can lead to a whole new life.

By saying that the problem can be found in how we see ourselves, we're saying that the problem lies within us. It's not in the outer circumstances or events we encounter. This is because information from the outside world must first pass through our internal filter of "who we think we are" before we can react to it. In the job loss example, as the knowledge that we've been laid off enters our consciousness, the mind tries to make sense of it. It can only do this by examining that information within the context of what it already knows. What it already knows is how we have experienced similar situations in the past. The mind thus uses our past experiences to build up and/or reinforce our self-image and that self-image then becomes the filter through which all new data must pass. By processing the information in this way, the mind assigns a meaning to the current situation and it is to this meaning which we react.

Of course, all this happens very quickly – within milliseconds. Yet it can be proven by the simple fact that our reactions will be different depending on how we see ourselves. Let's look again at the job loss example. As we've already said, if how we see ourselves is as someone who can handle the situation, we'll have one reaction. If "who we think we are" is someone who can't, we'll have a very different one. It's the exact same event – i.e., losing our job – yet we have different reactions based on our internal filtering process. Thus, we can say that:

How we react to something is always determined by how we see ourselves rather than by the thing itself.

Again, this is really important since we often can't change the situation. But we can always change how we see ourselves.

I said earlier that many of us have resistance to the idea that we create our own misery. Whether in good times or in bad we've been conditioned to look outside ourselves for the source of our experience. As a result, we're usually certain someone or something else needs to change in order for us to feel OK.

Think about your own life for a moment. Identify a difficult relationship. Have you ever *not* thought that the problem lies with the other person and that they have to change before you can feel better? Have you ever remotely considered that the cause of your unhappiness lies within you rather than within them? As we'll discuss in the next chapter, it's the almost universal unwillingness to take responsibility for our own thoughts and feelings that creates much of the drama and conflict in our lives. It's also this unwillingness that leaves us powerless to have a different experience.

Past performance is not indicative of future results.

A moment ago I said that our self-image is the result of the mind interpreting our past experiences. When we're confronted with a difficult situation in the present, the mind relies on who we were in the past in deciding how to react. In an evolutionary context, this makes sense. It's important to identify and assess present dangers based on past experiences. For instance, primitive man may not have gotten many chances to learn that fire is harmful. Or that it's not a good idea to wake a sleeping Saber Tooth Tiger ("*Here kitty, kitty...*" Chomp! ☺). Thus, learning in this way can be quite adaptive. Yet, as we'll discuss in Chapter Four, primitive man's fear of Saber Tooth Tigers has been replaced by modern man's fear of his boss, mother-in-law or the

IRS. Therefore, within the context of how we live our lives today, relying on past experiences in understanding current situations may hold us back as much as it can help.

Saber Tooth Mother-In-Law's aside for the moment, the bigger problem lies in the fact that most of us believe who we *are* today is who we *were* in the past. (And actually, an even bigger problem lies in the fact that who we were in the past was completely made up – more about that later.) Deep down inside, we don't think we can change how we see ourselves. *"Yes,"* we may say, *"it's important to have a positive self-image."* But when confronted with our own negative thoughts and beliefs, we immediately follow up with the quotes I mentioned earlier: *"Well, that's just the way I am,"* or *"I'll never change,"* or *"You can't teach an old dog new tricks,"* etc.

The bottom line is, many of us don't think we can change who we are. For example, if we've always felt anxious speaking in public, we're sure we'll continue to feel that way in the future. Or if we've always struggled with math, well, there's nothing we can really do to change that. And so on. While our past is often hard to ignore, prior experiences aren't necessarily determinative of future ones. For instance, as I mentioned in the Introduction, I changed my relationship with public speaking pretty dramatically. I went from someone who absolutely loathed and freaked out at the thought of doing it, to someone who now absolutely loves it. Thus, I believe if we keep repeating the same experiences over and over, it's not because that's just the way we are. Rather, it's because we haven't changed how we see ourselves in that situation.

Many of us are also convinced we are the way we are because of what the world – and especially other people – have done to us: *"I am this way because of how my boss treats me."* Or *"If my mother had been nicer I wouldn't be so uncomfortable around women."* Or *"I'm afraid to take risks because my older brother always beat me up if I failed."* And so on. While our interactions with others can definitely have an impact on us (especially as children), it's my belief that it's still possible to become whoever we want to be in life. This is in spite of what other people did or didn't do to us, or what may have otherwise happened in the past.

Dressing for success

If most of us judge "who we think we are" based on our past experiences, then negative past experiences can effectively limit how high we go. Yet when I was contemplating what successful people might be doing differently than the rest of us, it occurred to me that – perhaps without even realizing it – they see themselves as being able to handle situations *irrespective* of what happened in the past. They approach life from a place that says "*I got this*," even if they have contrary prior experiences. They consciously or unconsciously ignore anything negative (other than to learn from it) in determining how they see themselves. Thus, what happened before doesn't limit them.

They also probably trust they will get any additional skills or help necessary to get the job done. This belief in themselves, as well as in their ability to positively interact with others, is what *confidence* is all about. I'll have more to say about confidence later, but for now note the confidence I'm talking about is probably not what most people think confidence is. Moreover, without this particular type of confidence, it's almost impossible to have a profitable business, a successful relationship – or even a happy life.

As I said, the successful person may not even realize they're doing all this. But if they consistently produce positive results (which is how most of us would define a successful person), then somehow, someway, consciously or unconsciously, they must have chosen to see themselves as being able to handle whatever life is sending their way. And in many cases, this may even extend to deliberately overlooking any past negative experiences.

Adam Ant

Let's take a look at an example from my own life that illustrates how "who we think we are" relative to a situation determines our experience of it. Now this is definitely *not* an inspiring tale of bravery or courage. In fact, it's just the opposite.

But it is a good example of how "who I thought I was" influenced my experience with some household pests several years ago.

DISCLAIMER: KIDS – ALWAYS GET YOUR PARENTS' PERMISSION BEFORE USING HOUSEHOLD CLEANING PRODUCTS – ESPECIALLY FOR ANYTHING OTHER THAN CLEANING

When I was first considering the idea that how I see myself determines everything, I was looking for a concrete example of that. Staring down at the ground – at the concrete no less – I saw a bunch of little red ants scurrying around on the sidewalk. I thought, "*I see myself as being able to take care of myself in relation to these ants. I don't feel threatened by them. Rather, I see myself as powerful. I know that in less than a second I could crush them under my heel and not think twice about it.*"[3] Here, I thought, was the perfect example of how "who I thought I was" relative to a particular situation determined how I reacted to it.

Well it's funny how life works sometimes (actually it's not so funny as you'll see in a minute). A few weeks later I was in my kitchen and I noticed a couple of red ants walking along the counter. I didn't think much of it and got on with what I was doing. The next day I woke up and saw a bunch more. Now my kitchen is usually pretty clean – there definitely wasn't much to attract these little critters. So I thought to myself, "*This is just an anomaly – a seasonal thing – they'll be gone in a couple of days.*"

Well the next day came and there were ants everywhere – walls, counters, floor. I'm not a bug-a-phobe, but this truly freaked me out. I started to panic. Because I don't normally kill bugs, I don't keep any insect spray in the house. So I grabbed the only spray I had: window cleaner. I sprayed the $hit out of those little guys, until nearly half the bottle was gone. [Un?]Surprisingly, it turns out glass cleaner works pretty well as an insecticide and eventually most of the ones who weren't already dead, scattered for higher ground.

---

[3] Before people get upset about me killing things, just so you know 1) I never touched these little guys, and 2) I have no less than four empty plastic yogurt containers strategically placed around my house so whenever I see a stray bug inside I can gently scoop them up and place them outside unharmed.

Now I'm not telling you this story to convince you window cleaner is a good way to get rid of bugs. What I want you to see is how, in that moment, the idea that I could take care of myself *vis-a-vis* the ants went out the window. My panicked and highly upset internal reaction shows my lack of certainty that I would be OK. "Who I thought I was" in that situation, was basically, "*Screwed!*"

The point of this sad, somewhat silly story is they were still the same little ants that I had seen scurrying around on the sidewalk a few weeks earlier. The ones I was so confident didn't pose a threat to me. Yet now, because I saw myself differently in relation to them, this time I had a whole different reaction.

You might be thinking, "*well, wait a second – there lot's more ants. It's not really the same situation.*" And I would say, perhaps. But consider this: regardless of how many ants there were, there are people in the world who would not have been freaked out by them. They might be entomologists or they might be exterminators. But not everyone would have the same reaction I did. This is because how we see ourselves in a given situation determines how we react to it. If the situation were responsible for our reactions, then everyone would react the same way. So if even one person responds differently, this shows pretty clearly that it's "who we think we are" that drives our experience – not what seems to be going on around us.

Of course, I'm not saying we have to live with ants – or anything else we might consider to be a problem. It's OK to resolve whatever issues we are confronted with in life. The thing we don't want to do, however, is let our negative reactions run the show. If we're freaking out, chances are pretty good we won't make the best decisions. We may actually end up doing more harm than good (note to self: don't spray blue glass cleaner on white kitchen curtains.)

Another reason I am bringing up this example now is, as we'll discuss in detail later in this book, many of us rely on negative emotions to take care of ourselves. In particular, we use anger to get through difficult situations and as a form of protection. Imagine that if instead of ants, my problem was with another person. In my frantic attempts to "solve the problem," I grabbed the glass cleaner and started spraying that person. Harmless (perhaps) and also kinda funny. But probably not a good solution. Now imagine that if instead I grabbed a loaded gun. Thousands of people every year employ this kind of "solution" when they see themselves as powerless and threatened. As in my example, how they react is determined entirely by how they see themselves – i.e., "who they think they are" – in that situation.

Change your thinking, change your life

We can't change something if we're not aware of what it is. So it should be obvious that if our thoughts and beliefs about ourselves are the source of our problems, it's probably important to become more aware of them.

A helpful method to notice our thoughts is meditation. I started meditating many years ago and have done it on and off since. While I have used several different techniques, when I started it was mostly sitting quietly for 20 to 30 minutes. During those meditations I never saw God or had any other mystical experience. Yet I did begin to notice my thinking. After a short time I could see certain patterns arising. For instance, I became aware that I would often have arguments inside my head with other people. I felt like I was on-trial, defending myself for the things I did or didn't do. Sometimes these encounters were with people I didn't know and/or would never meet (e.g., politicians, sports figures, etc.) It was really amazing – and kind of crazy – to see how, when left to its own devices, my mind would consistently default to such negative patterns of thinking.

I can see now that this particular type of thinking was related to my subconscious feelings of guilt and unworthiness. I had been challenged a lot as a kid to explain myself – why I had or had not done something. This was generally a negative, shaming experience, and I guess I continued those patterns on my own. Without even realizing it, I was recreating my childhood in my own mind as an adult. So the point is, if you're at all like me, your mind may not be your friend. You could be reinforcing all kinds of negative thoughts and beliefs about yourself without realizing it. Thus, however you choose to do it (meditation, journaling, therapy, Facebook – oops), becoming more aware of your negative, repetitive patterns of thinking is important. This awareness is a necessary first step in the process of turning our minds – and our lives – around.

Simple, but not easy

I'm the first to admit that changing how we see ourselves may be simple, but it ain't always easy. I've been at this for years and many days I still act as if "who I think I am" is a frightened, little kid. Now it wouldn't be so bad if our unconscious thoughts and beliefs about ourselves were positive. Walking around with a subconscious program of empowering internal messages might completely eliminate the need to read this book! Sadly, however, for many of us that's not the case. We focus almost entirely on our perceived flaws and shortcomings. We maximize what we think is wrong with us, while minimizing what we think is right.

The basis of this negative internal self-image is often found in our childhood experiences. In particular, how we were treated as kids – especially by our parents and older siblings – greatly influences "who we think we are" as adults. If we experienced a lot of negativity (such as scolding, punishment, teasing, shaming, scape-goating, verbal/physical abuse, etc.), eventually we internalize it. We can end up seeing ourselves as imperfect, unworthy, and perhaps even unlovable. In addition, the fact that we can't protect ourselves against such negativity impacts our sense of safety and security in the world.

This negative self-image can become so deeply ingrained that by the time we reach adulthood, we just accept that that's who we are. Yet because it's so painful for us to think of ourselves in this way (especially as children), we *dissociate* from those thoughts. We'll talk more about "dissociation" later, but the end result is we can literally become unconscious of how we see ourselves. Our lives are essentially run by our negative thoughts and beliefs – yet we're almost completely unaware that that's what's happening.

As a consequence, being afraid of life and/or beating ourselves up for our mistakes seems normal. We avoid the people and things we're afraid of, while internally addressing ourselves with cruelty rather than kindness. Such a mindset is highly destructive. It's impossible to achieve anything extraordinary when we're afraid of life and/or hating ourselves. Both steal the energy we need to move forward.

An example of this is when I started working as a photographer. I was completely unaware of how my negative thinking was affecting me. All I knew was that it was very hard for me to get anything done. Days and weeks would go by and I was still right where I started.

Eventually I saw I was terrified of rejection and criticism. I lived in fear of other people thinking poorly of me and my work. I also noticed I was very hard on myself. My mind was filled with thoughts like: *"Your photos suck," "No one is going to hire you," "You don't know what you're doing," "Why bother; nothing is going to come of this,"* and so on. My negative thinking was draining my life energy. It was literally taking the wind out of my sails when it came to moving forward with my life. It wasn't until I identified my negative beliefs and then began to undo them that things began to change.

"Deal with reality kid"

Limiting thoughts can sometimes manifest as "dealing with reality." For instance, someone might say, *"I consider myself a somewhat capable person, but I'll never be Vice President of my division,"* or *"I just don't have the talent to solo for my choir,"* or *"That attractive blonde in accounting? She would never say 'yes' to a date with me."* We all pretty much define our limits based on "who we think we are" and rarely do we try to reach beyond those limits.

Now it's true that just saying positive affirmations in and of themselves may not be enough to help us reach our goals. We might need additional skills, training, financial resources, etc. In my case, it took several years of learning photography before I had the knowledge and experience necessary to be able to work as a professional. If I just walked around telling myself, *"I'm a great photographer, I'm a great photographer,"* but never learned how to actually do it, the whole thing would have been a joke. So sometimes, in order to change how we see ourselves, we need to do things beyond just cultivating a positive self-image. Yet I can also say that all the talent and skill in the world won't help someone who believes they're no good. I've met several photographers and/or artists who, though highly talented, can't get out of their own way when it comes to putting their work out there. Their negative self-image holds them back.

So the idea is to foster a highly positive self-image, while also being realistic if there is something else we need to do to achieve our goals. I also think it's clear that the more we see ourselves in a positive light, the more we'll be able to do what it takes to get any additional resources we might need. For instance, if I need financial support or technical knowledge, I probably won't even seek those things out if my predominant thought is, *"Why bother, nothing is gonna come of this."*

We're making it all up

So far, I've tried to show that many of us are either unconscious of our negative thoughts and beliefs about ourselves, or if we are aware of them, we're convinced they're true. In terms of the latter, we all have our ways of expressing this – *"I'm just not smart enough to make more money," "I've always been unattractive," "I'll never be able to hold a job,"* and so on. Then even if we do realize it's our negative self-image that's holding us back, we don't see any way to easily change it. So we spend all our time and energy trying to change the situation. This, in turn, usually means trying to change other people. If you're married, over 30, or have kids at any age, well you know how trying to change other people goes...

A moment ago I introduced the (probably obvious) idea that much of our self-image is the result of our childhood experiences. We come into the world as blank slates. As our brains grow and mature, our life experiences become imprinted in our gray matter. We eventually build a picture of ourselves and this picture becomes "who we think we are."[4]

Children are literal – they take everything at face value. Children are also highly ego-centric – they believe everything that happens is about them. So if a parent is upset and tells the child he or she is bad, the child believes them. Being yelled at or scolded on a regular basis reinforces this belief. It also teaches the child that it's their fault when someone else is upset. Eventually the child gets the message he/she is not good enough to be loved the way they are.

Because children don't have the mental capacity to understand their interactions with others, when those interactions are negative, the child can be left hurt, confused or even traumatized. With no way to process those encounters, the child buries them deep within the subconscious mind and they become part of the automatic, habitual way the child reacts to life. They also directly shape who the child thinks he or she is in the world. Unfortunately, most of us don't outgrow this negative self-image and we end up carrying it into our adult lives.

The point is this negative self-concept is borne out of the mind of a child. It has within it all that child's inherently limited understandings and capacities. So in essence, many of us are relying on the conclusions of a six year old in determining "who we think we are" as adults. The fact is, this self-image is *totally made up* – it has little or no basis in reality. It's primarily the result of the conjecture and limited understandings of a child.

By the way: none of this is meant as an indictment of our parents – or us as parents. Parenting is hands down the toughest job on the planet. It's easy to make mistakes in raising children. Yet I think it's helpful to mention the issue here because our childhood experiences can so deeply impact our ideas about ourselves. The very short answer is we ultimately have to forgive all that happened to us as kids if we want to be free of it. So

---

[4] Some studies suggest our personality is almost fully formed by the time we reach First Grade. https://www.livescience.com/8432-personality-set-life-1st-grade-study-suggests.html

children: forgive your parents. Parents: forgive yourselves. Of course, like many things in this book, this may be easier said than done. But you're not without help – I've devoted the entire last chapter to the topic of "Forgiveness," so stay tuned for that.

Childhood trauma aside for the moment, even our negative or unpleasant experiences as an adult don't have to define "who we think we are." Everyone has, at some point, suffered at the hands of another person's unmindful or unloving words or deeds. Likewise, we've all perpetrated our own harmful ways – intentionally or unintentionally – on others. Our own or another's poor choices and decisions don't have to form the basis for our self-image. Yet for many of us it seems natural to do this. We either define ourselves as the helpless victim of someone else's wrongdoing. Or we put ourselves down and make ourselves wrong for our own mistakes.

In terms of seeing ourselves as victims, we'll talk more about this in the next chapter. For now note that it usually doesn't serve us to think of ourselves in this manner. And in the case where we're the bad guy, saying, *"I need to be hard on myself so I'll do better next time,"* doesn't serve us either. Wanting to do better isn't the problem. Thinking we have to beat ourselves up to get there is. I will argue later that self-recrimination is a primary source of fear in our lives. It's ultimately one of the main reasons that many of us fail to realize our goals and dreams in life.

Becoming our own BFF

I mentioned earlier that in the last few years I have won many awards for my photography. I've also had my photos published in newspapers and magazines around the world. My work has been shown in exhibitions as far away as Spain and South America. Plus I've sold signed, Limited Edition prints to Collectors in places as far off as Australia. And I did all this without ever taking a photography or art class.

Now you may say, *"Good on you! I'm sure you've worked hard to get there."*

While that may be true, before 2012, I never won an award for anything. Even as a kid, I never got one of those little plastic trophies you get for being on the 14th place soccer team. And before 2012, hardly anyone ever saw my work. I was barely able to post my photos on social media, much less imagine them being published in a major newspaper or magazine. The idea that someone half-way around the world would want to purchase one of my photos never even remotely entered my mind.

This was all because of how I saw myself at the time. "Who I thought I was" was someone who lacked talent and ability – whether as a photographer, artist, or anything else. I was certain I didn't have what it took to win a contest or an award, much less more than 70 of them. I was terrified of rejection and criticism. The result was I never entered any contests or submitted my photos for publication. I also thought I had to be perfect in order to participate at all as a creative person. And I was sure I wasn't that. Thus, these negative ideas about myself conspired to keep my life very small, safe and unhappy.

So what changed? As I mentioned in the Introduction, it started by me waking up to the fact that what was holding me back in life wasn't all the competition from other photographers. It wasn't my lack of any formal education as an artist. Or the fact that I didn't have the best or most expensive camera equipment. It wasn't all the haters that I thought would be out to get me on social media. It wasn't even the recession or tough economy that started in 2009. It was always and only my own unloving thoughts and beliefs about myself. My negative self-image, and the hurtful ways I treated myself as a result, were the only things standing between me and everything I wanted in my life.

All of this all came into focus (pun intended) around 2012. I realized I needed to be a different person if I wanted my life to change – especially in terms of "who I thought I was" as an artist and photographer. So I started to question all the limiting thoughts and beliefs I had about myself. As I noticed one, I tried to replace it with something more positive. This was tough going at first. Like we said earlier, those negative thoughts can seem so familiar that that's just who we think we are. I had to become super-aware of what I was thinking and/or saying to myself almost on a moment-by-moment basis. When a negative thought would pop up, I would try to question whether or not that thought was true about me. In fact, on more than one occasion I stopped what I was doing and said out loud, *"Is that really true?"* In those moments, I'm sure if anyone was in my vicinity they would have thought I was a lunatic. Yet this is exactly what I needed to do to stop the crazy train that kept making unscheduled stops in my brain. It also got worse before it got better. The more I paid attention to my thinking, the more I could see how dark it was. Yet I stuck with it and eventually I realized it was possible to counteract my negative self-image with more positive ideas about myself.

The end result was I was able to take many of the actions I had feared to do before. For instance, I began entering shows, contests and exhibitions. I also began submitting my work for publication. I posted regularly on social media and started doing everything I could think of to get my photos seen and myself work as a photographer. I went from being totally paralyzed by fear to almost being fearless when it came to putting myself and my art out there.

If I could summarize the biggest change that's taken place over the last few years it's that I've begun to see myself differently. I've changed "who I think I am" from an unworthy, talentless person, to a worthy, talented person. I've also stopped being so hard on myself. I made a conscious and deliberate choice to go from being my own worst enemy to my own best friend. The sum total is, I've accomplished many things that I would have never thought were possible. Not everything has gone perfectly. And I still have many challenges, both personally and as an artist. But I have been able to marshal enough energy and enthusiasm to get stuff done that before was difficult, if not impossible.

As an example, I went from having only a few dozen, somewhat average pictures, to now having a body of work of more than 1,500 high-quality, publication worthy images. These are photos that can be sold as prints, licensed for commercial use, and/or published on editorial pages. In addition, as I mentioned earlier, I've created two Collections of abstract designs, several of which were licensed by a large home décor company. And as I'll describe in detail in Chapter Four, I did a ton more to push through my fears and build my commercial photography business. All of this has happened since my "awakening" and all of it took tremendous time, effort and energy. And none of it would have happened if I was still beating the heck out of myself for being less than perfect.

A final example of how seeing myself in a new way has positively impacted my life is the fact that I'm even writing this book. Like the not-so-nice person in the story at the beginning of this chapter, there's still a voice in my head that says, "*Who do you think you are to write a book like this?!?*" This is not a friendly voice and it doesn't help me move forward in life. But now, being aware of its true nature, most days I am able to say to the voice, "*Thank you for sharing.*" Then I take out my computer and get to work.

The fear of self-recrimination

I briefly introduced this subject earlier and will have more to say about it in later chapters. But I wanted to mention here that no one likes to feel judged, criticized or rejected. Deep down we all want to be loved for who we are. Yet what few of us realize is that when we feel hurt, it's because of our judgment and rejection of *ourselves*. Remember: we're always and only reacting to "who we think we are" in any given situation. When someone else criticizes us, that information must past through our internal filter. If our internal filter says we're bad or unworthy and so on, we'll react one way. If our internal filter says we're good and valuable and worthy, we'll react another.

Later in this book we'll discuss how what we call "insecurity" is really just a lack of love for ourselves that we project out onto other people. As a preview, think about how you react to someone else's unpleasantries when you feel good about yourself vs. how you react when you don't. Is there a difference? (This is one of the exercises at the end of this chapter so you'll have time to suss it out for yourself then.)

In my case, I originally assumed the insecurity I felt about showing my photos was caused by a fear of other people's criticism of me. I was certain I was worried about what other people thought. Then one day I realized:

It wasn't their rejection or criticism I was afraid of; it was my own.

This was literally one of the biggest "ah-ha" moments of my life – the understanding that what had kept me paralyzed with fear was *my own rejection of myself*. In all the time that I struggled with moving forward, it never occurred to me that the source of my fear was my own self-recrimination. I also realized that I tried to cope with that fear in many different ways. For instance, I often pretended that showing my photos wasn't important to me. If you asked why I didn't submit my work to a particular show or contest, I would probably say something like, "*I just wasn't into it.*" Thus, in the past, my way of coping meant I would eventually give up on my dreams. Thankfully now I have a whole new way of dealing with all this.

Compare and despair

Related to our self-inflicted insecurity is comparing ourselves to others and then feeling bad when we come up short. When I was just beginning photography as a hobby around 2004, I had loads of enthusiasm but lacked the technical knowledge and skills most good photographers have. I'm actually being nice here – the truth is, I stunk. I didn't have a clue. But – neither do most people when they are starting out on something new. Of course, I thought I was supposed to already know everything before even having a chance to learn it. So when I would compare my photos with more accomplished photographers, I always came up short. Then I would beat myself up for it.

Comparing our work to others' can be a good way to learn and grow. But only if we're nice to ourselves about it. For me, when I came up on the short end of the stick, I would use the rest of that stick to beat the heck out of myself. I thought certain people were born with talent and if I didn't have that innate ability, I shouldn't even try. It sounds crazy as I write this, but that's how I saw it.

Luckily, my intense love for photography allowed me to continue to learn and grow despite my crazy thinking.

This is not just the way I am

I mentioned earlier that a lot of us came to certain conclusions about "who we think we are" as the result of our negative childhood experiences. For me, I arrived at the belief that there was something inherently wrong with me. I felt unworthy in almost every situation I encountered and this created a lot of pain and sorrow within me. Feeling unworthy preceded and went far beyond my photography. It affected every aspect of my life. I became convinced this was "just the way I was" and found all kinds of crazy and unhealthy ways to compensate for it. The worst part though is I ended up hating myself for being this way.

What I didn't know (and what I think most people don't know), is how much it hurts to hate ourselves. I'm of the mind that self-hatred is really the most painful and deeply damaging thing we can do. In my case, I believe the pain of this self-hatred, along with a general fear of life, gave rise to certain addictive/compulsive behaviors in me. I'll talk about this in Chapter Five. It's also true that some people can take the pain of not loving themselves and turn it into violence against themselves or others.

If you suffer from negative thoughts and beliefs about yourself like I did, the good news is you can begin to move from being your own worst enemy to your own best friend. You no longer have to beat yourself up for being less than perfect. Or sit around, wondering why you can't move forward in life. You also don't have to live in fear of other people's opinions of you. As we've already seen:

The only person's opinion of us that really matter is our own.

Of course, this is good if we have a high opinion of ourselves and maybe not so good when we don't. But as I've shown, even if we have a negative self-image, it's possible to turn that around.

Will it take work if we want things to change? Absolutely. We have to do things differently to enjoy a bigger life. In particular, as we'll see in the next chapter, we have to start taking responsibility for every aspect of our lives. We must own *all* our actions and reactions – in each circumstance and with every person. Taking responsibility is a prerequisite for changing who we are in the world. When we do this we have a much improved chance of loving the life we have so we can have a life we love.

TAKEAWAYS:

1. *"Who do you think you are?"* is the most important question we can ask ourselves since this is exactly who we'll end up being in life. It informs every decision we make and it's those decisions that determine how our life goes.

2. Another way of saying "who do you think you are?" is "H*ow do you see yourself?*" Everything we think, feel, say and do is grounded in our internal self-image. Therefore we must shift this self-image before our lives can change.

3. In each moment we're deciding "who we think we are" in relation to every situation we encounter in life. The fact that we may be unaware we're doing this doesn't mean we aren't doing it.

4. If you want to know how you see yourself in any given situation look at the way you describe it to yourself or others, as well as your internal thoughts and feelings about it.

5. While it's important to learn from our mistakes, self-recrimination can add even more stress to what may already be a difficult situation. Just being nicer to ourselves can sometimes make a huge difference in how things turn out.

6. The problem is never the situation but always – and only – how we see ourselves in that situation. It's usually much easier to change "who we think we are" than it is to change the situation itself.

7. Information from the outside world must first pass through our internal filter of "who we think we are." The mind then gives that information a meaning based on our past experiences and we react to it. Thus, all our reactions are based on how we see ourselves, not on the external events or circumstances.

8. Past performance is not indicative of future results. You *can* teach an old dog new tricks.

9. Stress comes from focusing on things we have no control over.

10. Successful people see themselves as being able to handle situations irrespective of their previous experiences. They approach life from a place that says "*I got this,*" even if they have contrary evidence from their past.

11. Many of us have a lifetime of deeply ingrained negative thoughts and beliefs about ourselves. We maximize what we think is wrong with us and minimize what we think is right.

12. It's not someone else's rejection or criticism we fear; it's our own. Self-recrimination is a primary source of fear.

13. Comparing our work with the work of others can be a good way to learn and grow. But only if we're nice to ourselves about it.

14. Positive affirmations in and of themselves may not be enough to help us reach our goals. Yet if our predominant thought is, "*Why bother – nothing good will come of this,*" we might not even attempt to seek out the additional resources we need.

Likewise, all the talent and skill in the world won't help someone who believes they're no good.

15. Because children take things at face value and believe everything is about them, negative experiences can lead to a negative self-image. The child may end up seeing himself or herself as imperfect, unworthy, helpless and perhaps even unlovable. These beliefs can be so painful that we dissociate from them.

16. Most of the negative stuff we believe about ourselves is made up by the mind of a six year old. As such, it's not a solid foundation for deciding who we are as adults.

17. Parenting is the toughest job on the planet. Children: forgive your parents. Parents: forgive yourselves.

18. Most people have no idea how painful it is to hate themselves. It is the pain of self-hatred that gives rise to compulsive and/or addictive behaviors as well as violence against ourselves and others.

19. The good news is we can move from being our own worst enemy to our own best friend. We no longer have to beat ourselves up for being less than perfect, or sit around wondering why we can't move forward in life.

20. The only person's opinion of us that really matters is our own.

EXERCISES:

1. So, "who do you think you are?" Pick three uncomfortable or stressful situations in your life. Use the form on the next page to guide you in identifying how you see yourself in those situations. (A blank form that you can use appears in the Appendix)

Situation	How do I describe the situation	What are my internal thoughts and feelings about it	Who do I think I am
Being passed over for a promotion at work	"They screwed me" "They don't appreciate me" "I'm too old/young/not the boss's son" "This is the last straw" "I'll show those ungrateful SOB's"	Life is not fair. No one appreciates me. I work hard for nothing. I can't trust people. I'm angry. I'm sad. I'm afraid I'll be stuck here forever.	Unappreciated Treated unfairly A victim Powerless Not valuable Disrespected Justified in being angry

2. In the situations you identified in #1 above, describe how it would be easier to change who you think you are in that situation as opposed to trying to change the situation itself.

3. Review one or more stressful situations from the past few weeks. Write about if you were focused on things that were outside of your control and how that created stress. Then describe how things would have been different if you shifted your focus to things that you could control. Go over it again in your mind and replace any negative thoughts with "*I got this!*" "*I can handle this*" "*This will be OK,*" etc. Repeat these phrases several times until you feel your energy shift.

4. "*The situation is never the problem; the problem is always – and only – how I see myself in that situation.*" Agree or disagree? Why? Give examples.

5. Describe at least three places where you feel stuck in your life. Identify any negative thoughts or beliefs about yourself, such as "*I'm not good enough,*" or "*I don't have what it takes,*" or "*No one is going to like me,*" etc. Write about how changing "who you think you are" in those situations will help you move forward.

6. Begin to think about the internal filtering process we described in this chapter. Look at three recent events in your life. See if you

can discern how information from each event was processed within your own mind. Can you see how your self-image formed the basis of the meaning you gave each event? Can you see how you reacted to that meaning rather than to the event itself? Discuss.

7. Identify at least three major limiting thoughts or beliefs about yourself that stem from your childhood. Begin to question whether those thoughts or beliefs are true. Then replace each of them with more positive ones. Can you see how those old thoughts were never really the truth about you?

8. "Dealing with reality" – Identify at least three limiting thoughts or beliefs you have about yourself that fall into the category of you "dealing with reality." (Review this chapter for some examples.) Then identify whether seeing yourself in this way is serving you, or if you need to adjust your ideas about yourself to help you move forward. Also note if any additional skills, training or resources are needed to achieve your goals. Identify any limiting thoughts or beliefs that are holding you back from pursuing those resources.

9. Begin a regular practice of journaling, meditation or some other technique to help you identify your negative thinking. We can't change what we're not aware of so our goal is to become the observer of our minds. Look for patterns or habitual ways of thinking that don't serve you. Also begin to question all your negative thoughts as you become aware of them. Ask yourself out loud, "Is that true?" when you notice a negative belief about yourself.

10. What many of us call "insecurity" is really just a lack of love for ourselves that we project out onto other people. As was mentioned in this chapter, think about how you react to someone else's unpleasantries when you feel good about yourself. Now think about how you react to those unpleasantries when you don't. Is there a difference?

11. Become your own best friend. Write at least three full paragraphs about why you are such a wonderful, talented, amazing person. Say all the things you wish other people would say to you. Go through your past achievements and offer to support yourself on your future adventures. End by telling yourself that you love yourself just the way you are!

Chapter Two
Taking Responsibility

"The price of greatness is responsibility."
- Winston Churchill

Another thing I heard about writing a book is you should make your points as impactful as possible. Grab the readers' attention with a powerful statement of truth. Light 'em up early – and often. So here's mine:

I am totally responsible for my life.

"OK...," maybe you're thinking, *"Thanks for sharing!"*

Well I believe *you're* totally responsible for your life too! *How you like me now?*

What I mean is we're each responsible for how we experience life. This includes all our actions and reactions, as well as how we see ourselves and who we think we are. We're responsible for these things regardless of what happened in the past, what's happening now or what may happen in the future.

Still with me?

Respond-ability

You may have seen this before: the word "responsibility" can be read as "respond-ability", i.e., the ability to respond. The ability to respond implies that we have a choice as to how we deal with life, including how we react to any situation we may be faced with. There are four primary ways we respond to life: through our thoughts, feelings, words and actions. Thus, when I say we have the ability to respond, I'm saying we get to decide what we think, how we feel, what we say and what we do in each and every moment of our lives.

Now this is really important because it turns out there is a significant relationship between these four things: our thoughts lead to our feelings; our feelings lead to our words and actions; and our words and actions lead to the outcomes we experience in life. So, for example, if I start with crappy thoughts, I am going to have crappy feelings. If I have crappy feelings, I'm going to speak crappy words and take crappy actions. If I speak crappy words and take crappy actions, the odds are good I'll eventually experience crappy outcomes in my life. The opposite would also be true, i.e., positive thoughts eventually lead to positive outcomes, a point we'll revisit later. The significance of this cannot be overstated:

Every thought we think has the potential to manifest as an outcome in our lives.

A key concept of taking responsibility is to *own* all our thoughts, feelings, words and actions. Ownership implies that we're responsible for that thing. By owning everything that emanates from us in terms of how we respond to life, we take our power back. This also means if we don't own it, we condone it!

"You make me feel"
The problem is, very few people have been trained to take ownership of how they respond to life. This is particularly true with regard to feelings. There seems to be an almost universal agreement that our emotions are the result of what's happening outside of us. *"You/it/they make me feel..."* is a familiar refrain for most people. For instance, someone gives us a gift and we feel happy. Something interrupts us while we're working and we feel mad. In both cases, because we feel differently before and after the event, we think the event caused us to feel the way we do.

Yet... that's not true. As I'll show in this chapter, *no one and nothing makes us feel anything* (and by extension, think, say or do anything.)

The fact that there's no causal link between external events and our internal feelings is not necessarily intuitive. This is why I said previously I thought most people would resist the idea that they were the cause of their own misery. As we said in Chapter One, information about an external event passes through our internal filter of "who we think we are." The mind compares that data to what it already knows, i.e., who we've been in the past in similar situations. Once this comparison is made, the mind then assigns a meaning to the event. It's to this meaning that we react. Prior to this filtering process, the event has no meaning at all. It's always our subjective interpretation based on "who we think we are" that leads to a particular response. Moreover, it's this internal filtering process that breaks any causal connection between what's happening outside of us and how we feel inside.

Let's look at a hypothetical example: Suppose you just submitted an expense report for a recent business trip. Moments later your boss rushes into your office. He has an angry look on his face. He starts peppering you with questions about the expenses. You increasingly feel fear and anxiety. Your body tightens and your senses narrow. You become so tense that you can't speak – instead you just stutter and stammer your way through his questions. He grows more and more agitated and storms out of your office as quickly as he came. Flying down the hall, he promises to send someone else on the next business trip to Las Vegas.

What caused you to react the way you did? The short answer is, you did. Starting from the beginning, when your boss entered the office with an angry look on his face, your mind took this information and immediately ran it through the filter of what it already knew – who you were in previous situations with your boss. Since those prior encounters were usually negative, your mind gave this situation a similar negative meaning (*this is going to be unpleasant, something bad is about to happen*, and so on.) Accordingly you reacted with fear and trepidation. Moreover, since your thoughts lead to your feelings and your feelings lead to your words and actions, those negative thoughts about the situation gave rise to the fear and anxiety you experienced. This in turn resulted in your negative reactions, i.e., the stuttering, stammering and tense body. Finally, those negative reactions led to a negative outcome – you falling out of favor with your boss and him sending someone else on the next trip to Vegas.

Now of course all this happens very quickly – too quick to be the product of your conscious mind. You probably have a long history either with this boss, or bosses in general. That history solidified who you thought you were in this situation. Thus, you came to your subjective, internal conclusion almost instantaneously and your emotional and physical reactions followed. Because it all happens so quickly, we assume the cause of our reactions is outside of us. Yet this is not true: no matter how fast they seem to unfold, our reactions are always about how we see ourselves and not about what someone else is saying or doing.

With regard to this last point, what if you saw yourself differently? Imagine you were confident in your relationship with your boss and who you thought you were was his equal. Even if he looked upset when he came into your office, might your reaction have been different? Might you have calmly responded to his questions? Is it possible you could quickly find the receipts and satisfy his inquiry? Same people, same situation, different reaction. What changed? Only the meaning you gave the situation based on how you saw yourself.[5]

Because when we're upset we usually assume the problem is outside of us, that's where we go to try to correct it. In the expense report example, this might mean attempting to change your boss and/or his reactions. You might try to distract him – *"Hey, congrats on closing that big sale last week!"* You might lie to him about the receipts. It might even cross your mind to hide

---

[5] Some of us try to get around this by saying that the other person *triggers us*, or *pushes our buttons*. Taking responsibility means we own our buttons. It means we take responsibility for our triggers – not blame the other person for them.

under your desk or make a run for the rest room (hey – we've all been there.) Yet obviously none of these are healthy or functional solutions.

So to take responsibility, we start by letting go of the notion that other people and/or external events are the cause of our reactions. We understand and accept that what we think, feel, say and do is the result of how we see ourselves, not what someone else is saying or doing. The way to do this is to be as aware as possible in each moment of our actions and reactions. We then take that awareness and try to intentionally change "who we think we are" in a way that will result in a more positive outcome. This may seem like a tall order, but it is possible to do this. I know from my own experiences, some of which I will describe in later chapters. Bottom line is, we can't continue to blame other people and/or the events and circumstances of our lives for what we think, feel, say or do, and expect anything to be different.

You may be familiar with the work of Dr. Joe Dispenza.[6] He says it's our personality that gives rise to our personal reality. He reminds us that we can't think the same thoughts, feel the same feelings, speak the same words and take the same actions day after day and expect our lives to change. We literally have to become someone new if we want to have a different experience.

It should be obvious it will take effort as well as conscious awareness on our part to achieve this. This is why I spent time in the last chapter explaining that it's actually possible to change who we are in the world. I emphasized that most of our negative thoughts and beliefs are just made-up fictions. Yet if you think thoughts like, "*I'll never change,*" "*This is just the way I am*", and so on, you're dead in the water. You'll never even bother to take the first step in becoming a new you. Thus, you must begin by seeing that change is possible. If you really want your life to be different, you'll have to find a way to believe that you *can* teach an old dog new tricks.

Many people believe change is possible – just not for them. They may have a long history of trying to be different in certain

---

[6] https://drjoedispenza.com/

areas of their lives but never reaching their goal. This leads them to conclude they can't make significant or lasting changes. While it may be different for everyone, I think people who have reached this point are really saying they can't handle any more disappointment. Whether it's changing who we are in certain situations, or actually pursuing a particular goal in our lives, we try and try but something always seems to get in the way. At a certain point the disappointment becomes too much. We eventually give up on our dreams simply because it's too painful to continue to try and fail.

Dealing with disappointment has been an ongoing challenge in my own life. I still wrestle with it at times and will describe later what I have learned in terms of overcoming it. For now I'll say it seems like failure is a natural part of almost everyone's journey to success. In interview after interview that I've read with successful people, they all had to deal with their share of things not working out. And some of them failed quite publicly. Few people are successful the first – or even the tenth – time out. So if you want to achieve anything significant in your life, you better figure out – in advance – how to deal with the inevitable setbacks and disappointments. In my case, the pain of disappointment was often compounded by the agony of self-recrimination. Being more forgiving of myself has been a huge first step in undoing the hex disappointment had cast over me.

Becoming more aware

We now know the importance of becoming more aware of the thoughts and feelings that drive us every day. This is especially true in terms of taking responsibility for our lives. There are several things we can do to help raise our awareness of the thoughts and beliefs that don't serve us:

1. Slow down – In the last chapter I mentioned the benefits of meditation. For me, this is a powerful way to become more aware of our thoughts. Yet few people take the time to do this. Instead, we rush through our day, racing from one task to the next. Rushing becomes a way to avoid being in the moment and does

not foster contemplative living. There's no way around the fact that if we want a more peaceful and productive life, we need to take responsibility for how we manage our time. This includes slowing down and making room in our schedules for things like relaxation and meditation. The more frantic our lives, the less chance of becoming aware in the moment of "who we think we are."

2. Identify patterns – Begin to look for habitual or repetitive ways you react to certain people and/or situations. When I started doing this I was shocked. For example, as I'll discuss in Chapter Seven, I've had many challenges with neighbors over the years. In one case I found that every time they turned on their shower or flushed their toilet, I had an extreme negative reaction. This reaction stemmed from the fact that whenever they did this, I experienced a precipitous drop in water pressure and temperature. On more than one occasion, this interrupted my ability to complete my own shower or finish washing the dishes. The problem was my reaction became so conditioned that I would experience negative emotions even if I wasn't using my water at that moment. This habitual reaction continually reinforced the resentment and powerlessness I felt in that living situation. Noticing patterns means we can anticipate future situations better and make changes before things become a problem (an example of that in a minute.)

3. Stop the blame & complain game – We said earlier we can't continue to blame other people, situations and/or circumstances for how we feel and expect our lives to change. So as soon as your mind goes to *"You/they/it make me feel..."*, flag it. This means you're not taking responsibility for your feelings. Sometimes it's not obvious when we're blaming others. Muttering *"Jerk..."* (or worse) under our breath when another car cuts us off means we just blamed that driver for how we feel. It doesn't matter what they did or if they were right or wrong for doing it. We take the focus off others and keep it on ourselves when we take responsibility for our lives. The moment we blame someone else

for how we feel and/or focus on what they are doing or not doing, we're giving our power away.

Likewise, constantly complaining about what other people are doing to us announces that "who we think we are" is a victim. Continually telling others how the world has hurt us reinforces the idea that we're poor helpless victims. Even if someone else was initially at fault, every time we repeat the story we're actually reinjuring ourselves. It's like picking at a scab – we reopen the wound rather than letting it heal. Moreover, complaining to others can ruin that person's day. It's tantamount to dumping our emotional baggage on them. It's often an (unconscious) attempt to elicit sympathy and/or agreement that we're right and the person who harmed us is wrong. We're selfishly looking for allies in our crusade for self-pity; yet what we're really doing is pulling the other person down into our own quagmire of unhappiness. Whatever the motivation, complaining to others about others is never an empowered way to live.

4. No more excuses – We said being responsible starts with owning all our choices and decisions. Making excuses is the opposite of that. So for instance, be on the lookout for when you say something like, *"Well I have no choice - I have to do this because of what [name of person] said or did."* What's actually happening is we're using someone else's behavior as an excuse for a choice that we're about to make. *"You make me do,"* is a close first cousin to *"You make me feel."* Neither are true.

Similarly, notice when you claim you're doing something out of *"obligation,"* or when you feel like what you're doing is a *"sacrifice."* Both imply that you're doing something because you "have" to, rather than because you want to. Truth is:

No one ever does anything they don't want to do.

What we call obligation is really a decision like any other – we expect to gain from doing it, though the nature of that gain may not be so obvious. A basic law of human nature is we do everything we do because we think it will confer some benefit upon us – otherwise we'd never do it. So saying something like we're attending a family or work function out of obligation is to deny our true motivation. A benefit to us of attending such a function might be to win favor and/or avoid a conflict with another person. For instance, you may complain to others about having to go to your boss's weekly karaoke night at the local YMCA. Yet deep down you know attending will keep you in his good graces. So you're actually choosing to participate because of the benefit you think you'll get by doing it.

Likewise, sacrifice implies we're giving up something that's important to us. But if I'm giving it up, I must think I'm getting a thing of equal or greater value in return. What we call "sacrifice" therefore can often be us trying to look good in front of others (*"He's such a good husband – look at all he sacrifices for his family"*). Or it may be an attempt to make others feel guilty. For example, constantly telling your kids how much you do for them could be your way to make them feel bad for what you perceive as their ingratitude.

I'm not suggesting we shouldn't do things for others. Devoted and selfless service is good for us as individuals as well as for our families and our nations. And of course there are many people who have made tremendous sacrifices for their fellow citizens and their country. What I'm talking about here is making excuses by claiming we're doing something we really don't want to do. Taking responsibility means owning all our choices and actions, rather than hiding them behind the veil of excuse, obligation or sacrifice.

5. Turn off the TV – Messages from the entertainment, news and advertising media often reinforce the belief that something outside causes us to feel or act a certain way. For instance, look at the average blockbuster movie. The good guy is always justified in blowing up the bad guy because of what the bad guy did – stole the good guy's money, ran over his cat, started a nuclear war – you know, the usual bad guy stuff. All these things make the good guy feel and act a certain way. It's the bad guy's fault that the good guy reacts the way he does.

For this reason, we love conflict and drama – both in our own lives and on our screens. It arises out of one character blaming the other for how they feel. You've never heard anyone on a soap opera say, *"Clarence, I understand you're leaving me for the gardener. But I get to decide how I feel and I choose to not be upset about this."* That show would be off the air in two minutes!

Similarly, most advertising tells us we need to buy a particular product to feel a certain way. The (sub)text is, *"You can't feel that way without buying this product."* Given this propensity of the entertainment or advertising industries, to be fully informed, consumers we need to separate out the sales pitch from the facts. Actually, what we really need to do is to stop looking outside ourselves for our answers. We are the cause of our experience and can thus create whatever experience we want. More about that in Chapter Three.

6. Working backwards – In the last chapter we said it's not always obvious how we see ourselves in a given situation. We have to pay attention to things like how we're describing the event to ourselves and others, as well as what internal thoughts and feelings we are experiencing. Moreover, sometimes a significant amount of time can go by before we realize how we reacted was a problem. In those cases, we have to become like forensic investigators and work backwards. We ask, *"How would I have had to see myself in order to think, feel, speak or act that way?"* We try to uncover an unhealthy self-image by looking at our reactions to past events. This type of inquiry can help increase our awareness and set change in motion for the future.

An illustration of this can be found in the expense report example. Imagine if before you submitted the report to your boss, you thought about past interactions with him. You recognized that they didn't always go very well and so instead of blaming him, you wondered how you would have had to have seen yourself in order to react the ways you did. You become aware that you often gave your power away by being fearful and seeing him as more powerful or important than you. So this time, before submitting your report, you spend five minutes seeing yourself differently. You decide to let go of the idea he has power over you and instead envision yourself as his equal. You then choose to focus on some new, empowering thoughts about yourself, such as, *"I'm an honest person and good employee," "I am trustworthy," "I always do my best to comply with company policies,"* and so on. (Of course, we have to assume this is actually true – if you're ripping off your employer, all the positive thinking in the world won't undo the underlying guilt.) You also decide not to beat yourself up if things don't go well in your meeting with him. Do you think if you did all this before he came into your office your experience would have been different? Changing our mind about ourselves has the power to change everything in our lives.

Check in time

Let's take a brief break and check in with what you are thinking and feeling right now. Notice if you are agitated by what I am saying. Take this as an opportunity to do exactly what we're talking about and to begin to become more aware of "who you think you are" in this moment. Our goal is to increase our recognition of any unconscious beliefs so we can take back control of our lives. The thoughts and feelings you experience while reading this book are as good a place as any to start.

You may be thinking, *"Well, it's impossible to be aware of all my thoughts and feelings all of the time. Plus, I'll be spending so much time being aware, I won't have time to actually get anything done!"* I understand why you might think this, but in my own experience, that's just resistance. It's the mind's attempt to justify not having to change. Look – we all make time for the things we consider important to us. This means making time to break through the wall of unconsciousness most of us live behind. Like it or not, if our lives are not working, *we have to be different*. If we think the solution is that someone or something else needs to change, we are probably setting ourselves up for more disappointment and resentment.

Consciously changing "who we think we are"

It should be obvious the reason we want to be more aware of what we're thinking and feeling in any given situation is so that we can change those things if they're not serving us. The goal is to eventually have conscious control over all our actions and reactions. We want to be able to intentionally choose what we're thinking, feeling, saying and doing in each moment.

I mentioned earlier successful people probably have a self-image that says they can handle any situation that comes their way. I would be willing to bet that they've learned to deliberately see themselves in a way that empowers them, to the point that they can disregard negative past experiences. Even the largest challenges can be approached more effectively when "who we think we are" is someone who is capable of dealing with those challenges. Yet for most of us, it's not natural to see ourselves in this way. Instead of, *"I got this!"*, we default to *"There's no way I can deal with this!"*

And while it's very important to learn from our mistakes, that doesn't mean we need to crucify ourselves for them. I'll say many times throughout this book that beating ourselves up for anything never makes us better people. Thus, letting go of self-recrimination is a necessary ingredient in the recipe for being truly successful in life.

As we said in the last chapter, what makes all this so difficult is even if we're aware that our self-image isn't serving us, we just assume that's the way we are. We feel powerless to change long standing habits and behaviors. The thing to remember is, with what I'm saying we don't have to try to change our habits or behaviors. That's like trying to change the effect rather than the cause. Instead, what we need to do is to become determined to see ourselves differently. We can question "who we think we are" in any situation and then change that if our current beliefs aren't serving us. The end result is our habits and behaviors will change automatically – without us even trying.

The six methods I mentioned above are a helpful first step in uncovering and/or detaching from our negative thoughts and beliefs. Having done this, we then need to come up with a new, more empowered way of seeing ourselves. As we saw in the updated expense report example, taking the time to shift "who we think we are" *before* a difficult encounter can change how we respond to it. In this case, as we change how we see ourselves, our actions and reactions will change of their own accord.

In terms of seeing ourselves in a new way, there are five methods I have used in the past that have been really helpful. There may be other methods out there as well so you're encouraged to do some investigation on your own.

1. Positive affirmations – we've already touched on this. We want to come up with some new, empowering things we can say to ourselves, either in advance of, or during a challenging situation. These may be written down or just ideas we carry in our head. Affirmations should be first person "I" statement, such as "I am this," "I have this" and so on. They should also be present tense where possible – "*I am healthy*" vs. "*I will be healthy*." It's also helpful that our affirmations be believable to be most effective. I'll speak more about this, as well as give some examples, later in this chapter.

2. Vision Statements – this is taking positive affirmations to the next level. Write out several paragraphs describing "Who you want to be" in a given situation, or in your life in general. (I have included an example of my Vision Statement in the Appendix.) Basically you want to write out your vision for yourself in a way that's both empowering and believable. Three or four paragraphs are sufficient, though you can do more if you wish. Like with affirmations, your statement should be written in the first person ("I") and present tense.

The key is to read this statement to yourself every day. You can print it out or keep it on your phone or computer. I usually read mine in the morning just before my meditation. You can read your Statement out loud, and if you're really daring, do it in front of a mirror. It is helpful to read it more than once per day if you have the time since it is repetition that reprograms the subconscious mind. If you think about how often you repeated negative thoughts to yourself in the past, then taking a few minutes each day to read your Vision Statement doesn't really take much effort.

3. Guided Meditation/Visualization – here we take our Vision Statement to the next level. You have a couple of options: first, you can read your statement right before you go into your meditation. Then during the meditation, visualize yourself being that person. See yourself as this new you in your mind's eye. Spend 20 minutes or more imagining what it would be like to be this person. How would you feel? What would you say to yourself and others? What would the rest of your life look like?

The second option is to record your Vision Statement and/or positive affirmations in your own voice on your phone – or even better, with a high quality microphone on your computer. Then listen to the recording while you're meditating. If you want to get really fancy, you can record your voice over a piece of music.

In both cases, the goal of the meditation is to get your emotions going. You want to feel powerful, positive emotions while imagining yourself in a new way. Our conscious thought of "who we want to be" sends the intention out, while our emotions bring the vision back as an experience. The more excited you are about being a new you, the faster and more powerfully it will manifest in your life.

4. Vision Board – the idea here is to create a visual representation of your goals. You can do this for anything from a new car to a new you. In the old days, we would clip photos from magazines. Today I was say download a bunch of images that represent the thing you want to change or achieve in your life. Then use the images to create a collage that embodies your vision. For instance, if you want to see yourself as more successful, find images that hold this meaning for you and arrange them in a way that empowers your vision. You can have different Vision Boards for different aspects of your life. When you're done, either print out your boards or keep them on your phone or computer. Like the written Vision Statement, the key is to refer to your Vision

Board(s) often – several times per day if possible. This will help keep the new you top of mind.

5. Mind Movies™ (www.mindmovies.com) – Mind Movies are a motion-based, visual and auditory representation of the new you. It's animating your Positive Affirmations, Guided Visualizations, Vision Statement and Vision Board all in one with video clips, still images, text and inspiring music. It's your own little movie of how you want your life to be. It's a powerful way to influence your subconscious mind to a new and elevated self-image.

In terms of sharing your work around changing how you see yourself with others, it's important to use discretion. Make sure whoever you share your idea for a new you with can support it. Nothing has the potential to take the wind out of your sails faster than someone you trust or look up to poo-pooing your goals and dreams in life.

Responsibility re-defined
OK, so let's back up a bit and look again at what it means to be "responsible." Dictionary definitions include:

- *the opportunity or ability to make decisions;*
- *the state or fact of being accountable for something;*
- *being the primary cause of something.*

With respect to the last definition – being the primary cause of something – when we deny responsibility we're saying we didn't cause that thing. Rather, it was caused by a force outside our control. We must learn to see ourselves as the origin or source of all our experiences. Earlier we said it's the internal filtering process within our minds that determines our reactions to a particular event or circumstance. We use that process to assign a meaning to the situation and then we react based on that meaning.

If you're still not entirely (at all?) convinced that this is how things work, consider this: has there ever been a time when you reacted one way to a certain person or situation, and then at another time you reacted to the same person or situation differently? What accounts for the difference? Only the meaning you gave the event based on who you thought you were. Let's look at an example.

Suppose your teenage son leaves his soccer cleats on the carpet after a game. You express your frustration by yelling at him and threatening to throw the cleats out if he leaves them there again. Yet the following week, when he does the exact same thing, you simply scoop them up (with Playtex® gloves and a dust pan of course) and place them in the garage where they belong. You do all this without saying a word or feeling any negative emotions.

If your son was the cause of your reactions, those reactions would have been the same. The fact that you reacted differently means something else is going on. Yes – of course we're often responding to our external environments. But the *nature* of that response is the result of our internal process of assigning meaning based on "who we think we are." Therefore, we're actually the cause of all our actions, reactions and experiences.

Let's look a little closer at what may have been behind the difference in your reactions. We said we're always and only reacting to "who we think we are." The first time your son left his shoes on the carpet perhaps you saw yourself as his maid or housekeeper. The meaning you gave the situation was that you were unappreciated and/or your things (house, carpet) weren't important. I would submit that it was this negative interpretation that gave rise to your angry feelings – not him leaving his shoes on the carpet. You were actually mad at the subjective meaning you gave his actions within your own mind. He may in reality love, respect and value you very much. He was just focused on something else when he got home. It was the fact that you took his actions personally and gave them an entirely made-up, negative meaning within your own mind that caused your unhappiness and angry reaction. How you felt actually had very little to do with him.

How do we know? A week later you weren't upset by him doing the exact same thing. What changed? Only "who you thought you were." For instance, suppose in the intervening time, your son out of the blue, surprised you with a card and flowers. He was expressing his gratitude for all you do for him (hey – it could happen.☺) So now, instead of seeing yourself as an unimportant housekeeper for an ungrateful son, you see yourself as valued, loved and appreciated. This explains the difference in your reactions – that difference was based entirely on how you saw yourself in the situation.

Now we're still not done. You seeing yourself as valued, loved and appreciated in the second instance changed your experience. Yet, it was still based on something happening outside you – the fact that your son suddenly discovered Hallmark greeting cards. What if you could see yourself this way without needing cards or flowers? What if you could consciously and deliberately think positive and empowering thoughts about yourself irrespective of what your son or anyone else does? Would that be a whole new way to live?

Changing who we think we are in any given situation doesn't mean we become a doormat (pun intended) for someone else's inconsiderate behavior. In the above case, it may still be appropriate to set some boundaries regarding your son's undressing habits. Yet self-care aside for the moment, the purpose of this book is to show all of us – myself included – that it's possible to consciously and deliberately change how we see ourselves in every situation so we can begin to have a new experience of life. No more drifting through our days half-asleep, blaming everyone else for how we feel. Rather, it's vital to embrace the idea that we are the one and only cause of our experiences in the world. Until we're willing to take responsibility for all of it, we can't change any of it.

Truth or Consequences [7]

Every choice or decision we make has a consequence. Being the cause of something means we set the train in motion. The consequences of that train then flow back to us, sometimes quickly, sometimes slowly, but always inevitably. Thus, in a very real sense, our lives are the result of all the decisions we've made, along with all the consequences that flow from those decisions. In fact, that's what life *is* – an ongoing process of making choices, experiencing the consequences, and then making new choices. Denying responsibility for any of our choices is thus to deny that we are creating our lives.

When we create we bring something into being by deciding amongst alternatives. A painter chooses her paint, her brushes and her canvas. When she begins to paint, each stroke represents a choice of how much of the canvas will be covered. Decision upon decision, stroke upon stroke eventually leads to a finished painting. Like that painting, our life is the sum total of all the choices and decisions we make. Taking responsibility means we see ourselves as the cause of each stroke in the painting of our lives. This may be difficult for us, especially at first, so be easy on yourself. Yet, which picture do you think will be more appealing and beautiful to behold – the one we create through our subconscious, dysfunctional ways of being? Or the one that results from us intentionally guiding the brushstrokes of our lives.

Awareness, Accountability and Action

As we can see in the second definition above, being responsible for something is closely associated with being accountable for it. For this reason, I often refer to "Responsibility" as the three "A's": Awareness, Accountability and Action.

1. *Awareness* - Awareness is just that: being aware of how our actions and/or reactions affect ourselves and others. We are

---

[7] Little known fact: Legendary TV Game Show host Bob Barker made his TV debut in 1956 as host of "*Truth or Consequences*". https://youtu.be/UkAMm2iJuZk

conscious of "who we think we are" in each situation and adjust that image of ourselves accordingly. It's no longer living life on autopilot.

2. *Accountability* – Being accountable is where we take ownership for our part in things. We become willing to account to ourselves or another for the effects of our behavior. We acknowledge those effects and are ready to set things right if we've harmed or damaged ourselves or another.

3. *Action* – Action is the "setting things right" part. This may mean going to the person(s) we have harmed and apologizing or making an amends. It could take the form of a simple apology, or it could be as complex as making financial or legal restitution for any damage we have caused. It also means not repeating harmful behavior in the future. If down the road what we do is the same damaging things as what we've done in the past, our apologies are meaningless.

We'll speak more about making an apology or amends in Chapter Seven when we talk about "Forgiveness." For now I will mention that for most of my life I was terrified to admit the things I had done wrong. After all, wasn't this just more evidence that I was a bad person? I couldn't see how admitting my mistakes and shortcomings could be a good thing. What I have since learned is that – as always – the problem is with how I was seeing myself. No one would want to admit their mistakes if "who they thought they were" was bad or guilty. As I began to see myself differently and to understand that my poor choices didn't make me a bad person, I could approach the amends process in a whole new way.

Today, instead of feeling bad, it actually feels good when I can admit I was wrong. Going to a person I have harmed and offering to make things right actually lifts my self-esteem. Taking responsibility in this way frees me from the guilt of my past. (It also has the potential to "mend" the relationship – although the other person has to be onboard for that. More about that later.) In this way, taking responsibility is a gift I give to myself. I actually now see it not as a negative thing, but rather as an act of self-love.

Respond-ability vs. react-ability

When we speak of taking responsibility I think it's helpful to mention the sometimes subtle, sometimes significant, difference between "responding" and "reacting." "Reacting" implies a lack of consciousness or deliberateness. We are usually acting out of habit, and chances are also good that we are "reenacting" our past. "Responding," on the other hand, implies some level of awareness and/or intentionality. It's probably more purposeful and calculated. Pausing before we respond, even for a moment, can put some distance between our internal decision-making process and the external situation. This may be enough to shift how we see ourselves and thus give us a chance of dealing more effectively with the situation at hand. Responding rather than reacting also suggests we own whatever choices or decisions we make. In effect, we say, *"I am choosing to respond this way,"* rather than being a slave to our knee-jerk reactions and whatever else seems to be going on outside of us.

When we respond instead of react we refrain from judging others and/or taking what they say or do personally. We look only at our part in the situation, understanding that we are the "primary cause" of our experience. We accept their actions at face value and don't feel compelled to judge them for those actions. Yes, we take care of ourselves, but we do it without taking someone else's inventory. "Judgment" will be covered in detail in Chapter Six. For now note that not only are other people not the cause of our experience, but most of the time, we don't really know what's motivating them to act the way they do. The guy who just cut me off on the highway may be a real turd - or he may be racing a loved one to the hospital. We're not making excuses for other people's inappropriate behavior. But making someone else wrong – with or without knowing all the facts – keeps us stuck in an unhealthy, and unhappy place. Judging someone else for their choices is usually a way we reaffirm that we are a victim of those choices, and is thus an expression of powerlessness rather than power.

"I Am Not A Victim of the World I See"[8]

When most of us think of a "victim," we think of someone who is harmed or injured through no fault of their own. That person's distress is caused by someone or something outside of them. Yet as we said earlier, everything we think, feel, say and do is the result of our own internal filtering process. This means we're always responding to our subjective interpretation of an event, rather than to the event itself. This further means, at the most basic level no one and nothing outside of us can make us feel anything.

The problem with seeing ourselves as a victim is that it usually means blaming someone or something else for how we feel. We take things personally and feel hurt as a result. Our minds can become preoccupied with how unkind, inconsiderate and thoughtless other people are, or how unfair life has been to us. As a result, it's easy to end up being consumed with resentment, self-pity and despair. Taken to an extreme, we can even feel justified in hurting others, especially if we think those people hurt us first.

So while bad things *can* happen to good people, we have to stay out of victim mode. It may be true that someone or something has caused us harm through no fault of our own. Yet as we'll see in a minute, we don't have to be a victim to take care of ourselves in the situation. Beyond that, in my own life every time I've felt victimized by another, when I was willing to look closer I almost always had a part in how things played out. In one way or another I contributed to the situation. Taking responsibility means owning our actions and reactions, irrespective of what someone else did to us. Even if we're totally innocent, we're still responsible for how we respond (our thoughts, feelings, words and actions) in that situation.

Seeing one's self as a victim is usually a coping mechanism. It's an attempt to feel powerful when we feel powerless. There's a rush of energy that comes with pointing an accusing finger at our wrong-doers. This feeling can be amplified by the sympathy and cries of encouragement that we may get from others. Yet seeing

---

[8] *A Course in Miracles* Lesson 31

ourselves as victims means we're giving our power away. It also leads to a life filled with unhappiness (it's very tough to be happy when "who we think we are" is a victim.) Thus, there are definitely more empowered ways to deal with harm or injury – even if that harm or injury came through no fault of our own.

In terms of becoming more aware of when "who we think we are" is a victim, be alert to the following: taking things personally; feeling angry or resentful because of someone else's inconsideration; taking umbrage to supposed slights or insults; complaining about what others did to us; feeling justified in lashing out or getting even because they did something first, and so on. In general, notice when you're complaining and/or blaming others for how you feel. It's OK to stand up for yourself and expect others to make things right when they've done something wrong. But we don't have to see ourselves as victims to do that.

"Fake It 'Till You Make It"
So we've already talked about the importance of replacing our negative thoughts and beliefs with more positive ones, and that Positive Affirmations, Vision Statements, Guided Visualizations, Vision Boards and Mind Movies™ are all good ways to do this. In terms of affirmations, two of my favorites are, "*I got this!*" and "*I'm a good person and it's OK for me to have a good life.*" But remember: affirmations only work if they're believable. If they're not, they may actually make things worse since our mind now tells us that we're kidding ourselves. The same may be true of our Vision Statements and/or Visualizations. The key is to see ourselves in a positive way that's also believable to our subconscious mind. Try starting small. Instead of, "*I can handle anything life sends my way today,*" say, "*I know it may be tough at times but eventually I'll get through this,*" or "*I am taking small steps toward resolving this in a positive way for everyone involved.*" If you go too big without really believing in the affirmations your mind may try to derail you.

If there's still resistance to making up positive thoughts about yourself, consider what we said earlier: all the negative stuff most of us believe about ourselves is made up too. Our negative self-image is usually the conclusion of a six year old and likely has little or no basis in reality. Therefore, positive affirmations such as, "*I can handle this*", or "*I trust myself to make good choices and decisions*", are no more false than, "*I'm a screw up,*" or "*I'll never amount to anything.*" For me, there was a great sense of relief when I realized all the bad stuff I thought about myself might not be true. This realization gave me hope that my future could actually be different from my past.

You might be thinking, "W*ell, I get that as kids we misinterpret a lot of things. But what about the stuff I've done as an adult?*" While it's true grownups can act in less than enlightened ways (even though they "should know better"), making mistakes or even doing harmful things to ourselves and others doesn't invalidate us as people. What we want is more self-forgiveness rather than more self-recrimination. Remember – there's a difference between what we do and who we are. Yes, it's very important to take responsibility for our actions, especially when those actions negatively impact others. Yet we don't have to hate ourselves to do this.

Regression analysis

In terms of seeing ourselves differently, I realized several years ago that I would often regress back to being like a little kid in certain situations or with certain people. When I perceived someone as an authority figure or otherwise having power over me, I became afraid to speak up for myself or risk upsetting them by expressing a contrary opinion. In this vein, for many years one of my biggest fears in life was that a client was going to call me up and yell at me for doing something wrong. This resulted in me feeling anxious, overwhelmed and defensive. Needless to say it wasn't much fun to be trapped in such emotions. I also certainly couldn't do my best work for clients when I was feeling this way.

The above is a really clear example that the problem is with me and not with other people. Living in fear of getting yelled at is only possible when "who I think I am" is a little kid. When I see myself as an adult, I don't have the same reactions. Even with a person with a difficult personality, I'm able to discuss problems and resolve conflict. Thus I have an entirely different experience when how I see myself is as a grown-up.

When I first became aware that I was regressing, I would literally stop what I was doing and remind myself that I'm not a little kid any more. Consciously taking a pause allowed me to respond rather than react. I would tell myself that I have ways of taking care of myself that I didn't have as a kid. "*Heck,*" I thought, "*if it really gets bad, I can just get in my car and drive away.*" That wasn't an option when I was five or seven or whatever age. But we have to be conscious enough in the moment to realize when we're regressing. Without this awareness, it's very difficult to disengage from our past. This is why it's helpful to spend some time identifying our unconscious patterns of thinking and behaving *before* engaging with difficult people or in difficult situations.

Talk is cheap

Taking responsibility for our lives means getting into action. It's one thing to say, "*I can handle whatever comes my way today.*" It's another to pick up that phone and call the prospect we've been avoiding for the last three weeks. Or to apply for the job we've been putting off for the last three months. Or to submit the manuscript we've been making excuses about for the last three years. A new, positive self-image is important. But to be effective, that new self image must be accompanied by action.

This is where the rubber meets the road. Action is an expression of desire and desire is how we attain our goals and dreams in life. We'll discuss the relationship between "action" and "desire" in Chapter Four. For now note that weak desire = weak action = weak results. I'll also be talking about how getting into action changed everything for me in terms of my photography career. In this regard, something that was very helpful for me was having an Action Partner. This was someone I spoke with on a regular basis (usually daily) who supported me in taking the actions necessary to move my business forward. I provided the same support for them. Mastermind Groups may also be helpful in this regard. Of course it may take a while to find the right people to partner with. But I never would have accomplished what I did with my photography if I tried to do everything on my own.

The good news is, eventually new actions will lead to new experiences and new experiences will lead to a new self-image. This positive feedback loop will reinforce the idea that we can change who we think we are and that we are able to handle a lot more than we thought we could. The "fake-it-'til-you-make-it" affirmations have now become reality and we have shifted "who we think we are."

Responsibility is not the same as blame

I'm going to end this chapter with what I think is the biggest thing most of us need to learn about taking responsibility. I mentioned earlier that, in my own life, I have at times been reluctant to admit when I did something wrong. This is because I was afraid it was just more evidence I was a bad person. As a result, dodging responsibility became a bit of an art form for me. I don't think I am alone in this: I bet at one time or another, nearly everyone has been tempted to avoid owning up to one or more of their misdeeds. I believe the reason this is so is because most of us equate responsibility with *blame.* We think it means *liability.* We see being responsible as the same as being *guilty.* Thus, even simple mistakes can become proof of our unworthiness. The more we judge ourselves for our shortcomings, the less likely it is we'll want to take responsibility for them.

So once again the problem lies with "who we think we are." Many of us see ourselves as bad or guilty without even having done anything. We often unknowingly carry this burden of guilt, and as a result avoid anything that might reinforce these negative feelings about ourselves. We also talked about how we can engage in self-recrimination when we mess things up. This doesn't help either when it comes to taking responsibility. We'd be much more likely to admit our mistakes if we loved ourselves no matter what we did.

Some people say, "*It's important to feel bad when we do something wrong. If we don't, there's nothing to stop us from doing it again.*" They think feeling guilty is a check on their bad behavior. While I agree it is important to have a moral compass, guilt isn't that compass. Remember this always:

"Guilt" is just another word for self-hatred.

No matter what anyone says, feeling bad about ourselves for anything does not make us better people.

A better way to think about responsibility is the "Three A's" we discussed earlier: *Awareness, Accountability* and *Action*. We want to be *aware* of what we did that may have created a problem. We want to be *accountable* for any harm or damage we caused. And we want to take *action* to make things right. Notice there's nothing in there about feeling guilty or beating ourselves up. Even feeling remorse isn't necessary if we are continually aware of our actions and then jump in quickly to set things right. In this way, as I mentioned earlier, taking responsibility removes the guilt we might otherwise feel. Making things right builds our self-esteem rather than diminishing it.

That's a wrap!

In this chapter we looked at the importance of taking responsibility for our lives. We said being responsible means owning all our actions and reactions, and doing what's necessary to set things right when we've done something wrong. It also means not being a victim or blaming other people, events or circumstances for what we think, feel, say or do. In the next chapter we're going to extend these concepts and look at what I call "True Power." It turns out there's a very important relationship between responsibility and True Power. Yet I sense very few people are aware of exactly what that relationship is.

TAKEAWAYS:

1. We're all totally responsible for our lives. This means we're each responsible for all our actions and reactions, as well as how we see ourselves and who we think we are. This is true

regardless of what happened in the past, what's happening now or what may happen in the future.

2. Thoughts lead to feelings; feelings lead to words and actions; words and actions lead to the outcomes we experience in life.

3. No one and nothing outside of us makes us think, feel, say or do anything. External events must pass through the internal filter of "who we think we are" before we respond to them and this filtering process breaks any causal connection between what's happening outside and how we feel inside.

4. If we want to change our lives, we have to become conscious of what we are thinking, feeling, saying and doing in each moment. When we are unconscious, it's easy to believe that the direction of our lives is caused by something outside of us.

5. To become more alert to what we're thinking, feeling, saying and/or doing in each situation:
   a. Slow down
   b. Identify patterns
   c. Stop the blame & complain game
   d. No more excuses
   e. Turn off the TV
   f. Work backwards

6. A basic law of human nature is we do everything we do because we think it will confer some benefit upon us. This means no one ever does anything they don't want to do.

7. "Responsibility" is about Awareness, Accountability and Action. We are *aware* of how our actions and/or reactions affect ourselves and others. We choose to be *accountable* for our part in things. Then we take *action* to "set things right."

8. There's a difference between "responding" and "reacting".

9. Seeing ourselves as victims is usually a coping mechanism. It's an attempt to feel powerful when we feel powerless. Anger and resentment are ways we try to take care of ourselves when we feel threatened or damaged by others.

10. Positive affirmations will only work if 1) we believe we can change how we see ourselves, and 2) the affirmations themselves are believable. The key is to find a way to see ourselves in a positive light that's also believable to our subconscious mind.

11. Beating ourselves up for anything never makes us better people.

12. Be aware of when you're regressing. Many of us can default to seeing ourselves as little kids when we're in challenging or difficult situations. Living in fear that someone is going to yell at us tells us we're seeing ourselves as a child.

13. Talk is cheap. Taking responsibility means getting into action. It's one thing to say, *"I can handle whatever comes my way today."* It's another to take the actions we've been avoiding for the last three days, weeks, months or years. A new, positive self-image must be accompanied by action.

14. Responsibility is not the same as blame; "Guilt" is just another word for self-hatred. Feeling guilty does not make us better people. Awareness, Accountability and Action do. We'll be much more likely to admit our mistakes if we love ourselves no matter what we do.

EXERCISES:

1. *"I am totally responsible for my life."* Agree or disagree? If you agree, explain what it means to be "totally responsible." If you disagree, explain who is responsible for your life if not you.

2. Pick four different situations in your life, two positive and two negative. For each, write how your thoughts affected your feelings, how your feelings affected your words and actions, and how your words and actions affected the outcomes you experienced.

3. Identify at least three different areas of your life where you have been making excuses or blaming someone or something outside yourself for how your life is going, or what you're doing or not doing. Write about:

     a. how you would need to see yourself in order to take responsibility for your current state; and

     b. What actions you need to take to turn those situations around.

     c. Then go out and do those things.

4.   a. *"I am not a victim of the world I see."* Agree or disagree? What does being a victim mean to you?

     b. *"No one does anything they don't want to do."* Agree or disagree? Why?

5. Pick two or three difficult situations that happened in the past. Briefly describe each and then identify the meaning you gave the situation, e.g., *"I'm screwed"*, or *"they don't love me"* or *"there's no way I can compete"*, etc. How did that meaning influence your reactions? How would your reactions be different if you had given

the situation a different meaning? Write out a more empowered way of seeing yourself in similar situations in the future.

6. Put together a list of positive affirmations. Review this list daily and keep it handy for any challenging situations that might turn up.

7. Write out your Personal Vision Statement. Review the Statement daily. Read it out loud to yourself. Then take the Statement into your meditation and turn it into a guided visualization.

8. "Responding" vs. "Reacting" – pick three recent situations where you reacted rather than responded. Write about how those situations would have been different if you had responded instead.

9. Describe three different times where you felt like:

   a. you had to do something because you had no choice;

   b. you were acting out of obligation; or

   c. you were sacrificing something important to you for someone else's benefit.

Turn each of those around so you are taking full responsibility for your actions. Note the true reason you were doing or not doing that thing.

10. Identify any recent situations where you may have regressed to acting or feeling like a child. Write about what you were thinking, feeling, saying or doing. Without making yourself wrong, describe how if you saw yourself as an adult you would have handled the situation differently.

11. Apply the Three A's – Awareness, Accountability and Action – to at least three situations where you caused harm or damage to someone (including yourself). Contrast this with what would have happened if you avoided responsibility for causing the harm or damage. If you actually did avoid responsibility was it because you were afraid of feeling bad about yourself?

12. Write about the difference between "responsibility" and blame, shame or guilt.

Chapter Three

True Power & True Happiness

"Power is the ultimate aphrodisiac."

-Henry Kissinger

Power tends to be a big deal in most human societies. Some people will tell you knowledge is power. Others say power corrupts. In physics, power is the ability to use energy to do or change something. When the average person talks about power they may be thinking of political power, economic power or military power. Most of my life I thought power was about getting other people to do what I wanted them to do. When there's a military conflict, whoever has the most power usually wins. In our own lives, whether it's our boss, the government, or even the weather, it can seem like something outside of us has power over us.

True Power

What I will be calling "True Power" is something entirely different. In the last chapter we said "responsibility" can be read as "respond-ability", i.e., the ability to respond. This means we choose who we are and how we're being in relation to all the events and circumstances of our lives. We also said responsibility is about taking ownership of all our thoughts, feelings, words and actions, and that if we don't own it, we condone it.

In contrast, when we deny responsibility for something, we lose our ability to change or control it. If we can't change or control it, we have no power over it. Likewise, when we blame something outside of us for our actions or reactions, we're saying that thing has power over us. It somehow has the ability to control what we think, feel, say or do.

The point is, denying responsibility for something renders us powerless to change it. This is for the simple reason that we can't control what we aren't causing. Likewise, by blaming someone or something else for our thoughts, feelings, words or actions, we're giving that person or thing the power to decide our internal state for us. Of course, as we've already discussed and will discuss further below, nothing outside of us can choose what we think, feel, say or do. Yet each of us, in our own way, has regularly believed and/or acted as if our actions and reactions were determined by someone or something outside of us.

Accordingly, I see "True Power" as the means by which we exercise control over our internal state of being, as well as how we react to the external world. It is the process whereby we consciously choose who and what we want to be in a specific situation and in our lives in general. Thus, I define "True Power" as:

The ability to choose and/or change our thoughts, feelings, words and actions.

Notice that by consciously choosing these things we can create the lives we want. Notice too, that by *not* consciously choosing these things we leave the direction of our lives to chance or fate. Three important points arise from this definition:

1) No one but us can choose and/or change what we think, feel, say or do. This means no one has power over us;

2) We cannot choose or change anyone else's thoughts, feelings, words or actions. This means we're powerless over others; and

3) Our thoughts, feelings, words and actions are the only four things we need power over to create the lives that we want.

Let's look at each of these in turn:

#1 – We spent a lot of time in the last chapter looking at how there's no causal link between what's happening outside of us and what we think or feel inside. We pass external events and circumstances through the internal filter of "who we think we are" and arrive at a conclusion about what that event or circumstance means. We then respond or react accordingly. Thus, since this is an internal process, no one and nothing outside of us can cause us to think, feel, speak or act in a certain way. This means that other people, as well as the events and circumstances of our lives, are essentially powerless over us.

#2 – One of the biggest moments of relief in my own life came when I started attending Codependents Anonymous meetings in the late 1990's.[9] The written materials for the First Step in that program said I was powerless over others. Up until that time, in one way or another I felt responsible for other people's psychological and/or emotional well-being. I was convinced I was the cause of many of their actions and reactions, at least as those things related to me. Of course, this idea was absurd – yet I truly believed it. Needless to say, it created a lot of stress and, at times, profound confusion, shame and unhappiness in my life. Now I see that what other people think, feel, say and do is *always* about them and never about me. I am accountable for my own behaviors (i.e., my words and actions), but I am never responsible for how anyone else thinks or feels, or how they act or react. I also finally

---

[9] For anyone not familiar with codependency, a couple of books to get you started are: "Codependent No More: How to Stop Controlling Others and Start Caring for Yourself" by Melody Beattie, and "Facing Codependence" by Pia Mellody. The Codependents Anonymous website is also a good place to get information – visit www.coda.org.

understand that I can't change other people. Only they can change themselves.

#3 – We are the creators of our lives. We do this by making choices and decisions. As we said in the last chapter, every choice or decision has a consequence. It is the sum total of our choices and their corresponding consequences that make up the content of our lives. Thus, by consciously and deliberately using the power of choice each day, we mold the clay of our existence in a way that serves us. Eventually, "who we think we are" becomes "who we want to be."

The power of choice

To choose is to decide among alternatives. Yet to make an effective choice, we have to know what it is we want. Thus, the first step in exercising "True Power" is to be clear on our goals and priorities. Equally important, however, is that we have to believe it's possible for us to achieve those things. This is the biggest obstacle many of us face in terms of realizing our dreams: we don't believe it's possible for us to do or have the things we really want. We either think it's too hard, or we think we don't deserve those things. All the negative thoughts and beliefs about ourselves that we discussed in the first two chapters tend to reinforce one or both of these beliefs.

The end result is we don't even try to get the things we really want. We either give up entirely, or settle for something less than what would make our hearts sing. Thus, for those of us who think this way, we have to change what we think we're capable of and/or what we think we deserve from life. In short, we have to change "who we think we are." We can't continue seeing ourselves in the same old way and expect things to change.

I'm not sure if I'm the first person to say, "*If you can believe it, you can achieve it.*" But I will also say, it may take some work to get to the point where we actually believe it's possible to achieve what we want. That's why being conscious and aware of all our thoughts and beliefs is so important. In fact, the not so good news is, if you want to know what you currently think you're capable of or what you deserve from life, look at what you already have. Remember: it's impossible to act in a way that's inconsistent with our predominant thoughts and beliefs about ourselves. This includes having or not having what it is we really want. If you're still wondering how you see yourself, simply look at your life. What you see says, *"This is who I think I am."*

Now of course, as we said in the first chapter, we may need additional skills, training and/or resources to get to where we want to be. Pure, positive affirmations, while helpful, may not be enough. But as we also said we probably won't even attempt to go after those things if we have a pessimistic outlook about ourselves or life in general.

I'll speak later about breaking down our goals into small, easily achievable steps. This makes our progress more obvious and helps reinforce a sense of success. Accordingly, doing this increases both our positive outlook and the idea that it's possible to achieve the things we want. But it's still up to each of us to initiate the actions necessary to get to where we want to be. The Action Partner or Master Mind Group I mentioned in the last chapter may provide some much-needed support with this.

The idea that we deserve to have our goals and dreams in life is one of the main points of this book. Seeing myself as deserving and worthy has been a long, and at times difficult, process. Themes from my own journey in this regard include the self-love and self-forgiveness I've already mentioned. Likewise, doing my best to become my own best friend and biggest cheerleader have also been helpful in this regard. You may already be there. But for those who aren't, we each have to discover our own path to realizing our sense of worth and value. If you're like me, you may end up finding you're the only one who ever doubted those things – other people probably already see and love the wonderful, worthy person that is you. ☺

If we're doing it, we're choosing it

By now we know that taking responsibility means we stop making excuses and blaming others for our choices. In terms of "True Power," we can add that we're consciously and deliberately choosing what we think, feel, say or do. All this means that if we're doing it (or thinking, feeling or saying it), we're choosing it. Now for some people, this may seem a bit unfair. After all, don't we sometimes have to do things we really don't want to? We covered some of this in the last chapter when we spoke about doing things out of "obligation" or as a "sacrifice." Here I would add, where does the "have to" come from? If we're the only ones who have power over our actions and reactions. And if no one outside of us has the ability to choose what we think, feel, say or do, then there's nothing present but our own will in everything we do or don't do. Now I would agree we may not always like the choices we are faced with. And I also get that, at times, life seems unfair. But it doesn't matter if we don't like the alternatives, or even if life actually *is* unfair. This doesn't change the fact that if we're doing it, we're doing it because we choose to.

At this point you might be thinking something like, *"Well what if someone holds a gun to our head? Are we doing what we do because we choose to?"* My response is the same: it doesn't matter the situation or circumstances. If we're doing it, we're choosing it. Let's say you decide to act in accordance with the gunman's wishes. You're still choosing to do what you do. I would remind you there have been many people in history who, despite having a gun to their head, refused to comply with their captor's wishes. Hopefully none of us will ever be faced with such a distressing situation. Yet living an empowered life means taking full responsibility for *all* our actions and reactions – period.

And while the gun to the head is an extreme example, as most people figure out sooner or later, you can't really force someone to do something they don't want to do – at least not with consistent or positive results. Rather, you need to show them that there's some benefit in doing what you want them to do. That's what good bosses, leaders, sales people and parents do. Yet to convince them of this, you must have taken their best interests into account. Most people see through manipulations. You may fool them once but usually not twice. And eventually, deceiving others will always come back to you. Likewise, telling the other person they can avoid punishment by complying with your wishes is not the kind of benefit I am talking about. Threatening others is always an attempt to control their behavior; not enhance or improve their lives. Like deceit, control has a way of coming back to haunt us.

At the beginning of this chapter we talked about how the world at large sees "power". A lot of people confuse force, coercion and/or manipulation with it. They think "true power" is having power over others. I'm here to say "True Power" is having power over *ourselves*! When we acknowledge that we are the primary cause of everything we do or experience in life, we are embracing our True Power. Yet most of us do the opposite: we spend our days bouncing around like billiard balls. We're constantly reacting to what appears to be going on around us, rather than creating our lives from within. We rarely stop and say, "*What do I want to experience in this moment?*" and then make choices designed to create that experience for ourselves. Bouncing around at the effect of life and other people is a sign that "who we think we are" is pretty powerless. We're talking about "Reactors" vs. "Creators:" when we "C" correctly, we move from the former to the latter – and our whole life has the potential to change.

Giving our power away

In the last chapter we briefly discussed giving our power away. We said any time we're blaming other people, being a victim, reacting rather than responding, or, as we'll see in the next chapter, acting out of fear or other negative emotions, we're giving our power away. This means we no longer have control over what we think, feel, say or do. As we've said, when we place responsibility for these things outside of us, we lose our ability to change them. Doing this consistently makes for a very disempowered and unhappy life.

Of course, we can't really give our power away. As we've said a few times already, no one and nothing has power over us. Thus, we're still choosing everything we think, feel, say and do. But now we're just blaming other people or the situation for those choices.

We all do this in one way or another, at one time or another. Yet I hope you're beginning to see that this doesn't really serve us.

A good example from my own life is public speaking. There was a time I was terrified to speak in public: my hands would shake and I would sweat just thinking about being on a stage.[10] When I got up there, I would freeze: it would literally feel like my mind had stopped working. I would stutter and stammer and generally have a miserable time of it. Of course, I blamed the situation (and other people) for my reactions. I was convinced it was because I was on a stage in front of an audience that I felt the way I did. I could point to the fact that when I was off stage, I didn't have so many issues. This was proof that the situation was making me feel the way I did. The result was for years I routinely avoided anything that involved speaking in front of a large group of people. I was letting the situation dictate for me what I thought, how I felt and what I said or did.

Yet, based on what we've said over the last 70 pages or so of this book, it should be clear that the situation was not the cause of my reactions. *I* was the cause of my reactions. In particular, how I saw myself in the situation dictated all my negative feelings. I ran what was happening through the internal filter of "who I thought I was" and arrived at a not so positive meaning for the event. In my mind, I was incompetent,, inept and unattractive on stage. These negative thoughts generated negative feelings (intense fear and anxiety). The negative feelings in turn generated negative bodily sensations (shaking, sweating, stammering, freezing up) as well as avoidance behaviors (I shied away from public speaking). The result was, I experienced negative outcomes (I bombed when I did speak in public and I missed out on opportunities to expand my business and personal life by addressing large groups).

Today, I have a totally different relationship with public speaking. I routinely speak to groups and really enjoy it. One particular week in the Summer of 2017, was just awesome. I was

---

[10] Depending on who you ask, fear of speaking in public (Glossophobia) is in the top five fears for most people right up there with fear of heights, dying or losing a job.

invited by a college in Colombia, South America to visit and speak to the students during their "Semana Internacional" ("International Week.")[11] I ended up giving seven lectures to nearly 1,000 students at three different colleges while I was there. And I freakin' loved every minute of it. I literally couldn't wait to get up on stage.[12]

So what changed? At a certain point I realized the problem wasn't with the situation – the problem was with me. I became aware that by avoiding public speaking I was giving my power away. I was letting the situation decide for me how I felt. So I began to consciously and deliberately change how I saw myself. I believed in my mind that I was competent, capable and even – dare I say – attractive while on stage! Seeing myself differently was my way of taking my power back and no longer letting the situation dictate my experience.

As a side-note, recall what I said earlier about becoming our own best friends and biggest cheerleaders. For a long time, I beat myself up and made myself wrong for almost everything, including my fear of public speaking. I had very little compassion for myself or any real understanding of the childhood difficulties that were behind my reactions. I thought I was just supposed to be able to get up there and do it. And when I couldn't, I was very, very hard on myself.

Today, I can see that it was this self-recrimination that was the real source of my fear. I notice that when I decided to stop beating myself up so much there was a lot more I could actually do in my life. I increasingly have compassion rather than contempt for my shortcomings – and by extension, the shortcomings of others. I am not a bad or defective person because I had fear around public speaking. I've also found that the less I beat myself up, the more likely I am to take responsibility for my actions and reactions. The

---

[11] https://www.peteralessandriaphotography.com/blog/2017/9/colombia-south-america-2017

[12] Actually, I like to come down off the stage and speak to the audience at eye level. I even sometimes walk to the rear of the room to better connect with the folks hiding out back there. It drives the event's audio/video personnel crazy but it really works for me.

more I take responsibility, the more I embrace my True Power and am able to make lasting changes in my life.

Applying our power

So why aren't more of us using our True Power to create our lives the way we want them to be? Four main reasons:

1. The bad news. It turns out we actually *are already* creating our lives the way we want them to be. As I alluded to earlier, since we're all living in accordance with our predominant thoughts and beliefs about ourselves, we get (and have) as much as we think we deserve from life. If my life is filled with problems and disappointments, at some level that's what I'm choosing. Admittedly we're not doing this consciously. But again, that doesn't mean we aren't doing it. This is also another example of why the question "who do you think you are?" is so important. Whoever we think we are is exactly who we'll end up being in life. And who we're being determines what we achieve or don't achieve and what we have or don't have.

2. Playing the victim. We discussed this in the last chapter. For many people in many situations, "who they think they are" is a victim. From noisy neighbors to financial problems to people breaking up with us by text message, we often see ourselves as the helpless victims of a hostile world. The best we can hope to do is stave off disaster one more day. Yet if we saw ourselves as having complete dominion and control over our lives, this would all change.

However, seeing ourselves as the creators of our lives means *giving up* the emotional and/or psychological payoff of being a victim. We talked about the rush of energy that comes with accusing someone else of hurting us, as well as the potential sympathy and attention we receive from others. Victims also get to "be right" and see themselves as better than the one(s) who they think harmed them. These are all rewards we get by identifying ourselves as victims. We'll talk more about this later, but don't underestimate the emotional and/or psychological payoff many of us get by playing the victim.

Also, there's often great resistance to letting go of a self-image which we hold dear. When we see ourselves as a victim long enough it becomes a part of our identity. Thus we may actually have trouble answering a question like "W*ho would I be in this situation if I weren't a victim?*" Any strong identification with a particular self-image can make changing "who we think we are" in that situation very difficult.

3. No one else is doing it. As a practical matter, there's not a lot of support out there in the world for the idea that we have the ability to choose our own thoughts, feelings, words and actions. Very few people live as if they are the creators of their own lives. Reactors, yes. Creators, no. Imagine someone cuts you off on your drive to work. No one I know (including myself) says, "*In this moment, I am choosing to be upset that that driver just cut in front of me.*" Instead it's more like, "*You f'ing a$$hole! Learn how to drive!*" Strong emotional outbursts are a good sign that we're not in control of our reactions.

Likewise, most of the world's messages reinforce the idea that we are powerless over how we feel. They tell us we need someone or something outside ourselves to change our inner experience. For instance, we're bombarded all day long with advertising that says, "*You need to wear these clothes/ take this drug/ buy this car,*" and so on to feel good. The implication is we can't feel good without outside intervention.

As I said in the last chapter, seeing oneself as a victim is an attempt to feel powerful when we feel powerless. Based on my observations over the past 30 years, it seems to me that both as individuals and as a race, we have a huge investment in seeing ourselves as powerless. Our minds are filled all day long with thoughts about what life (other people, events, circumstances, etc.) is doing to us. Now along comes a book which says not only do you have the power to create what you want in life, but that you're *already* doing it! All the stuff you complain about and claim you hate, you actually love (or at least *value* – we'll talk more about the difference later.) Once I get my workshops and classes up and running, I anticipate some fun times trying to help certain people see that they're totally responsible for their lives. Most of us only want to talk about what the outer conditions of our lives (such as the economy, the stock market, the weather) and especially other people (friends, family, strangers, the government, our bosses) are doing to us. We don't want to hear about what we're doing to ourselves.

4. An apparent lack of control. To the average unconscious person ☺, it seems that stuff just happens quite randomly in life. People, events and circumstances seem to come and go as they will. This seeming lack of control over what's happening outside of us makes it easy to conclude that we have no power over our internal experience either. This is compounded by the fact that most of us still see the external world as the source and cause of our experiences. We have no clue that how we see ourselves is what really determines how we experience things. So this apparent lack of control over our lives discourages taking conscious control of our actions and reactions, and thus claiming our True Power.

Power equals responsibility

At the end of the last chapter I teased that it was my feeling that most people were unaware of the nature of true power. We've already covered this at length, but I also teased that most of us were probably unaware of the relationship between power and responsibility. I want to address that now. We know that when we deny responsibility for something, we lose our ability to change it. This is because we see its source as outside of us. Likewise, when we take responsibility for something, we get our power back since we can now change or control it. Thus, if power is the ability to choose or change something, and if that ability is contingent on us taking responsibility for that thing, then it becomes clear that:

Power and responsibility are the same thing – you can't have one without the other. They're two sides of the same coin.

It's only when we take ownership of something that we can change it. In practical terms, this means we can't alter any part of our lives that we're not willing to take responsibility for. As long as you believe that it's your mother's fault, or your teacher's fault, or your boss's fault, or the government's fault, that you are the way you are, you're powerless to change things. Of course the converse is also true: by accepting responsibility we can have a whole new experience of our lives.

The courage to change

Just because we have the "ability" to do something doesn't necessarily mean we're going to do it. Even after years of working on myself, I still sometimes (often?) act in accordance with my old, habitual ways of being. I've found that for me, breaking old habits and making new choices requires *courage*. Why? Because *change is scary*. We're potentially entering the unknown and the unknown can be very frightening. My life may be miserable and I may be in terrible pain – but at least I know what to expect each day. Fear of the unknown can often overpower the pain of the known.

Related to this is the fear many of us have around the loss of a particular identity. I mentioned this earlier in relation to seeing ourselves as victims. The unhappiness and/or self-pity many of us associate with being a victim can become an integral part of "who we think we are." The result is there may be great resistance in our subconscious mind to letting that self-image go. This issue is further compounded by the fact that it's common in our society to define ourselves, and/or to relate to others, based on our negative life experiences. For instance, we may bond with others on the basis of our illnesses, failed romances, missed career opportunities, broken family relationships, etc. (If you think I'm overstating this, the next time you talk to a friend that you usually commiserate with, refrain from saying anything negative about your life and see how long the conversation lasts!) A long history of relating to others based on our negative self-image and life experiences can make changing "who we think we are" very difficult. Thus, becoming a "new you" may require greater conscious intention than you think.

"Don't worry, be happy"[13]

OK – so we've covered "True Power" – now it's time to talk about the idea of "True Happiness".

If you ask the average person what they want out of life, most will say they just want to be happy. But they say it like there's something that's preventing them from being that. What most of us don't realize is that happiness is not something that just happens to us (although it can seem this way when we're not consciously creating our lives.) Rather, happiness is a *choice*. It's a *decision* to experience life in a certain way. Thus, if we want to feel more happiness, we have to deliberately choose thoughts, feelings, words and actions that are consistent with it. This means, for instance, letting go of fearful, angry or depressing thoughts. Likewise, it's impossible to feel good if we're beating ourselves up all the time. The insanity is many of us choose unhappy thoughts all day long and then wonder why we're unhappy. That's how out to lunch we are in terms of creating our own lives!

Jerry and Esther Hicks (Abraham-Hicks Publications)[14], who teach what is commonly known as the "Law of Attraction," have this to say about "happiness":

> *"[Y]ou have absolute and utter control about [feeling good] because you can choose the thought that makes you worry or the thought that makes you happy; the things that thrill you, or the things that worry you. You have that choice in every moment."*

This is consistent with what we've been saying – if we want to feel happy it's our responsibility to choose happiness. We do this by thinking happy thoughts. Although we're probably not aware

---

[13] https://youtu.be/d-diB65scQU
[14] https://www.abraham-hicks.com/

of it most of the time, we're constantly deciding how we feel by the nature of the thoughts we think.

As I said in the Introduction to this book, *"people who are truly happy are probably happy* despite *the events and circumstances of their lives rather than* because *of them."* We have to want to be happy no matter what's going on around us. This means if we're waiting for our boss to acknowledge us for a job well done, or our teenager to say "thank you" for anything before we can be happy, we may be in for a very, very long wait. And as we'll see in a moment, happiness that's contingent on anything outside of us is not True Happiness anyway.

The fact is most people have no idea what True Happiness is. We often mistake "satisfaction", "relief", physical pleasure and/or fun times with friends or family for happiness. For instance, getting something we want is great – but it usually produces *satisfaction*, not True Happiness. We know this because eventually the good feeling fades. True Happiness never fades. Likewise, when a problem is solved or a pressure removed (e.g., a financial burden is lifted), we may think we feel happy, but it's really just *relief*. True Happiness remains even if the pressure or problem returns, whereas relief – like satisfaction – eventually fades.

Similarly, physical pleasures and/or the joys of playing with others are also fleeting. Sure it feels good to feel good in our physical bodies. But whether it's a great workout, a great meal, or a great orgasm, by this time tomorrow the physical sensations will be long gone. The same is true of having fun with friends – when the game is over the fun soon goes with it. I'm not advocating the denial of physical pleasure or that we stop having fun; I'm just wanting to point out there is a difference between those things and True Happiness.

Some people might say True Happiness is closely related to feeling affection for family or friends, or being in love with another person. While it is true our bonds with family, friends and lovers can create intense feelings of affection and delight, I'm going to reserve further discussion of this point for now since we're talking about "love" as much as happiness here. In the next

87

chapter we're going to take a deep-dive into the subject of "love" – including what it means to truly love another person. For now I will say that True Happiness is more about loving ourselves than it is about loving another.

Friends, family and lovers aside for the moment, people might also ask, *"What about helping others? Don't we get joy from assisting our fellow man?"* While we can certainly experience feelings of contentment and even jubilation in being of service to others, I would still assert that True Happiness is different. Never turn down an opportunity to assist others. In fact, that's one of the reasons I'm writing this book and contemplating a career change from photographer to teacher. But it's also important to consider the following: Sometimes we may find, if we look deeply, in our desire to help others we're actually trying to feel good about ourselves. We may be doing all kinds of great things in the world, but if our motivation is accolades, recognition, or even just some appreciation from the people we're helping, our happiness may be short lived. On top of that, the reality is not everyone wants or needs our help. For instance, I know right now this book won't be the right fit for everyone (imagine that!).

If the source of our joy is others' needing our help, then we stand to lose that feeling when they don't. Likewise, if our happiness is dependent upon other people being in a state of trouble, lack or need, what would we do in a world full of whole and healthy people? Don't get me wrong: being of service to others is great and can represent a very high spiritual calling. Yet if our happiness is contingent on making a difference in the lives of others, we're still seeking that happiness outside ourselves. And that is not – as we'll see in a moment – the place to find true happiness.

True Happiness

OK, so what exactly is True Happiness? We've already gotten some clues. First, it's not contingent on what's happening outside of us. True Happiness is an internal decision that's independent of all external causes and conditions. We choose joy whether they love us or hate us; whether we're rich or poor; whether the outside world seems to be cooperating or not. It has nothing to do with how other people feel about us nor how much we achieve in life nor where we're going on vacation next year. Second, it's constant and never fades of its own accord. Unlike the pleasures and satisfactions of the world, True Happiness is not fleeting. We may choose it or un-choose it, as we decide, but it's always there if we want it. Thus, we can say "True Happiness" is:

An ongoing, internal decision to feel joy no matter what. It means being happy for any reason – or for no reason at all.

Now, given the way most of us currently view happiness, the problems with this definition should be fairly obvious. First, no one I know (including myself) thinks of happiness as coming from inside us. We're always looking for someone or something outside of us to fill our lives with joy. Second, we usually need an excuse to feel happy. The idea that True Happiness is based on any, or no reason at all, is more than a little confusing and hard to comprehend. Finally – and probably the biggest problem – this definition implies we're responsible for our own happiness. It says True Happiness cannot be given to us, nor can it be taken away. It's entirely on us to choose it – or lose it. Again, I don't know about you guys, but I've never been taught to think of happiness in this way.

If all that's not enough, here are a few more points to consider: First, True Happiness requires that we want to be happy more than anything else. We must desire joy more than the alternatives. This is because as we already said, True Happiness is a decision – it's not something that just happens to us when the stars align. Like all choices, a decision to be happy means we put aside all alternatives. We have to give up things like self-pity, fear, depression, worry, anger, etc., and choose joy instead.

Next, any choice (including the choice to be happy) is made on the basis of perceived benefit to us. That is, we choose what we choose because we *value* it. To value something means we accord it with a certain level of importance or worth. Thus, to be happy, we have to value happiness. I'll admit it sounds a little silly to say it like this. But I know in my own life, there have been plenty of times when I was happy being unhappy. I was valuing emotional pain or misery more than any of the more positive alternatives.

As we'll discover in Chapter Five, it is quite easy to value things that don't serve us. I'll give specific examples in that chapter, but note here that when we make choices unconsciously, we can end up experiencing lots of things we don't really want – or at least we *wouldn't* want if we were more aware of what we were choosing. For example, when we value unhappiness more than happiness, we usually do this because we perceive there's a payoff to being unhappy. Perhaps other people feel sorry for us so we get their attention and/or sympathy. Or they make excuses for us so we can avoid doing something we really don't want to do.

I know in my own life, I have used being unhappy as a way of getting back at others. For instance, for a long time I could never be happy around one particular person because I wanted them to know how much they had hurt me. Even though the circumstances surrounding the hurt were over a long time ago, I kept the misery going. The payoff I sought was trying to punish another person by making them feel guilty for what they had done to me. Yet all I really accomplished was keeping myself stuck in my own suffering. (Yes – that's how crazy I was.)

It should also be noted that (like all our feelings) happiness is a statement of "who we think we are." We have to see ourselves in a certain way before we can realize it. For instance, if "who we think we are" is unlovable, threatened, victimized, unappreciated, etc., it will be very difficult to choose happiness. In addition to giving up our negative feelings, we have to give up our negative self-image as well. This can be very difficult if we have an investment in seeing ourselves a certain way or if we see a payoff in a state of being other than happiness. It should be clear that it can be difficult to make headway in any of this without being super-aware of what we're choosing and why. Consciousness is the key.

All expressions of true power are arbitrary

As we prepare to close this chapter, I want to jump back to our discussion of True Power. Like True Happiness, all expressions of True Power must be based on our own internal decision-making processes. True Power choices cannot be contingent on what's happening outside of us. Instead, our decisions as to what we think, feel, say and do must be made solely on the basis of the internal reference of "who we want to be" in life. For the empowered, self-creative person, this is the sole criteria for every choice or decision.

What this means is, to be an expression of our True Power, all our thoughts, feelings, words and actions must be *arbitrary vis-à-vis* the external world. That is, our choices regarding these things are made solely from the internal reference I mentioned above. This may seem like a big leap from where many of us currently stand in terms of our decision-making. Most of our choices and decisions are made in reaction to what we perceive in the outside world. The difference now is these choices and decisions are inner-directed. "Who we want to be in this situation," becomes the sole basis of our decision-making.

This is a subtle, yet highly important distinction. For many of us, it's such a novel way of living it can be difficult to comprehend. The point to remember is that what's happening outside of us (including what other people are doing or not doing) *does not matter.* This is because those things have no power over us. The external situation is our cue or stimulus to make a choice – but not the basis for that choice. We'll have more to say about all this in later chapters.

Accordingly, tying our discussion of True Power and True Happiness together, it can be said that:

The greatest expression of True Power is True Happiness.

Being happy *despite* the events and circumstances of our lives rather than *because* of them means we are choosing what we choose altogether independently of the outside world and are thus invoking our True Power.

To sum up, True Power is the ability to choose our thoughts, feelings, words and actions. It's the direct result of taking responsibility for all our choices and decisions. When we own our power, we can create a life based solely on "who we want to be" in every situation, rather than letting the external circumstances and conditions of our life dictate that for us. Yet as we said earlier, having the ability to do something doesn't always mean we're going to do it. When it comes to creating the life we want for ourselves and the people we love, there's still something that can hold us back. It stymies us from exercising our True Power and realizing our greatest vision of ourselves. That something is the subject of the next chapter. That something is commonly known as F.E.A.R.

TAKEAWAYS:

1. When we deny responsibility for something we can't change it. It is, by definition, outside of our control. If we can't change or control something, that means we have no power over it.

2. "True Power" is directly related to taking responsibility for our lives. It is about consciously and deliberately choosing thoughts, feelings, words and actions that move us closer to who and what we want to be in life.

3. "True Power" is defined as *the ability to choose and change our thoughts, feelings, words and actions.* Three important points arise from this definition: 1) no one else has power over us; 2) we are powerless over everyone else; and 3) our thoughts, feelings, words and actions are the only things we need power over to create the life we want.

4. The biggest obstacle many of us face in terms of achieving our goals or getting what we want from life is we don't believe it's possible for us to have those things. We either think it's too

hard to get them or we don't deserve to have them. The end result is many of us don't even try to get what we really want.

5. If we're doing it, we're choosing it. Taking responsibility means we stop blaming someone or something else for our choices. True Power means we're consciously and deliberately choosing what we think, feel, say and do.

6. If you want to know what you currently think you're capable of or what you deserve from life, look at what you already have. What you see is the result of choices that say, "*This is who I think I am.*"

7. A lot of people confuse force, coercion and/or manipulation with power. They think true power is having power over others. We now know that "True Power" is having power over ourselves.

8. Any time we're blaming other people, being a victim, reacting rather than responding, or acting out of fear or other negative emotions, we're giving our power away. This means we no longer have control of what we think, feel, say or do. Doing this consistently makes for a very disempowered and unhappy life.

9. When we give our power away, we're forfeiting our right to decide how we think or feel and/or what we say or do. We're in effect saying, "*Situation, you decide these things for me.*" Of course the situation can't choose these things for us. All we're actually doing is denying we made a particular choice by blaming someone or something else for it.

10. From health problems to financial problems to family problems, we often see ourselves as helpless victims. There's a feeling of energy that comes with accusing someone else of hurting us. Being a victim is a way of gaining sympathy and seeing ourselves as superior to others.

11. To the average person, it seems that stuff just happens quite randomly in life. This apparent lack of control over what's happening outside us makes it easy to conclude that we have no power to control our internal experience either.

12. Power and responsibility are the same thing – you can't have one without the other. It's only when we own something that we can change it. In practical terms, we can't change any part of our lives that we're not willing to take responsibility for.

13. Making changes often requires courage. We're potentially entering the unknown and the unknown can be frightening. Fear of the unknown can often overpower the pain of the known.

14. If we want to experience happiness, we have to deliberately choose thoughts, feelings, words and actions that are consistent with it. The insanity is many of us choose unhappy thoughts and then wonder why we're unhappy.

15. Our current quandary around happiness is complicated by the fact that most of us have no idea what True Happiness is. We often mistake "satisfaction", "relief", physical pleasure and/or fun for happiness.

16. We choose what we choose because we *value* it. To value something means we accord it great importance or worth. Valuing emotional pain and misery more than happiness precludes us from experiencing it.

17. The reason why our positive feelings are so fleeting is that we tie them to the external events of our lives and when those external events change, so must our good feelings.

18. True Happiness is an ongoing, internal decision to feel good no matter what. We choose joy whether they love us or hate us;

whether we're rich or poor; whether the outside world seems to be cooperating or not, and so on.

19. True Happiness is the highest expression of True Power. We are happy for any or no reason at all.

21. All expressions of True Power must be arbitrary *vis-à-vis* the external world. Our decisions as to what we think, feel, say and do are made solely on the basis of an internal reference of "who we want to be in life."

EXERCISES:

1. How do you define "power?" Is there a difference between force, coercion and/or manipulation and power? Is there a difference between power over others and power over yourself?

2. Identify at least three situations where you routinely give your power away. Explain how and why you do it.

3. In the situations you identified in #2 above, write about how those situations will be different when you take responsibility and exercise your True Power. What new thoughts, feelings, words and actions will you choose for each situation?

4. Describe how your life would be different if you really believed you were powerless over others and that others were powerless over you.

5. Identify at least three things you want to achieve in your life. Discuss whether or not you believe it's possible to attain those things and whether or not you think you deserve them. If you come up short on either, describe how you would change "who you think you are" to make attaining those things possible.

6. "If you're doing it, you're choosing it.." Give at least three examples in your own life where you originally claimed you were doing something you didn't want to do. Then turn it around so you are now taking full responsibility for your actions and reactions.

7. Talk about the relationship between "power" and "responsibility". Pick at least three examples from your own life of how denying responsibility left you powerless to change something. Then write about any situations where when you took responsibility you were able to shift an outcome.

8. Write about any negative identities or labels you use in terms of defining yourself. For instance, do you label yourself by an illness or other experience? Come up with a definition of yourself free of any labels. Carry this new idea about yourself into your relationships with others.

9. "True Happiness"

   a. Describe what thoughts, feelings, words and/or actions you would have to change in order to be truly happy right now. Identify any unloving or fearful thoughts and what their correction would be.

   b. Do you *want* to be happy? Is there some payoff to being unhappy that is holding you back? If you have to give up all thoughts of victimization and unfairness to get there, are you ready to do it?

   c. What things in your life have you valued more than happiness? Did that serve you?

   d. True happiness is being happy for no reason. Write about a time when this was true for you.

10. All expressions of "True Power" must be arbitrary *vis-à-vis* the external world. Our sole criteria for all decisions as to what we think, feel, say and do is "who we want to be in life." Choose three upcoming events. In each case, write about who you want to be in each of those situations. In the time leading up to these events, keep reminding yourself of this ideal self-image. Then when it comes time for the actual event, be that person!

Chapter Four
From F.E.A.R. to L.O.V.E.

"The only thing we have to fear is fear itself."
- Franklin D. Roosevelt

As the above-quote from F.D.R's first inaugural address reminds us, there's only one thing that stands between us and everything we want in life: FEAR. Fear can derail a career, end a relationship or even terminate someone's life. As we'll see in this chapter, fear is not caused by something outside of us. Instead, like all feelings it's the result of "who we think we are." This means all it takes to alleviate our anxieties, worries and concerns is a new idea about ourselves. Of course, once again this falls under the heading of "simple but not easy." Yet until we understand the real source of the problem, it will be difficult if not impossible for us to change.

There are a couple of popular acronyms associated with the word "F.E.A.R.": One is "False Evidence Appearing Real." The other is "F@#k Everything And Run." (Cute, right?)

While both are worth thinking about, let me give you my own definition of fear:

Fear is an emotional response to a perception of ourselves as powerless and/or unlovable in a given situation.

How's that for a mouthful! Let's break it down.

"An emotional response..." You've probably heard it said that "emotion" equals *"energy in motion."* Think about when you feel good emotionally. Do you have more energy? Is it easier to get stuff done? Compare that to when you're not feeling so good emotionally. Lower energy? Tougher to get moving? Thus it can be said that there's a direct correlation between our emotional and physical states. Since it takes energy to accomplish things in life, it's good to know that our energy levels are affected by how we're feeling emotionally. We can improve our physical state by changing our thinking and thus our feelings. As a result, we can become more productive and effective in whatever we're attempting to do by being more aware of our emotions.

Generally speaking, fear is a paralyzing emotion.[15] When we're gripped by worry, anxiety, dread etc., it can be very difficult to take action or get things done. The physiological effects of fear in the body mimic the emotional ones: we hold our breath, tense our muscles, our stomach tightens, and we move more slowly. There's a general contraction in the body, accompanied by a marshalling of energy in anticipation of having to run, hide or fight.

From an evolutionary perspective this response is quite adaptive. When an animal is in danger, being prepared in this way can save that animal's life. But what may have served us in our nascent past in ancient Africa, probably has less value today. While there are certainly potential pitfalls associated with living in the modern world, it's unlikely we'll be confronted with the same or even similar dangers that our ancestors faced. Thus, true "fight or flight" situations, at least as measured by what primitive man had to deal with, are quite rare these days.

Yet the limbic brain in modern humans remains as vigilant as ever. It's constantly on the lookout for danger. Except instead of scanning the plains of the Serengeti, it scans our home, work and social environments. And instead of finding Wooly Mammoths or Saber Tooth Tigers, we're set on edge by an encounter with our

---

[15] Fear is behind the "fight or flight" response, so obviously fear can also get us going. But with those few exceptions where a burst of energy is needed to survive, fear mostly shuts us down.

boss, mother-in-law or the IRS. (When I was a young attorney and a senior partner walked into my office unexpectedly, he or she may as well have been a Saber Tooth Tiger or Wooly Mammoth. No offense to any of the senior partners at the firms I worked for.) Obviously in the appropriate situation, the "fight or flight" response can be a life saver. But most of us enter fight or flight mode without ever being in real physical danger. This results in the response being way over-utilized. False-positives release stress hormones into our bodies, which over the long term can actually damage the body's tissues, organs, and immune system.

Fear vs. caution

For this and other reasons, I like to remind people that there's a difference between "fear" and "caution." Caution means a common sense approach to life – we take reasonable precautions based on an objective assessment of the situation. Caution says look both ways before crossing the street; get all the information before making that investment; wear a safety belt when driving, and so on. It's a rational response to the vicissitudes of life and represents a reasonable and proportional attempt to mitigate risk.

Fear, on the other hand, is generally neither rational nor proportional. Whether paralyzing or adrenalizing, fear is often an intense reaction that has the potential to do more harm than good. Fear can take many forms including, anxiety, terror, panic, worry, concern, foreboding, dread and so on. We can spend a lifetime (metaphorically speaking at least) hiding under the bed in one or more areas of our lives because of some irrational form of fear.[16]

(Back to my definition of fear) "... *to a perception of ourselves*" – As we've been discussing throughout this book, a perception of

---

[16] Developmental psychologists tell us children are born with only two fears: fear of falling and fear of loud noises. These reactions make sense from an evolutionary standpoint. But what's important is that this means all our other fears are *learned*, i.e., they are not natural. Fear of criticism, fear of rejection, fear of shame or humiliation, even fear of death, are all learned responses. The good news is this means they can be unlearned.

ourselves is "who we think we are." It's the mostly made-up, mostly negative self-image that many of us carry from childhood. It results from the story we tell ourselves about our past experiences. The good news is any perception is just a way of seeing something. This means it can be changed. As we've already said, our goal is to move from "who we think we are" to "who we want to be." This is accomplished by consciously and deliberately choosing thoughts, feelings, words and actions that are in alignment with our new idea about ourselves. The more we do this, the more our perception of who we are changes.

"*... as powerless and/or unlovable...*" – Like all emotional reactions, fear is the result of passing an external event through our internal filter of "who we think we are," and then assigning a meaning to that event. Thus, as the following explanation makes clear, if we're reacting with fear, we're likely seeing ourselves as either powerless and/or as unlovable.

- "Powerless" means "who we think we are" is helpless. We see ourselves (often unconsciously) as unable to take care of ourselves or to get what we think we want or need. The specific feelings of fear arise when we think we will be hurt by someone or something, and that we will experience pain, injury, loss, damage, etc., as a result. The meaning we give the situation is that we can't protect or defend ourselves from these things.

- "Unlovable" literally means "we are not able to be loved." We believe there is something about us that is inherently not OK. We may see ourselves as bad, unworthy, guilty, unattractive, and so on. In this case, the fear arises from the idea that we will be met with punishment, rejection, humiliation, loneliness, etc., for being this way. We are certain we will feel bad or hurt as a result, and are equally certain there's little or nothing we can do to avoid feeling this way.

"*...in a given situation.*" Fear is mostly situational. Yes, we may experience an overall sense of dread or foreboding in our lives.

But acute feelings of fear usually arise in relation to specific people and/or circumstances. As you already know, the problem is never the situation, but always and only how we see ourselves in that situation. Thus, our normal response of trying to change the external circumstances when we're afraid won't be of much help. We may get some temporary relief, but eventually the fear will resurface elsewhere because we haven't addressed the root cause of it, i.e., "who we think we are" in that or similar situations.

My two problems

Dovetailing off the last few paragraphs, I realized a long time ago that I only have two problems in my life: I perceive myself as *unlovable* and I perceive myself as *powerless*. These two primary core beliefs have caused all kinds of pain and misery in my life. Yet because they were buried deep within my subconscious mind, I was almost completely unaware that they were running me.

Seeing myself as unlovable meant I had an unusually difficult time dealing with other people. For instance, it was tough for me to make friends or feel like I was part of a group. When I met someone new, I would often try to impress them by embellishing the truth about something I had done, or even lying to them about my accomplishments. Trying extra hard to get people to like me was my way to compensate for the "fact" that I was unlovable. I also either avoided social situations, or got so wasted I didn't care. I worked off the assumption that once people got to know me, they wouldn't like me. The few times I did let other people get close, my insecurities would usually lead me to abandon or sabotage the relationship so they couldn't reject me first.

My poor self-image also affected my work life. My first job after law school was with a large firm in Los Angeles. Because I felt so unworthy and inept, my primary goal was to hide out as much as possible. I avoided work assignments out of fear that if I didn't do them correctly I would feel humiliated and ashamed. Arriving late, leaving early and lying about doctor's appointments soon became the norm. Then of course, I had to pad my time sheets to make up for all the missed hours.

When I actually did attempt a work assignment, I could never ask for help. I thought I was supposed to already know everything and asking for help was proof that I didn't know what I was doing. I also avoided most of the firm social functions. As a result, few people got to know me and I quickly developed a reputation for having a bad attitude. What they didn't know – and what I didn't know – was that I was just terrified of being rejected or making a mistake and having it proved to me – and everyone else – that I wasn't good enough. The end result of seeing myself as unlovable was lots of trouble – at work and in my personal life. Not because I wasn't smart. And not because I wasn't a nice person. But because "who I thought I was" was incapable, incompetent, unlovable and someone who didn't deserve to be helped.

Seeing myself as powerless similarly created a lot of problems for me. It meant I didn't think I could cope with life. It manifested as feeling helpless and inept. This came up a lot in both my business and personal relationships. When there was a conflict, I almost never stood up for myself. I had a long history of letting other people get their way with me (not a good personality trait for a lawyer by the way). I also lived in fear of other people's disapproval or upsetting them because I had no idea how to deal with someone else's anger. To get around all this, I would usually resort to manipulation and/or dishonesty to get my way.

Mostly, I lived in fear of criticism or rejection by others. I lacked any real sense of value or worth so the slightest hint of disapproval or criticism sent me reeling. I would make what I thought they thought of me more important than what I thought of myself (more about what happens when we do this later). I had no idea how to take care of myself in the face of someone else's critical remarks or outward rejection of me. So as a result I avoided almost all situations where this was a possibility.

Now before we all get too depressed about my depressing story, I want to say I feel very differently about myself today – and my life reflects that. I'm not perfect. But I have come a long way in how I see myself, and how I treat myself and others as a result. I also want to repeat what I've said a few times already: I was making all of this up. All of my negative core beliefs about myself were untrue. They were the simple but unfortunate result of my distorted childhood perceptions. Yes, I did build a life around those beliefs for a long time. But I can also say I'm not that same person today. I am living proof that it's never too late to change "who we think we are."

Danger, Will Robinson, danger![17]

Earlier we alluded to the fact that fear has evolutionary value. When you're living in the jungle it's good to be alert to possible dangers. Thus, from a biological perspective, fear gets our attention and lets us know there's a potential for pain out there. But as we also said, most of us no longer live in the jungle. Life has probably never been safer for us human beings, at least not in terms of our day-to-day lives within our modern societies.

In my own life, I notice I can't always tell whether the source of fear is real or imagined. Many times I've convinced myself that a situation was going to be painful – only to come out the other side to find out it wasn't. When we lack confidence in our ability to handle what life sends our way, we tend to see more potential threats and dangers. This makes it easier to slip into fear-based thinking. Yet as we begin to see ourselves differently – such as being able to take care of ourselves even in difficult or trying situations – we worry less and trust more. Now this is really, really important since the world hasn't changed; the only thing that's changed is how we see ourselves in it.

As I change how I see myself, I change how I see the world.

It's a shift in our perception of "who we think we are" that has the potential to help make the world a safer place. Traditionally, we've relied on things like having more guns or bigger bombs in order to feel more secure. We tried to solve our internal problems of personal and national insecurity by changing the external situations. There's nothing wrong with this. Yet, in this day and age of increasing technology, weapon proliferation and potential

---

[17] https://youtu.be/RG0ochx16Dg

agitators, I can't help but wonder if there's another way to address our problems. Changing "who we think we are" so we're more secure – whether as individuals or as nations – is an inside job. We each need to look within and discover a more powerful, loving and secure way of seeing ourselves.

She loves me, she loves me not

Speaking of real vs. imagined threats, we've come to one of my favorites: insecurity in our romantic relationships. Looking at our ancestral past, I don't imagine Neanderthal Man cared too much about what that cute – but probably really hairy – cavewoman thought about him. He was much more likely concerned with four-legged – but perhaps equally hairy – threats stalking him in his environment. For modern man, while we may have less body hair, we definitely have a lot more fear than our Neanderthal friends when it comes to romantic relationships. Let's look at a hypothetical example.

Suppose you've met Mr. Right (minimal body hair). The relationship appears to be going well but deep down inside you have an uneasy feeling. *"Does he really love me? Will he stick around for a while?"* Then one day out of the blue, your worst fears are realized – he cuts things off with virtually no explanation. Even worse, he does it by text message. Thoughts of rejection, unworthiness, anger and self-pity fill your mind. In short order your outlook goes from *"everything's great"* to *"life sucks."*

Now if you're like 99.95% of the human population you would probably assume that he was the cause of what you were feeling. Everything was great until he changed his mind; now your life sucks, so it must be his fault. Yet you now know the cause of your distress is not found in what he did or didn't do. You took his behavior, passed it through the filter of "who you think you are," and then came to a conclusion about what his actions say about *you*. It is to that conclusion that you are now reacting.

Despite being really, really upset, you're also a really good student. So you remember I said something back in Chapter Two about "working backwards." You recall that this is a technique we can use to discover how we see ourselves in certain painful or difficult situations. You flip back to those pages, review what I said, and then ask yourself the following questions: *"How must I see myself to feel so much pain and anger about someone leaving me? Who must I think I am for his actions to hurt me so much?"* As you ponder those questions, your mind begins to open: *"Hmmmm... maybe these feelings are more about me than him. Maybe I'm reacting to something buried deep within the recesses of my own subconscious mind. Maybe I need to look at who I think I am, rather than who I think he is..."*

Feelings of sadness or grief naturally follow any loss. Yet what may not be so normal – and what we therefore want to be on the lookout for – is when we're devastated, angry, vengeful, incapacitated, depressed, etc. In those cases, chances are pretty good that something else is going on. Such emotions transcend the normal feelings of sadness or grief that accompany the loss of something special.

I would suggest that the true cause of our emotional pain in a situation like the one I outlined above (once we've accounted for the normal sadness of a relationship ending) is the result of our own negative beliefs about ourselves. The idea that we're unlovable, unworthy, not good enough, etc. This is the true source of our pain and is far more agonizing than someone simply leaving the relationship. Seeing ourselves as unlovable or unworthy is tantamount to abandoning or rejecting ourselves. Thus, it's our own self-abandonment or self-rejection that gives rise to the extreme feelings many of us experience when someone breaks up with us – not what the other person did or did not do.

This is true even if they lie to us or cheat on us or break up with us by text message. Again, we're not making excuses for someone else's unloving or inconsiderate behavior – people can be jerks (or worse) in relationships. Yet, we're learning that if we want our lives to be different, our focus must be on ourselves. We have to look at how we can take responsibility for our own feelings. We also know we can't change another person's behavior. All this means regardless of what they say or do, our feelings are about us.[18]

When deep feelings of anger, rage, emotional pain and/or unworthiness follow a breakup, I'm going to suggest it's not because of how little the other person seems to think of us; it's because of how little we think of ourselves. This means that if we're insecure in any relationship, the source of our fear is not that we'll lose *their* love; it's that we'll lose our *own*. This is true because no one can really love us if we don't love ourselves. It's also true because no one can hurt us when we do.

If all this is hard to believe, think about it this way: was there ever a time you weren't upset about a relationship ending? What was different in that situation? Only one thing: you didn't see yourself as unlovable – you didn't take their leaving as a sign that you were worthless. It was the exact same situation, but because of how you saw yourself (and by extension how you saw them), you gave the situation a different meaning. Thus, instead of being devastated, you were nonplussed. You might have actually even been relieved to see them go.

True Romance

I'm not sure if what I'm about to say is good news or not – I'll let you decide for yourself. If it's true the reason we feel bad in relationships is because of how we see ourselves, then it must also be true that we feel good in relationships for the same reason. Let me explain: as I've been saying for the better part of the last four chapters, no one makes us feel anything – good *or* bad. All our emotions originate within us. We're always reacting to the meaning we give a particular situation based on our internal filtering process. This means the head-over-heels "I-can't-wait-to-eat-Jello-while-wearing-her-socks" state of mind is only

---

[18] Have you ever considered feeling compassion for a person who has to lie or cheat their way through life? Someone who has so little faith in themselves they have to deceive others to get what they want? How happy and secure could someone be who has to mislead people to get involved with them in the first place? I know what it's like to be that person from first-hand experience. It's not a happy existence.

about us. Like the fact that we're the source of our misery when a relationship ends, we're also the source of our joy when we think things are good.

Now – and this is probably more bad than good on the news front – what we're feeling in those situations isn't really love. The good feelings are actually an egoic emotional reaction based on the thought that someone special likes us. That is, our positive feelings arise from the ego's idea that someone who we perceive as valuable or important has taken a shine to us. Since being "special" is the lifeblood of the ego, someone special liking us means we must be special too. This is the basis for the good feelings we experience in such a situation. (We'll discuss the "ego" in great detail in Chapter Six.)

Of course, those feelings can quickly change when we think the other person no longer likes us. Thus, both the head-over-heels-in-love feeling and the gut-wrenching sense of loss and despair actually come from within us, not the other person, and are based solely on what we think someone else thinks of us.

The problem is most of us are unaware that this is what's going on. We're certain those amazing feelings of chemistry and attraction are "true love" (or at least they'll lead to it sometime soon.) While it's possible the chemistry may eventually morph into something more, it's not very likely. This is because the ego isn't really interested in love. Its primary concern is what it can get from others. Thus, the ego's real interest is in what that hottie can do for us in terms of proving we're more special than anyone else. Accordingly, when someone we think is special thinks we're special, the ego is in heaven. When the other person no longer sees us this way, the ego is in hell.

If getting is the ego's primary motivation, when the getting stops – i.e., the other person no longer thinks we're special – negative emotions such as unworthiness, self-pity, anger and despair quickly follow. People feel these feelings when they think something has been taken away from them (watch two or more five year olds play for any amount of time and you'll soon see this in action.) When a relationship ends and we feel any of these emotions to an extreme, the ego is reacting to the idea that it is now being deprived of something it wants. It will always look outside itself and blame someone or something else for this loss – and direct its displeasure accordingly.

Now some people will dispute they're only out to get something in their relationships. They might say, *"What about all I give to other people? I'm constantly doing for my spouse/kids/parents, etc."* The very short answer is, the ego only gives in order to get. This is why we react so negatively when we feel unappreciated or when people don't recognize or reciprocate our kindnesses. Many people will also say it's only fair to get something back from the people we've given to. Each person needs to decide for themselves what's fair. But I will say True Love is only concerned with what it can give – not with what it can get. For the ego, it's just the opposite.

The reason this may be good news is, we really don't need anyone else liking us to experience the kind of emotions we often feel when we first get involved with someone new. Conceivably at least, we could generate these feelings within ourselves. However, that's not the way the ego works. We'll almost always seek outside ourselves for a reason to feel the way we do – good or bad. Just like we blame others when we feel bad, we blame that special someone when we feel good. Yet in both cases, no one makes us feel anything. We're always and only reacting to ourselves.

The other thing to remember is that like "True Happiness," "True Love" never fades of its own accord. We may abandon either or both True Love or True Happiness, but they never abandon us. This means falling in and then out of love with someone is a misnomer. If we truly love someone, that feeling never fades. We may no longer choose to be in relationship with that person for any number of reasons. But the feeling we would call True Love remains. While feelings of anger or despair may seem normal when someone leaves us – especially in what we consider a cruel or thoughtless way – this only tells us we never really loved that person. Rather, we loved what we thought they were giving us. With the realization that's been taken away, the ego is now either really pissed or feels really sorry for itself (or both!)

I'm guessing more than a few people will be upset with me for bursting their whole notion of romantic love. (Hey - I'm not particularly happy about all this myself.) Yet, short of physical illness and death, I can't think of anything that creates more pain and anguish in many peoples' lives than the loss of a romantic relationship. Unless we begin to view all this differently, that pain and misery will continue. (In case you've forgotten how this all feels, recall how your first marriage started – and how it ended.)

The value people feel as adults is directly related to the value they felt as children. This is why it's crucial to instill a sense of self-worth in our kids while they're young. There's nothing more important – not what school you send them to or what you put in their lunch box everyday – than building a child's self-esteem. How we treat a young child day-after-day is what teaches them whether they're a lovable person. The more they feel valuable inside, the less they'll seek a sense of value and specialness outside of themselves when they're adults. All the education in the world can't compensate for a child's lack of self-esteem.

I know some (many) people these days are worried we're over-esteeming our children. Those little plastic trophies for the last place field hockey team notwithstanding, it's how we interact with our kids on a daily basis that forms their sense of worth. Regularly shaming, blaming, scape-goating them and so on, will impact them much more than giving them trophies or not. This is made even worse when one minute we're telling them we love them, and the next minute shaming them for getting handprints all over the refrigerator.

In terms of valuing our children, actions speak louder than words. I personally don't think it's possible to over-esteem a child. I also don't think telling them – and more importantly, acting as if – they are valuable and important to us will make them less able to cope with life. A sense of entitlement only comes from people who *lack* self-esteem and are trying to compensate for it. People who are really full of themselves in a positive, healthy way only want to give of the abundance they already feel. These are the people who do great things in the world.

Unequal partners

For most of my life, my relationships (especially the romantic ones) were characterized by inequality between the parties: I either thought I was better than them or they were better than me. When I thought I was better, I saw myself as more important, worthy or valuable. When I thought they were better, the opposite was true. Seeing inequality in any of my relationships is highly codependent and a sign of immaturity.[19]

If I think somebody is better than me, I will usually have an investment in being liked by them. This is because I will feel more valuable if someone I think is more valuable than me, likes me. If we're in a relationship, it's also likely I'll live in fear of them leaving me. This is because if they do, my worth as a person will be diminished – I will, quite literally, be *"worth-less"* if someone worth more than me, leaves me. Obviously this is an insane way to live – yet for me personally, I spent many years drowning in such insanity.

It actually doesn't matter what kind of relationship it is – work, romance or even a friendship. When we see inequality, it destroys any chance of real intimacy. Attempting to improve our sense of worth by associating with others who we think are more worthy than us can only result in pain, unhappiness and anxiety. This is because, as I mentioned above, our own sense of importance will seemingly rest in the hands of that other person. It thus has the potential to change at any moment when what we think they think of us changes.

Of course, all we're really doing in these situations is giving our power away. We're making another person responsible for how we feel. But since they can't control our emotions and thus aren't actually the cause of any of our feelings, we're just blaming

---

[19] Pia Mellody actually refers to codependence as the "disease of immaturity. *Facing Codependence* https://www.amazon.com/Facing-Codependence-Where-Comes-Sabotages/dp/0062505890

them for how we (subconsciously) feel about ourselves. It's hard to enjoy a peaceful or loving relationship while under the grip of this type of thinking.

Celebrity worship

Related to this is the love affair – and obsession – many of us have with celebrities. We want to be just like our favorite movie star, reality TV personality or sports hero. Because we often judge celebrities to be more valuable and important than we are, we think emulating them will make us more important too. This is why celebrity endorsements are so highly sought after by advertisers. People think owning the same products as their favorite celebrities will somehow make them more valuable and worthy too. It's for similar reasons many people are obsessed with certain *brands* – clothing, cars, hotels, electronics, etc. They think owning that particular brand makes them more valuable as a person than those who don't.

Whether we engage in celebrity worship or inequality in relationships with people we actually know, this is a reflection of our belief in our own inherent lack of worth and value. This is actually true anytime we look outside ourselves for something to inflate our sense of self. This is also another good example of why it's so important to uncover our negative core beliefs about ourselves. If I see myself as inherently valueless, I will unconsciously seek ways – including leaching off other peoples' celebrity status – to feel more valuable. It's these mostly unconscious negative core beliefs that run us.

Sure it's fun to have public figures that we look up to and who inspire us to succeed in life. And what would Halloween be without us dressing up as our favorite politician or superhero? But "worth by association" thinking, whether in our personal relationships or with respect to the celebrities we idolize, does not serve us. So knock it off! (By the way, George Clooney drives an Audi and so do I. ☺)

With respect to relationships with people we actually know (that poster of Kim Kardashian in your man cave does not count!), many of us can be obsessed with what we think other people think about us. Yet since we're always reacting to our own opinions of ourselves, worrying about what other people think of us is never time well spent. Add to that the fact that other people don't have the power to make us feel anything anyway and, well, this whole idea of living in fear of other people's opinions is just a huge waste of time. Thus, it's helpful to keep the following saying in mind (put it on a sticky note on your refrigerator):

What other people think of me is none of my business.

Of course, for this to work, we have to be willing to take responsibility for our own thoughts and feelings. Living in fear of what someone else thinks of us says we don't know that we actually have the power to decide how we feel about ourselves. As I mentioned in the example of the people with no body hair falling in love, if I experience negative emotions at any time during a relationship, it's because I am judging myself as unlovable. Any anger or despair is caused by my own negative self-image – not by what the other person thinks of me, or has or has not done. Accordingly, here's another really important sticky note for the refrigerator (outside, not inside):

No one has the power to hurt me unless I give them that power.

Now I'm sure not everyone is on-board with this. As we discussed in the last chapter, we often have an investment in seeing ourselves as victims, especially in our personal relationships. Thus, someone might say, "*What about being married for 15 years only to find out your spouse has been cheating on you with your best friend. Is that not supposed to hurt?*" My reply would start with that I'm sorry you had that experience – no one deserves to be treated that way. Second, I would say I understand how that could be shocking and trigger feelings of loss, sadness and grief. But then I would also add that, if after the initial shock wears off, you still feel hurt or betrayed, there's something else going on. It probably means you're interpreting their behavior in a way that says you're worthless, unimportant or unlovable. But since they can't make you feel anything, it's actually you thinking of yourself in this way that is the real cause of your pain. Recall what we said earlier about the case where we don't feel upset when someone leaves us. We haven't taken their actions personally and so we don't doubt our own worth and value. Because we still feel lovable, we don't feel hurt by them leaving us. Instead, as I said, we may even feel relieved or happy that they're gone.

Also, it's important to be conscious of giving our power away in a situation like this. Other people can only hurt us if we believe they're right about us not being good enough. (I'll give a pretty elaborate example of this in Chapter Six. As a preview, you should start brushing up on your archery lessons.) If we truly loved and accepted ourselves, we might feel surprised, perhaps even shocked and some sadness when we find out they've been cheating – but we won't feel betrayed. It's always how we see ourselves – rather than what they did – that determines how we feel.

It's also really important to keep in mind that we have a part in how every relationship plays out. First, we're responsible for the people we pick. They may be cute and sexy as hell. But that doesn't mean we don't do our own due diligence. Marrying a psycho is on us, not them. You should also listen to everything they tell you. I once had a woman I got involved with tell me on our first date that she had left every relationship she had ever been in. Of course, I convinced myself that this time it would be different – until she left me for someone else six months later. ☹

Next, it's our job to take care of ourselves in all our relationships. This means that even if we miss their obvious-to-everyone-else sociopathic tendencies, it's up to us to get the heck out of Dodge if their behavior is truly harmful or inappropriate. We can't continue to ignore warning signs and then try to pin all our emotional distress on them.

Finally, being loving towards another doesn't mean we stop loving ourselves. We bear responsibility for turning a blind eye to someone else's bad behavior. Being kind doesn't mean letting someone else walk all over us. This actually isn't good for either party. We get more proof that other people are jerks. And they get the message that their inappropriate behavior is somehow OK. Thus, holding others accountable for their harmful behavior is good for us – and them. In Chapter Seven, we'll talk more about how we're responsible for teaching others how it's OK to treat us. If we put up with other people treating us poorly, that's our part in the situation.

Fear of the loss of identity

We've already mentioned this a couple of times but I think it's worth looking at a little more in-depth here. We said earlier that changing who we think we are can be scary. Our life may be a mess, but we're still resistant to doing what needs to be done to change it. This is probably because we're uncomfortable moving towards the unknown. While this may seem trite, even ridiculous, consider the following types of questions and see what kind of response they stir up in you:

Who would I be without my anger?
Who would I be without this depression?
Who would I be if I weren't a victim?
Who would I be without financial problems?
Who would I be if I wasn't sick?
Who would I be if everything always went my way?
Who would I be if people were always kind and considerate of me?
And so on.

I don't think we consciously desire negative things in our lives. Yet just like the fact that many bad habits are difficult to break, many deeply ingrained, negative ways of seeing ourselves can be tough to let go of. In addition, there's almost always a subconscious *payoff* to seeing ourselves in a certain way. For instance, as we mentioned in the last chapter, there's often a payoff to seeing ourselves as victims. With something like constant financial problems or continuing bad romantic relationships, the subconscious payoff may be that it affirms we deserve to suffer and struggle in life because we're bad people. We unconsciously value the negative experiences because they validate and confirm the subconscious version of "who we think we are."

Defensiveness

In our relationships, fear often manifests as defensiveness. Many of us feel like we have to constantly defend ourselves against attacks by other people and by the world. Even worse, we feel woefully inadequate to do so. In addition to our human relationships, we often feel we have to defend ourselves against all manner of threats from outside us, such as germs and disease, job loss or financial insecurity, environmental and climate threats, and so on. Most of us, most of the time, see ourselves as under constant siege by forces outside our control. Yet in all instances, I would argue our perceived need to protect and defend ourselves arises from "who we think we are," not from what's happening around or outside of us.

We said earlier no one has the power to hurt us unless we give them that power. Yet who lives that way? For most of us, it's just the opposite – we're constantly on-guard, ready to defend against the next blow. If I'm spending my time and energy trying to protect myself from being hurt by you, it doesn't leave a lot of room for intimacy or joy in our relationship. It also reaffirms that I think you have power over me and that I'm not in charge of my own feelings.

Changing "who we think we are" in any relationship or situation is the fastest way to reduce our feelings of insecurity and defensiveness. Unfortunately, many individuals and nations seek to lessen feelings of threat or vulnerability by building weapons and stockpiling arms. Instead of attempting to internally change our image of ourselves, we try to change the outer circumstances with walls, weapons and other so-called "defenses."

In this regard, it's helpful to understand that in both personal relationships, and in relationships between races and nations, defensiveness begets defensiveness. That is, defensiveness on one side often triggers it in the other. This can make the finding of a solution difficult, if not impossible. Yet if we understood that, like all feelings, defensiveness is based on "who we think we are", we could begin to move away from our traditional modes of dealing with conflict. Since I know the true source of my problem is within me, and since I am now more willing to take responsibility for my own actions and reactions, I can initiate an internal shift in my self-image before I engage (further) with you on the issue. The key is our willingness to take responsibility for all our feelings of threat, insecurity and defensiveness, rather than pushing them out on to the other party.

Defensiveness is actually a coping mechanism designed to deal with feelings of powerlessness. For instance, in my own life, I was conditioned from an early age to expect criticism. Since I had no positive tools to deal with someone else's disapproval or shaming, defensiveness became one of my mainstays. It was my (dysfunctional) attempt to take care of myself in difficult situations. Of course, acting defensively often back-fired, making things worse rather than better.

As an example, on several occasions when working as both a lawyer and photographer, I misinterpreted communications from my clients. I would get a call or an email that on first glance I interpreted as being critical of me and my work. Upset quickly followed and I often responded back very defensively. I was surprised to find that the client was surprised by my reaction. In my mind, they attacked me first, so I was justified in responding in kind. Yet in almost every case, after I had calmed down and I went over their original communication to me again, I could see I had totally misinterpreted what they had said. It was quite surreal to realize I was reacting to something that *wasn't actually there*. Because I felt so powerless to take care of myself in the face of someone else's supposed criticism, I was blinded by my own defensiveness. The result was I couldn't even read an email or listen to a phone call correctly. The fact that it happened more than once was a real eye-opener for me, and indicated clearly that the problem was within me and how I saw myself.

The subconscious thought that gives rise to defensiveness is that I am not going to be OK. My internal filtering process says I can't handle the situation, and that the end result will thus be painful. Accordingly, when I shift "who I think I am" and consciously choose to see myself as being able to take care of myself, this goes a long way in diminishing fear and thus defensiveness. As I change my idea about myself to something more positive, I react less and respond more. I also don't misinterpret other people's communications or question their motives. And today if I'm in a situation that actually does require me to defend myself, I'm better able to do so because I'm not starting from a place of fear or vulnerability.

Fear as the absence of love

According to *A Course in Miracles* we're only capable of two emotions – love or fear.[20] Love can be said to encompass all our positive feelings, while fear encircles all the negative ones. In terms of the relationship between these two emotions, *The Course* says, *"fear is the absence of love."*[21]

It's really interesting to think of fear this way. Basically it's saying the way to free ourselves of fear (or any other negative emotion) is to bring love to it. We don't have to fight against or resist fear (fighting or resisting anything always makes it stronger by the way). Rather we just need to bestow love upon ourselves or another and the fear will disappear. This is because a positive emotion can displace a negative one. The form the love takes may differ – could be understanding, forgiveness, compassion, tolerance, etc. But the result is the same. Let me give an example of how this has worked in my own life.

As I mentioned in the Introduction, the first two or three years after I transitioned from being a lawyer to a photographer not much was happening. I had my websites set up and got a few clients that way, but I wasn't doing anything really proactive to bring in business. I was actually sitting around watching TV and

---

[20] *A Course in Miracles*, pg. 246
[21] *A Course In Miracles*, Workbook for Students, Part II, Sect. 3

playing video games most of the day – not because I was lazy, but because, as we'll see in a minute, I was terrified of putting myself out there. I had some money saved from before I changed careers and was using that to supplement my income. As three years came and went, that savings had seriously diminished. I knew I was going to have to do something to generate business if I wanted to continue doing photography for a living.

So I decided I needed to do some marketing. An easy way to think of marketing is making your business visible. There are different methods, such as advertising, social media campaigns, networking, direct mail, email blasts, cold calls, etc.[22] The problem was most marketing efforts cost money and by that point I barely had enough to cover my living expenses. This meant I had to focus on low cost/no cost methods. I tried some networking events and asked friends and colleagues for referrals, but both of these were very hit or miss. Social media was just coming into its own, but because of my own judgmental nature, I had been resisting using Facebook. I also got started very late on Instagram.

So that left email marketing and cold calling. While I eventually did both, I'm going to focus on my experience with cold calling for now. It was good because it wouldn't cost me anything financially and since I wasn't working very much, I had the time. I had considered doing some cold calling for a couple of years prior, but my stomach turned in knots every time I thought about it. I found the whole idea too painful and frightening to really consider it a viable option. That was until now.[23]

We said earlier that fear is a mostly paralyzing emotion. But that in certain situations it can also be a motivator. While initially I resisted making calls, when I realized if I didn't do something soon I might be homeless, fear became a motivator. As preparation, I researched how to find prospects and what to say during a call. I wrote myself a little script so I wouldn't be

---

[22] If you are interested in some of the things I did to market my photography business check out this YouTube video - https://youtu.be/jYrPE2TvfvY
[23] The focus of my cold calling was my product photography www.greatproductshots.com and headshot www.superstarheadshots.com businesses.

fumbling for words (I fumbled anyway.) And soon I started making some calls.

Not many – only a few a day at first. But I was doing it. And it was mostly awful. Not because of the other people – they were usually quite nice and polite (nicer than I was to telemarketers who called me.) But because of me. I judged myself very harshly. I thought I sounded stupid on the phone. I questioned whether I was actually a good photographer and could provide anything of value to a potential customer. When I got off the phone I would routinely beat myself up for everything I just said and did. Even if the call went well, I would find a way to berate myself. Looking back I could see I was really merciless in my self-condemnation at times.

Not surprisingly, my fear manifested physically. Before almost every call my hands would shake and I would start to sweat. During calls my body would tremble and my voice often cracked. The physical discomfort mirrored the emotional discomfort. To make matters worse, I would usually beat myself up for being so afraid.

After a few weeks of making calls, someone actually said "Yes". I was totally surprised – shocked actually. So shocked that I asked them if they were sure they wanted to hire me and told them they could change their mind later. (Boy – did I beat myself up for that one!)

After booking that first client, I spent some time reflecting on the angst of the prior weeks. What I realized was profound: The fear I was feeling wasn't because of what someone else was doing to me – like I said, most people were quite pleasant. Not only did no one hang up on me; some had even gone out of their way to help me - they gave me the names of other people who might be interested even though they themselves weren't. Rather, what was causing all the fear and emotional turmoil was what I was doing to myself. Before and after nearly every call, I was *rejecting myself.* No matter how the conversation went, I would find a way to make myself wrong. Even when I got a positive result, I found ways to hate myself: *"You should have said this instead of that"*, *"Now they're gonna find out you don't really know what you're doing*", etc. On more than one occasion, my own self-hatred turned winning into losing!

The gift in this experience was realizing I wasn't afraid because of what they thought of me – I was afraid because of what *I* thought of me. As I mentioned earlier, it was the self-recrimination that was creating all my fear. It was awesome to see (and not in a good way) how much emotional turmoil my own lack of self-love could create in my life.

After this realization, I began trying to be nicer to myself, especially when making calls. I remembered that *A Course in Miracles* says *"fear is the absence of love,"* so I started trying to love myself more, both during and after calls. I stopped judging myself so much and tried to replace self-flagellation with self-congratulation. I attempted to learn from my mistakes instead of crucifying myself for them. I even praised myself out loud from time-to-time for a job well done. Not surprisingly, the nicer I was to myself, the more smoothly the calls went.

Looking back, I can see this shift in attitude toward myself lessened the fear. Nothing changed with the people I was calling – they were exactly the same as before. Rather, what had changed was I was being kind instead of cruel towards myself. The result was I had less fear. It was around this time that I also started submitting my fine art photos to shows and exhibitions, as well as for publication. As I mentioned in Chapter One, I had a tremendous amount of anxiety around submitting my work. Because I judged myself very harshly, I was paralyzed with the fear of rejection and criticism.

I decided to start by sending my photos to some small, local art shows. That first year I entered six shows. I had made a deal with myself to be nice to myself regardless of how those submissions went. While I was preparing each application, I monitored my thoughts and tried to be aware of any negative self-talk. When I noticed I was being unkind to myself, I consciously tried to counteract that with encouraging thoughts and words, sometimes saying nice things out-loud.

The result was I got into two shows that first year. Even more surprising was I won Third Place in one of them! Winning that award was a really life changing experience – in fact, it was the shock of my life! (I'll talk a lot more about that particular experience in my workshops and seminars, so if you want to find out what actually happened, sign up for a workshop soon!) As for the shows which rejected my photos, I didn't judge or beat myself up for failing. I also made a decision not to take it personally. That too, was a life changing experience. It sounds a little crazy when I say it now, but all those little efforts to be nicer to myself unlocked some exciting new doors for me.

What kind of doors? I mentioned previously all the awards, exhibitions and accolades I've received the past few years. I have had several great work opportunities come to me as well. One I haven't yet mentioned is that I became an Official Photographer for one of the preeminent fireworks performance companies in the world. I've made several national and international trips for them the past two and a half years photographing their fireworks displays, including four Guinness World Record[24] performances.

Looking back I can honestly say almost all my awards and achievements were made possible by me simply being nicer to myself. Yes, it took a lot of time and hard work to achieve what I've achieved. But none of this would have been possible if I was still more into hating myself than being nice to myself. It's pretty clear to me now that the hard work of building a business is so much easier when I'm willing to forgive my mistakes and shortcomings – rather than crucify myself for them. It turns out the best Business Plan for me – and anyone else who wants to run a successful business – is to love ourselves! More about this in Chapter Five.

"You Should Go and Love Yourself"

By making all these changes, I was knocking down the fear and putting self-love into action. For years I had heard how important it was to love yourself. Yet I had no idea what that meant or how to do it. Do I buy myself flowers? Do I take myself

---

[24] https://www.peteralessandriaphotography.com/blog/2019/2/guinness-world-record---official-participant

out on a date? (I actually did try those things back in the day – you gotta love those personal empowerment workshops in California in the '90s!) If not all that, what the heck does it mean to love one's self?

I see now that self-love can be as simple as saying encouraging things to myself, treating myself with understanding and compassion, accepting myself even with all my flaws, and being really kind and gentle with myself no matter what. It means treating myself the way I would treat someone I really loved. It turns out self-love means doing many of the same things for ourselves that we do for another person when we love them.

I will acknowledge it's often easier to love myself when I'm doing all the things I think I'm supposed to do. When I'm making marketing calls for my business, submitting my work to shows, working on this book, etc. The real test, however, is how I treat myself when I'm not able to do any of that stuff. Because there are still days when I'm not able to do any of that stuff. Thus, for me, the truest measure of success is:

How much I love myself when I least like who I'm being.

Can I be kind to myself when I'm frightened, distracted or depressed? Will I still be nice to myself on the days I can't get off the couch? Will I encourage myself when I don't even want to get dressed or leave the house? When I can do these things – and I'm not saying I always can – my life gets better. I am learning to replace fear and self-loathing with love and that's proving to be a very good thing.

Unconditional Love

In relationships, lack of love can take many forms. For instance, we may judge, criticize or physically or verbally abuse another. Or it can be more subtle as in ignoring them or withholding our approval when they're not being who we want them to be. Withholding love by withholding approval is a common form of punishment – parents do this with children, bosses do it with employees, spouses do it with each other – and I've done it with myself.

Yet, just like self-love means being willing to love ourselves when we least like who we're being, loving another means continuing to love them even when they present us with the worst of themselves. The kid who embarrasses us in public with a tantrum; the spouse who has been hiding gambling debts or an affair; the co-worker who takes credit for our hard work, and so on. Each of these is an opportunity to extend love rather than fear. Similar to the concept of "True Happiness" which we discussed at the end of Chapter Three, "True," or "Unconditional Love" means making a decision based solely on an internal reference. We make the choice to love irrespective of what the other person is doing or being. Turns out "unconditional" love is just that: there are no conditions under which we withhold our love, whether for ourselves or another. We offer love no matter what.

Many think loving another means we're approving of what they're doing or being. This is not so. Like "True Happiness," the choice to love unconditionally is an arbitrary choice *vis-à-vis* the outside world. It's made solely on our own internal reference of "who we want to be" in life. As such, it has nothing to do with the other person or what they're doing or being. While there may be consequences for that person's actions or attitude, our choices reflect only our own internal desire to be who we are being.

As I stated earlier, loving another doesn't mean we stop loving ourselves. Showing love for other people doesn't require that we tolerate their inappropriate or harmful behavior. But it does mean we don't attack back or punish them for what they're doing. We may decide to get the heck out of there – but we find a way to do it with love. People often react with anger or judgment when they don't like what someone else is doing. We'll discuss these emotions in Chapter Six. For now understand that both anger and judgment are an extension of fear. Anger is a way we try to make others feel guilty for what they're doing. Judgment is an attempt to make them wrong for who they're being. Making others wrong is a way we try to make ourselves right, and thus see ourselves as superior to them.

The last thing I want to say about unconditional love is it usually means letting go of our agendas for other people. For many of us, there is a fine line between caring about another person and trying to control their lives. While usually well-intentioned and born out of a genuine desire to help, we can at times seek to impose our own view of things onto another person. Because we think we can see the problem in a way the other person can't, we form an opinion on what's needed to help. Thus, when it comes time to help that person we can often have an unspoken agenda that says, *"I know better than you what's good for you."* That agenda then "flavors" any assistance we may otherwise render.

Now again, this is often birthed from a sincere desire to help. And it is true that we are sometimes too close to our own problems to see them clearly. Yet, as I said earlier, it's easy to slip from caring to control. When we try to help, we may end up pushing our views on to them, only to find out our opinions were not asked for nor welcomed. Thinking we know better what someone else needs to get their life together can be condescending and/or disrespectful – especially if they haven't asked for our opinion. It assumes the other person can't take care of themselves.

So then, how can we provide assistance to the people we love? Well for me, the first thing I try to do is let go of the idea that someone else needs my "help." The word "help" implies they have a "problem" and "problem" implies they need to be "fixed." It's up to the other person – not me – to decide if what they are dealing with is a problem or not. And it's certainly not up to me to fix anyone. Rather, I try to think of it as me offering "assistance", or even better, being of "service" to that person.

Now you may be thinking, *"What's the difference – these are just words – they all mean approximately the same thing."* I'll remind you first, this is just for me. If you have another way that works for you, great. Next, the idea is that I am actually only assisting someone else in solving their own issue. They are capable of taking the lead, I'm just there to render whatever assistance I can. Likewise, in terms of service, I am there to serve their own agenda for themselves. This is very different than pushing my agenda for what I think they need upon them.

The thing that's necessary when either offering assistance or being of service is I first have to find out what outcome they want to achieve in the particular situation. I can usually do this by asking. Then I have to decide whether or not I can serve that agenda. This is respectful of both them and me. I'm not pushing my solution on them. But I may also decide, after hearing what they think they want or need, that I can't support them – at least not in that way. Thus I may decline to render any assistance. Doing this little analysis is my way of taking care of myself.

Of course, the second part of the equation is not making them wrong for a plan we can't support. Judging someone else for anything is not loving them. Let's look at an example:

Suppose a close friend or family member is having financial problems. They come to you to ask for money. They have children they are responsible for and their lack of money is impacting their ability to care for their family. You are amenable to loaning or gifting them some cash – until you find out their plan. They want to take the money to the track and bet on a horse they believe "can't lose" (they think they have inside info from the horse's trainer and are thus sure they can triple the money.)

Now all of a sudden you have a dilemma. You love this person and want to be of assistance. Yet you feel strongly that this is not a sound use of the money (perhaps you have your own negative experiences with gambling, etc). You also realize that you don't actually know how things would turn out – this might actually go well for them (though you're pretty sure the bet panning out in the way describe is unlikely.) Beyond that, you also trust that something much larger is going on in your life and this other person's life. Thus, what seems to be happening right here and now may not be the big picture. For instance, it may actually benefit this person in the long run to have a negative experience with taking chances with their family's money like this. They could learn a very valuable lesson. On the other hand, since you've been reading this book, you know loving another doesn't mean you stop loving yourself. So it's up to you to take care of yourself (and your money) so you don't feel resentful of them (and actually yourself) later. Finally, you also know that whatever you choose to do, making either them or you wrong for your respective choices can't be part of it. So what to do...

You give the situation a lot of thought. You also speak to other people about it, but find none of their solutions would really work for you. (One person kindly – but naively – suggests moving the kids in with you until the adult gets back on their feet. The other person says they have their *own* insider tip on a horse that can't lose and that they can *quadruple* – rather than just triple – your family member's bet.) Eventually you decide to sit down again with the person you're trying to assist and propose the following: you tell them you really appreciate their desire to improve the financial situation for themselves and their kids. You also acknowledge them for trying to be innovative and for "thinking outside the box." But you then share your concern that this may not turn out to be a sound use of the money. In addition, you share your own experience in similar situations, acknowledging responsibility for your own poor choices or decisions. You then tell them you are respectfully going to decline giving them the money for their intended purpose, but that you have an alternative solution you'd like to present to them.

You then propose an option that would work for you. For instance, you might agree to setup a credit account at a local grocery store. This would allow them to buy groceries for the family, but you have decided to exclude particular items, such as alcohol or tobacco. And you may only agree to do this for a specified period of time. After that, they would need to find another way. Thus, while you have decided you can't support their original agenda, you propose an alternative that would work for you.

Now you have done very well: you didn't make them wrong or shame them for their idea. Instead, you acknowledged them for trying to be innovative and for wanting a better life for their family. You also took care of yourself by not agreeing to an agenda which you couldn't support. They may or may not accept your offer, but you have honored yourself while not making them wrong. Thus we can say:

Unconditional love means wanting for another what they want for themselves. And at the same time honoring ourselves and not making anyone wrong for their choices.

So is loving unconditionally easier said than done? As always. But what else is there for us to strive for? Has "conditionally" loving ourselves or another made our lives easier or more worth living? Does attacking others for their mistakes lessen conflict and bring more peace into our lives? Can we find serenity using anger to make others feel guilty or judgment to make them feel less-than? Real love is unconditional. "Conditional love" would be an oxymoron. This is for the simple reason that if it's conditional, it ain't love.

Taking our power back

In the last chapter we talked about some of the ways we give our power away, such as by blaming others, making excuses, seeing ourselves as victims, etc. We give our power away anytime we let an external situation or event dictate our internal state. It turns out that being afraid is the biggest way most of us do this. When we're consumed with fear we're in effect saying, "*External event or situation – you decide for me how I should think, feel, speak or act.*" Of course, we now know that nothing external to us can do this. Yet we have to apply that knowledge to take our power back. The best way to do this is to face our fears directly by getting into action.

For example, when I picked up the phone to make a cold call, I was taking my power back. Prior to that, fear was paralyzing me. I couldn't get myself to do anything and I felt terrible. Yet every time I pushed through my fear and made a call I experienced a surge of energy. I felt empowered by my action rather than disempowered by my fears. When we face what we're afraid of, we are literally changing "who we think we are." This is because we must see ourselves differently to do things differently. Taking on something that previously terrified us proves we're no longer giving our power away to our fear.

Yet if fear is the absence of love, then in any fearful situation the key is to love ourselves enough so we can take all the scary actions and push through our fears. Self-love makes it safe for us to do the often frightening things we need to do to overcome our fear. Whether it's starting a business, looking for a job, or asking someone out on a date, we have to love ourselves enough to feel safe so we can do it. Safe from what? In most cases, safe from our own self-recrimination. Recall that it was my self-recrimination that made cold-calling so difficult at first. It's very tough to accomplish anything extraordinary in life when we're mired in fear and self-loathing.

False Evidence Appearing Real

We started this chapter by talking about the difference between fear and caution. We said caution was a rational response to the vicissitudes of life, while fear is often an irrational, disproportionate reaction based on our own subjective perceptions. Thus, for reasons which should become obvious shortly, the last and probably most important thing we can say about fear is, *it's not real*. Being irrational, disproportionate and subjective, fear has no objective basis in reality. This is shown by the fact that each person's experience in a given situation will be different, being based entirely on how they see themselves rather than what seems to be going on around them. If everyone's experience is different, then none of those individual experiences can be real, at least not in an objective, true-for-everyone sense. Let's look at an example.

Suppose there's a building on your street that's engulfed in flames. You know there are people inside and your mind is racing as you try to figure out how you can help. After assessing the situation, you quickly come to the conclusion that this is probably way more than you can handle. You've already called the police but while you're waiting you're frozen in place. You're torn between the thought that the people inside need help right *now* and the fear you could easily lose your own life if you go into that building.

Thankfully, a moment later a fire truck arrives. Several fire men and women jump off the truck, throw on their protective gear and rush right into the middle of that burning building. They rescue all the inhabitants and eventually put out the fire. You stand relieved and grateful: the people inside were saved – and you weren't the one who had to do it.

Now there are a few important points to be gleaned from this little incendiary adventure:

First, whose perception of the situation was correct? You were paralyzed with fear; the firefighters apparently not so much. We could say the fear was real for you. But does that mean it was real in fact? This is especially true if other people don't seem as bothered by the situation. If the fear isn't shared by everyone, can we say it's real?

Second, and more importantly, hopefully by now you can recognize that your fear was based on how you saw yourself in the situation and not the situation itself. Your experience was the result of your subjective interpretation of "who you thought you were" *vis-à-vis* the fire. The rescue personnel's experience of the same circumstances was apparently very different. Because they saw themselves as being able to handle the situation their reactions were motivating rather than paralyzing. Yes, they may have felt some trepidation as they entered the building. And yes, it may have taken years of training and thousands of dollars worth of protective equipment for them to see themselves in this more positive way. But clearly their response reflected a very different concept of themselves than yours did.

Now with regard to this specific example, thankfully neither you nor I will probably ever face a situation where the stakes are so high. But in most cases we also won't need years of training and thousands of dollars worth of protective equipment to change "who we think we are." Rather, it will likely take much less to see ourselves as equal to the task at hand. Thus, the reason we can say fear is not real is because when we change "who we think we are" in a given situation, it will disappear. If something can be made to disappear so easily, can it be real? I'll leave that up to you to decide.

Why we do what we do

As we bring this chapter to a close, hopefully now we have a new way to address our fears. Seeing ourselves differently – as always – is the path to a new experience. We also said a few moments ago that changing "who we think we are" by getting into action is the best way to overcome our fears. So it's important to look closer at what motivates us to take action and do the things we do. It turns out that all our choices and decisions have a very specific purpose. The particular situations and thus actions may be different. But the purpose behind those actions is always the same. We'll take a closer look at what that purpose is in the next chapter.

TAKEAWAYS:

1. The only thing we have to fear is fear itself. Fear is based on a false image of ourselves.

2. Fear is an *emotional response to a perception of ourselves as powerless and/or unlovable in a given situation*. Generally speaking, fear is a paralyzing emotion.

3. Emotion = energy in motion. When we feel good emotionally we have more energy and it's easier to get stuff done. When we're not feeling good emotionally the opposite is true.

4. Our ancestors were well served by the hypervigilance of the limbic brain; modern man, not so much so. For many of us, the fight or flight response is way over-utilized. False-positives release high doses of adrenalin and cortisol into our bodies which over the long term can damage the body.

5. There's a difference between "fear" and "caution." Caution means we take reasonable precautions based on an objective assessment of the situation. Fear is generally neither rational nor proportional. Whether paralyzing or adrenalizing, reacting with fear often does more harm than good.

6. Fear is situational. Acute feelings of fear usually arise in relation to specific people and/or circumstances. Like all emotional reactions, fear is caused by how we see ourselves in a particular situation.

7. Many of us have one or two primary problems in life: we perceive ourselves as unlovable and/or we perceive ourselves as powerless. These two core beliefs can affect everything we think, feel, say and do. Because these ideas are usually buried in our subconscious mind we are often completely unaware that they are running our lives.

8. When we see ourselves as unlovable, we are rejecting and abandoning ourselves. When we see ourselves as powerless, we believe we can't take care of ourselves. Both ideas give rise to feelings of fear, sadness and/or depression.

9. A sense of danger means that "who we think we are" in that situation is someone who will suffer injury, pain, loss or death. Yet we can't always trust ourselves to objectively assess whether a danger is real or imagined because the limbic brain can easily slip into overdrive and see a threat where there is none.

10. If we're insecure in any relationship, our fear is not that we'll lose the other person's love; our fear is the loss of our *own* love. Insecurity can be a reflection of the fact that who we think we are is unworthy or unlovable. It's our own self-abandonment that is often the source of our emotional pain when a relationship ends.

11. Feelings of sadness or grief naturally follow any loss. The magnitude of the feelings will vary but if we're devastated, angry, vengeful or incapacitated by depression, something else is going on.

12. No one makes us feel anything. All our emotional reactions – both positive and negative – originate within us. The good feelings we associate with someone special liking us are actually feelings we generate within ourselves.

13. The ego is always out to get something and knows nothing of giving. We feel anger and/or self-pity when we think something has been taken away from us. The ego will always blame someone or something else for this sense of loss or deprivation and direct its displeasure accordingly.

14. The amazing feeling of chemistry and attraction we sometimes feel is not true love. When someone we think is special thinks we're special, the ego is in heaven. When we think the other person no longer sees us this way, the ego is in hell.

15. There is nothing more important than building a child's self-esteem. How we treat them day-after-day is what teaches a child whether they're a valuable and worthy person. The more they feel valuable inside, the less they'll seek a sense of value and specialness outside.

16. Regularly punishing, shaming, or blaming a child will impact them much more than giving them trophies or not. A sense of entitlement only comes from people who lack self-esteem. People who are full of themselves in a positive, healthy way give of their abundance.

17. When we see ourselves as "less than," we have an investment in the other person liking us. We will feel more valuable and worthy if someone we think is more valuable than us, likes

us. Fear of another person leaving stems from the subconscious belief that we will be "worth-less" if they leave us.

18. George Clooney drives an Audi® - and so do I!

19. What other people think of us is none of our business. No one has the power to hurt us unless we give them that power.

20. We're responsible for the people we pick. We can't continually ignore the warning signs and then try to pin all our emotional distress on the other person.

21. The loss of our identity can be scary for many of us. Fear of the unknown can be greater than the pain of the known.

22. Defensiveness is a form of fear. It is a way to deal with feelings of powerlessness and as such is a coping mechanism.

23. Defensiveness begets defensiveness. This can make conflict resolution difficult, if not impossible.

24. "Fear is the absence of love" – We don't have to fight against or resist fear; rather we just need to bring love to ourselves or another and the fear will disappear.

25. Self-love can be as simple as being kind to ourselves no matter what. It means treating ourselves the way we would treat someone we really loved.

26. It's easy to love ourselves when we're doing all the things we think we're supposed to do. The real test, however, is how much we love ourselves when we least like who we're being. (The same is true of how much we love other people.)

27. "Unconditional love" is just that: there are no conditions under which we withhold our love. This doesn't mean we

approve of what someone else is doing. But it does mean we don't attack or punish them for it. All true love is unconditional.

28. Unconditional love means wanting for another what they want for themselves; while honoring ourselves and not making either party wrong if you disagree.

29. We have to face our fears to take our power back. The best way to do this is by getting into action.

30. Fear is not real. It's a subjective interpretation of an external event based on "who we think we are."

EXERCISES:

1. Think of one or more situations where you are afraid. Write about how perceiving yourself as powerless and/or unlovable in each of those situations gives rise to fear. Then write how you would have to change "who you think you are" to overcome the fear.

2. Identify three additional situations where you feel fear (other than those you identified in #1 above). Write about how each would be different if you approached them with caution rather than fear.

3. Describe one or more situations in your life where your initial response was fearful but it later turned out there was nothing to be afraid of. How can you judge better next time whether the danger is real or not?

4. *"I only have two problems: I perceive myself as unlovable and I perceive myself as powerless."* Agree or disagree? Discuss.

5. Think about one or more relationships where another person left you and you felt rejected and/or betrayed. Write about:

   a. The basis of your feelings. Was it based on them abandoning you? Or was it based on you abandoning yourself?

   b. Did you see yourself as unequal to them? If so, how did that affect who you thought you were during the relationship and how you felt after it ended?

   c. Write about a relationship where another person left you and you did *not* feel abandoned or rejected. What was different about that situation?

6. Write 10 times on a large piece of paper or whiteboard:

   "What other people think of me is none of my business."
   "No one has the power to hurt me unless I give them that power."

   Repeat once each day for a week. Then place these messages on your refrigerator and/or bathroom mirror so you can see them every day.

7. Pick all that apply from the following questions and write out your answers (if none apply make up your own):
   Who would I be without my anger?
   Who would I be without my depression?
   Who would I be if I weren't a victim?
   Who would I be without my financial problems?
   Who would I be without this illness?
   Who would I be if people were always kind and considerate of me?

8. Describe three situations where you were defensive. Did being defensive help or hurt you in those situations? Did your

defensiveness trigger someone else's defensiveness? What effect did that have in terms of resolving the conflict?

9. If fear is the absence of love, describe at least three situations where you can see how bringing love to yourself or another would alleviate fear and/or help resolve a conflict.

10. Unconditional love – Describe three situations where you realize your love for another or yourself was conditional. How would you have to be different if your love in those situations was unconditional?

11. When it comes to helping others, do you often push your agendas on them since "you know better" what they need to do to improve their situation? Discuss.

12. What does it mean to love yourself when you least like who you are being? What does it mean to love another when you least like who they are being?

13. *"Fear is not real."* Agree, disagree. Why.

14. Facing your fears – Identify at least three places in your life where you are stuck because of fear. Write about what you would need to do to get your power back. What would you have to do (what actions do you need to take) to face your fears in each one of those situations?

Chapter Five
Decision-Making & The Desire To Feel Better

"I feel good!"

-James Brown[25]

We talked previously about taking responsibility for all our choices and decisions, as well as using our True Power to create our lives. In this chapter we're going to look at the motivation behind those choices and decisions. We're going to reveal the true reason for why we do what we do and want what we want. We can't make better choices if we don't understand the underlying basis for our decision-making.

"I'm OK; You're OK"
In his best-selling 1992 book *"Homecoming"*, the late John Bradshaw said every child needs to know two things: 1) that their parents are OK, and 2) that the child matters (i.e., is important to his or her parents). Both of these needs arise out of the child's survival instincts – if either isn't met, the child may not survive.

In terms of our parents being OK, the reality is all people, including most parents, have issues. Of course, some of us have more than others, but having issues is part of the human condition. Because the child's survival is dependent upon their parent(s) being OK, the child will naturally attempt to

---

[25] https://www.youtube.com/watch?v=B1wOK9yGUYM

compensate for their parents' dysfunction. This compensation can take different forms as we'll discuss below.

Likewise, while healthy parents are naturally attentive to their kids, even the best parents can sometimes ignore them or send mixed messages as to how much the child matters. The need to know their parents care is so strong that children who don't get enough positive attention may engage in disruptive or inappropriate behavior to get negative attention. This is their attempt to receive the assurance they need that they matter.[26]

In terms of counterbalancing their parents' not OK-ness, some things a child might do include: trying to be "perfect" so as not to upset the parent; denying their own needs and wants so they will be less of a burden to their parents; becoming their parent's therapist, confidante, "best friend" and/or surrogate spouse; or taking on the role of the family hero or scapegoat. There may be other strategies as well. The thing all these strategies have in common is that they are attempts to provide stability and emotional support for a troubled parent and/or for the family. Yet any efforts to compensate for a parent's issues always come at the child's expense. Most children are simply not capable of care-taking their parents' emotional, psychological or social needs.

Again, none of this is about blaming our parents. As I said in Chapter One, parenting is hands-down the toughest job on the planet. Our parents all did (and in some cases are still doing) the best they could. Even the most challenged parents can instill many great qualities in their children. Most are really good people, truly loving and infinitely patient, wanting only the best for their offspring. If you're a parent, go easy on yourself. You may not have gotten everything you needed during your own childhood so it may be difficult to give what you don't have.

I personally believe the best gift we can bestow upon our children (at any age by the way) is to model self-love and self-forgiveness, as well as resolving our un-resolved issues. So in addition to forgiving your own parents, if you are a parent, forgive

---

[26] Negative behavior may also be an expression of anger or resentment, especially in older children.

yourself early and often for any mistakes you've made. Then do your best to move through your issues and resolve your past.

Fear and self-loathing in Las Vegas

In Chapter Two, we said that children naturally believe what their parents tell them. They are trusting by nature. If told (by words or actions) that they are bad or naughty often enough, these ideas become a permanent part of the child's belief system. Likewise, every time a child is yelled at, blamed, shamed or hit, their self-esteem diminishes. The message they receive is they are not worthy of being loved the way they are. Self-hatred (*"I'm bad and deserve to be punished"*) can follow.

We also said many of our childhood experiences, both within the family and outside of it, can be terribly confusing and frightening. For instance, most kids don't understand why adults fight or argue. They only know all the screaming and yelling (and sometimes hitting) is really scary. As a result, a child can feel powerless and alone. Since their parents are the source of their discomfort, the child may not have anyone to turn to for support or to be consoled. Also, since many parents have not made peace with their own feelings, such as sadness, anger or fear, they shame the child when the child exhibits any of these emotions. Continually shutting down the child's expression of negative emotions – or even worse, shaming them for having those emotions – causes these feelings to become trapped inside the child.

The combination of fear, self-loathing and stuffed emotions inherent in the less-than-perfect upbringing many of us experience can create problems for us later in life. These problems include codependency, relationship problems, health problems, low-self esteem, depression and many types of addictive/compulsive behavior. Addictions and compulsive behaviors, in particular, are about coping with emotional trauma and stress. They can be an attempt to escape or soothe the pain brought on by our difficult childhood experiences. Mood-altering substances or behaviors are our dysfunctional way of easing the suffering of a damaged psyche and a frightened mind.

Having wrestled with addictive and compulsive behavior myself, I will say I have nothing but compassion and heartfelt understanding for those of us who are so afflicted. There are obviously many negative consequences associated with addictions and the addictions themselves can ultimately (inevitably?) become quite self-destructive. Acting out in the addiction itself often feeds the cycle of guilt and shame that further increases the need to mood-alter. The addict can easily hate themselves for being addicted. Eventually it becomes a self-perpetuating downward spiral of shame and self-loathing.

Twelve Step recovery programs have played a big part in helping me overcome certain unhealthy, compulsive behaviors in my own life. I also personally know dozens and dozens of other people who have similarly benefitted from getting into recovery. Twelve Step programs are a proven way to deal with an addiction and carry-on with a productive life. While I haven't personally experienced other, non-12 Step rehabilitation programs, they too seem to provide assistance to certain people with particular problems. The point is, if you suspect you may be suffering from an addiction or other type of compulsive behavior, help is available. Most recovery programs have websites and phone numbers where you can get information anonymously. So don't be afraid to reach out. The thing to remember is there is no shame in addressing a particular issue in your life that's causing you problems. Millions and millions of people around the world have benefitted directly or indirectly from the recovery process. Not only is the addicted person helped, but their family, friends, clients, co-workers and neighbors also often benefit when someone gets help with their problems.

At a certain point in the 12 Step recovery process, it is suggested we take a personal moral inventory of ourselves. This happens in Step Four. We look at our part in all the negative (and if we have an enlightened sponsor, positive) events and circumstances of our lives. This looking at our part is the precursor to taking responsibility for our own harmful behavior, both to ourselves and others. It eventually culminates in us making amends to those we have harmed. By admitting the exact nature of our wrongs and setting things right, we take our power back and free ourselves from the bonds of guilt and self-hatred.

We'll discuss this important question of *"what was my part in this"* in greater depth in Chapter Seven when we talk about Forgiveness. For now, note that it's a great question to ask any time there is conflict in our lives. This is true whether we're in recovery or not. It's a crucial inquiry in taking responsibility and thus getting our power back. Some people may say, *"What about their part in what happened? Don't other people need to take responsibility for the harm they've done to us? Why do we have to apologize to them before they apologize to us?"*

These are good questions. My answer is we each have to decide for ourselves what is in fact justified with respect to our part vs. someone else's. I can say from my own experience, however, if I'm sitting around waiting for someone else to apologize to me before I apologize to them, I may be in for a very long wait. I have also noticed that in my own life, especially before I got into recovery, I was convinced it was everyone else's fault that I did the things I did. This included, at times, getting even with them for their less-than-loving actions and attitudes towards me. Thus, I make an amends for any of my own wrongful behavior directed towards others – irrespective of what they did or didn't do "to deserve it."

Again, we're not making excuses for someone else's harmful or unloving behavior. Yet as we said in Chapter Three, when we deny responsibility for our own actions and reactions, we are powerless to change them. Whether you're in recovery or not, I would urge you to take responsibility for your side of the street. This means looking at what you've done that may have caused harm to another, and letting go of what you think they did to you. We can give that to a Greater Consciousness and allow it to work things out for the highest good of everyone involved. That said, I have noticed in my own life that when I offer another person an apology, they will sometimes take it as a cue for their own apology to me. This doesn't always happen and we can't make an apology for that reason. But I can say the more willing I am to take responsibility for my part, the more others seem to be willing to do the same for theirs.

Admitting to someone we have harmed the exact nature of our wrongs is a huge and often life-changing step. When we offer an amends, we are agreeing to make restitution and/or do whatever else is necessary to make things right. Yet restitution is not always enough – an apology would be quite meaningless if we eventually returned to our old ways. So, in addition to doing what's needed to set things right, we may also offer a so-called "living amends." This means changing our behavior, now and in the future, towards that person. In fact, a true living amends means we forever change our ways with respect to that issue towards everyone and anyone we encounter.

As I mentioned earlier, making an amends can be a very empowering process. However, this is contingent on us letting go of the shame and guilt we may feel for our harmful behavior. Most of us feel bad (guilty, shameful, remorseful) when we do something that injures another person. If we use any part of the amends process to beat ourselves up, we won't be healed. This is one reason I emphasized earlier that responsibility is not the same as blame. Self-forgiveness must accompany the amends process in order for our healing to be complete.

You often hear people in 12 Step programs speak about "the disease" or the "ism" (e.g., alcohol*ism*). This is the thing that plagues the addict and leads to unmanageability in their lives. For me, the true disease – the underlying cause of all afflictions – is *self-hatred*. It's the sum total of the negative core beliefs many of us have about ourselves that says we are bad or guilty or unlovable and thus we deserve to suffer. It reflects an idea that we are unworthy of being loved as we are. Thus, it's my belief that self-hatred is the ultimate source of pain from which we try to escape through our addictions. It's not uncommon for addicts to conclude that what they've done, both to themselves and others, places them beyond redemption. For many then, the addiction itself can become yet another reason to loathe and despise themselves.

I am of the mind that no matter what we have done, no matter how far down the scale we have gone[27], no matter what sins we may have committed, none of us is beyond redemption. This seems to be one of the hardest things for many of us to accept, both in and out of recovery. Most people crucify themselves for being less than perfect. "Who we think we are" is defined by our terrible thoughts, words and deeds. While no one gets to escape the consequences of their actions, those consequences don't have to include self-punishment and/or self-recrimination. I personally believe we're all good people, often plagued by difficult and sometimes frightening experiences, that have to learn how to make better choices in life.

I started out this book by saying the question of "who do you think you are" is the most important question we can ask. This is because whoever we think we are is who we will be in life. Thus, if we think we are unworthy, unforgiveable and beyond redemption, that will be our experience. Likewise, if we can begin to see the good in us, despite the unloving things we may have done, our experience of life can change. For me, it's not the harmful things we've done over the course of our lives that are the problem. Those can almost always be corrected. The true problem is that we hate ourselves for doing or being those things. I'll say again, hating oneself never helped anyone become a better person.

The ability to choose

In Chapter Three, when we discussed "True Power", I said we *always* have the ability to choose, and ultimately the ability to change, our thoughts, feelings, words and actions. That is, as long as we're alive, conscious and of a relatively sound mind, we have power over our actions and reactions. We may currently be making terrible, harmful or even self-destructive choices. But that doesn't mean we're not choosing.

We also said that no one and nothing outside of us has power over us. Our thoughts, feelings, words and actions are always

---

[27] *Alcoholics Anonymous*, pg. 83-84 (also known as the "AA Big Book")

dictated by our own internal decision-making process. And then we said no one does anything they don't want to do. Even with a gun to our heads, we're still choosing. This last position seems a little extreme – yet it *must* be this way if we are to have free-will. Anything less and we're heading down a slippery-slope of avoiding responsibility for our choices by blaming others. Every excuse robs us of some of our power.

In a moment, I am going to apply the ideas that a) we always have the ability to choose what we do, and b) that we do everything we do because we want to, to our addictive and compulsive behaviors. But before I do that, I want to say that I understand – deeply and from firsthand knowledge – how difficult it can be to overcome an addiction. I also understand and acknowledge that other people may have a different opinion from what I am about to say. So I want to remind you that I am speaking only for myself in the next few paragraphs. As they say in recovery programs, "*take what you like and leave the rest.*"

When beginning any 12 Step program, it is suggested we make an admission of powerlessness and unmanageability around the particular substance or behavior that is the focus of that program. This admission is necessary to break the denial that many of us carry regarding the severity of the problem. It's only when we admit "complete defeat"[28] regarding our ability to kick the habit or quit the addiction on our own, that we can take the first steps towards our recovery.

Now while I technically agree that we are powerless over anything that is not our thoughts, feelings, words and actions – including substances like drugs or alcohol – I have spent the better part of 140 pages trying to show that we are not powerless over our choices. This includes using substances or behaviors to escape from life. Again, I'll say that while we may be making terrible choices, this does not mean we are not choosing.

Thus, while I agree an addiction can be so strong that it *feels* like a substance has power over us, ultimately I think it is far

---

[28] *Alcoholics Anonymous*, pg 21.
https://www.aa.org/assets/en_US/en_step1.pdf

more helpful for me to take full responsibility for all my choices. This is true no matter how insane or self-destructive those choices may be. And because I've taken blame out of the responsibility equation, then when I take full responsibility for all my choices and decisions – even the self-destructive ones – I am actually empowering and loving myself.

Now again, I know other people hold a different opinion on this issue and I respect their point of view as valid for them. Yet, because as we'll discuss in a minute, whether as addicts or "normal people" we do everything we do for a very specific reason, it's preferable for me to look at things as follows: *I do everything I do because I choose to.* I prefer to take this approach rather than to imply that a particular substance or behavior has the ability to usurp my will.

Do I need help to make a new choice and see the insanity of my current behavior? For sure. Does that help come through other people and/or a Power Greater Than Myself? I believe so, yes. Yet I also believe it's only by taking full responsibility for my actions that I can be helped. Without my willingness and consent, a Greater Power cannot intervene on my behalf. Thus, it's by owning all my insanity that I ultimately get my power back.

Whether we're in a 12 Step program or not, most of us spend a good part of our lives blaming other people and/or circumstances for how we feel and what we do. For instance, someone might say, "*I drink because my spouse nags me/my kids drive me crazy*!" Yet we now know blaming others or making excuses means we're giving our power away. We also know that no one makes us do anything. When we give our power away long enough, we render ourselves powerless to change our own lives. This sense of powerlessness then leads to more fear and often to more craziness.

Of course, to the person who claims the source of their problem is outside of them, the belief that someone or something else is the cause of their behaviors seems very true. In their mind it's obvious that the discomfort they feel is not their fault and so they are justified in doing what they do. Since they have no other way to handle things, they've learned to rely on a substance or behavior to help them through.

When we're unaware that the true cause of our distress is what's happening inside of us, it's easy to see ourselves as helpless in the face of other people's choices. This sense of helplessness can drive the addiction as well as leaving us overwhelmed, angry and resentful. Yet it's only by becoming willing to accept full responsibility for our lives that we can get our power back and ultimately overcome the addiction. This is the purpose and goal of most recovery programs. But of course, this is impossible as long as "who we think we are" is a victim of someone else's choices or behaviors.

If there's resistance to saying, "*I do everything I do because I choose to,*" especially in relation to addictive or compulsive behaviors, I sense it's because of the shame and guilt many of us feel when faced with our own poor choices in life. When looked at through the eyes of an addict, we must be bad, f'ed up people to behave this way. "Normal" people don't have to drink or drug themselves to death. Again, I'll say responsibility is not the same as blame. It is not a sentence of guilt or evidence of unworthiness. We're not bad or even wrong (more about that in a minute) for anything we do – even if it's totally messed up and self destructive! Once again we're talking about "forgiveness." As we'll see in Chapter Seven, it's only by forgiving our own and other people's pasts that we can move into the future.

Why we do what we do

OK, so I keep saying there's a reason we all do what we do. Let's leave the topic of addictive and compulsive behavior behind for the time being (though we will come back to it shortly), and look closer at this question. The following covers any and every choice we can make as human beings. It includes everything from taking a shower to decorating our home to who we marry to what team we root for in the World Series. The two main things that motivate all our choices and decisions in life are:

we want to look good
and
we want to feel good.

Examine your own life – I bet you'll see one or both of these were behind every decision you've ever made. For instance, think about what you had for breakfast this morning. If you're like most people, this one is easy – we choose the food we eat because we enjoy it and/or because we think it will help us stay healthy. Enjoying it or staying healthy means we feel good. In fact, the choice to eat anything at all is based on the notion that eating feels good – especially when we're really hungry!

Likewise, why did you wear the clothes you wore today? If you're like me and were home alone all day (writing this book!), your choice was probably based on comfort. Comfort = feeling good. However, if you went someplace outside your home, you may have made your choice based on wanting to have a particular appearance. This may include choosing clothes that are stylish or that help you fit-in socially and so on. The choice to wear something that you think will make you attractive or acceptable is founded on the desire to look good.

Most advertising plays to one or both of these desires. "*Drive this car/take this drug/buy this product, etc., and you will look good and/or feel good.*" You could say our entire economy is driven by these desires. In fact, the desires to look good and/or feel good are so fundamental and so pervasive, you could say our whole world is driven by them.

But actually, all that I just said is not entirely true. There's more to it...

Most people want to look good because when they look good, they feel good. We get an emotional lift when we perceive ourselves as being attractive (or at least acceptable) in terms of our appearance. We also like to fit in with our peers, our friends and other social groups. So it feels good when we see ourselves as being attractive and/or conforming with our tribes.

"Looking good" may not necessarily be limited to our outward, physical appearance. We may desire to look good in terms of our career, our social status, our zip code, and so on. But the bottom line is we feel good emotionally, psychologically and maybe even physically when we think we look good.[29]

So there's really only one reason we all do what we do:

We want to feel good.

Of course, that's not exactly revelatory – philosophers, psychologists and high school gym teachers (oops, never mind) have been speaking about the *"Pleasure Principle"* for centuries.[30] All the way back to ancient Greece, Socrates noted that, as a species, we instinctively strive to find pleasure and avoid pain. This plays out in all societies and in all levels of society. There's even evidence of it in the animal kingdom.

And yet..., saying that we do what we do because we want to feel good is not entirely true either. There's still more to it.

It turns out "feeling good" is *relative*. We make the decision about what will feel good based on where we're at at the time we make it. Our determination is thus relative to our current experience. The decisions we make will be motivated by our subjective evaluation of what will raise the bar or move the needle forward relative to where we are right now. Therefore we can say the reason we do what we do is:

We want to feel better.

That is, everything we do or don't do, or want or don't want, is based in the notion that we're trying to feel "better" than we do right now. Whether buying a car, going out on a date or taking a drink, it's all the same: our choices will be motivated by whether or not we think we will feel better having or doing that thing. In

---

[29] As Billy Crystal says *"Darling You Look Marvelous"*
https://youtu.be/hXydX9p_ZxA

[30] The scholarly texts on Freudian Psychology define the Pleasure Principle as "the instinctive drive to seek pleasure and avoid pain, expressed as a basic motivating force that reduces psychic tension." Read more
https://en.wikipedia.org/wiki/Pleasure_principle_(psychology).

most situations, we would think that "feeling better" is implied in "feeling good." But that's not always the case. As we'll see in a moment, it is possible to feel "better" but still not feel "good," at least not in an absolute sense.

Let's look at the example of buying a new car. At some point we realize our current car isn't cutting it. Our mind says there's something lacking and the way to fix it, is to replace the car. The problem which a new car would solve will be different for different people. For instance, for some, their current car may be lacking in terms of reliability. For others, they might be wanting more room to accommodate their burgeoning family. For still others, a new car would represent an advancement in their income or career. And so on.

In each case, we perceive that replacing the vehicle will solve our particular problem. The existence of the problem creates a tension in our minds. When the problem is solved, the tension is released and we feel better. For instance, for the person who is concerned about reliability, replacing the car solves the problem of it breaking down and leaving them stranded. For the person who needs more room for their family, their choice for a bigger car would not only allow them to fit more people comfortably, but it would also lessen the conflict as to who sits where (which if you have more than one kid you know is not a small improvement.) Lastly, for the driver who wants to replace their car because it's old and unattractive, they think a new car will make them feel better on the social status/ public appearance front.

Of course, in real life, the decision-making process isn't always as simple or clear cut as my examples suggest. First, there are often competing desires to feel better that influence our choices (I'll give an example in the car context in a moment). Second, our assessments of the problem and/or solution may not be accurate, or they may be based on incomplete information. For instance, in the unreliable car example, a simple repair or two may be all that's needed to get the car road-worthy. Or, even if we're correct in our assessment that the car needs to be replaced, a new car may not necessarily solve the problem, as anyone who's ever purchased a "lemon" knows. This idea that a particular solution may not give us the result we want, speaks to the problem of "expectations." Whether choosing a new car, a new wardrobe or a new spouse, what we think will make us feel better may not always do so (sorry to any newlyweds out there!) We've all wanted things only to find out when we got them they didn't live up to our expectations. Accordingly, we can say:

Disappointment is when we are expecting something to make us feel better and it doesn't.

In terms of competing desires, in the car example, while a new vehicle may result in us feeling better relative to our current situation (whether on the reliability, kids fighting or social status front), it may leave us feeling worse on the financial front. Getting a new car can create lack in terms of our finances. Thus, the desire to feel better in one area may conflict with how we want to feel in another. There may also be other people involved in the decision-making process. Their desire to feel better may conflict with ours. For instance, you may be convinced a red car would make you feel better. But your spouse is convinced red car drivers get more speeding tickets – or red cars often indicate the driver is having a mid-life crisis. Good luck with that one! (BTW - now you know why I drive a red car and I'm single. ☺)

Of course, there's not one answer as to how to resolve competing desires, especially when other people are involved. And while it's important to do our homework before making any significant choice or decision, we still may end up being disappointed in our choices. This is especially true over the long term – who hasn't pined over a particular job/car/house/spouse (sorry again to any newlyweds!) and then after getting that thing, slowly watched the joy and/or satisfaction of having it slip away over time as other things encroached on your bliss.

But jokes about new spouses aside, there is another consideration, more important than any other, that impacts our perception of what will feel better. Hopefully you've guessed by now that, since "who we think we are" impacts every choice and decision we make, what will feel better in any situation is therefore a function of "who we think we are" in that situation. As an example, a car mechanic would see the car reliability issue differently than the average layperson. They may have confidence that if the car poops out, they can fix it. Thus, instead of being concerned or worried, they may see the old car as a challenge; a way to test their skill and ingenuity when it comes to car repairs.

This is not an argument that we should go to mechanic school rather than replace an older vehicle. But it does support the idea that "who we think we are" determines what will feel better in every situation, and thus impacts our choices and decisions in those situations. As we've also mentioned several times, it may be easier to change "who we think we are" in a given situation than to attempt to change the situation itself. This applies in the "feeling better" context as well as in any other. For instance, when I first started working in Los Angeles in the Entertainment Industry, I thought I needed a fancy new car to fit in with my peers. So I went out and leased a black BMW convertible. While the car was fine and a lot of fun, it was more expensive than I could afford and so created a lot of financial pressure. If, instead of approaching the problem from the place of looking outside myself to feel acceptable, I had changed who I thought I was to someone who was acceptable no matter what car I drove, I could have saved myself a lot of (financial) heartache. We'll look at another example of how changing how we see ourselves can influence a choice to "feel better" within a particular context below.

This is going to hurt me more than it hurts you...

So far my examples of making choices to feel better have been pretty obvious and fairly easy to digest. But we're actually talking about a continuum of feeling better. This may mean we're starting off on the low end of the scale – the low, low, low end of the scale. That is, we're trying to feel better in a really bad situation. The parent that screams at their child at the shopping mall may not feel "good" while they're doing it. But they are still doing what they do to feel better. The child may be making a scene which the parent associates with embarrassment. Or the child may be acting in a way which jeopardizes their own or someone else's safety. How the parent sees themselves (and by extension, how they see the child) in that situation will determine how they react. If they see themselves as overwhelmed, powerless and/or unable to control their child, then in an attempt to reduce their discomfort (i.e., feel better), they may lash out at the child.

Now the parent isn't bad or even wrong in this situation – they're just being human. To not lash out at a child under such circumstances may require a very high level of awareness and/or self-control. Yet by understanding why we do what we do, we can begin to do things better. For instance, the parent, being more aware of the true nature of the problem, can come up with a plan ahead of time as to how they will act if the situation comes up again. In the long run, if we want to be better people and live happier lives, learning how to control and/or consciously select our response in each situation is of vital importance. Planning things out in advance is one way to do this.

And even if we don't have time to put together an advance plan, taking a pause and remembering the problem is always how we see ourselves in a particular situation, rather· than the situation itself, can help change how we react in the moment. We talked about the difference between "reacting" and "responding." Sometimes taking a pause and bringing some conscious awareness to what we're about to say or do, may be all that's needed to achieve a more positive result.

As with all our actions and reactions, a decision about what will feel better has to pass through the filter of "who we think we are". So, again, in the unruly child example, if I see myself as powerless in the face of my child's outbursts, I am going to have one reaction. If I see myself in a more positive way, I'll have a different response. Thus, whether it's my kids, my job or just my drive to work, it may be helpful to take some time when things are not so heated to envision myself in a new and empowered way.

Returning to our discussion of addictive/compulsive behaviors, I can now say I did what I did because I thought I would feel better doing it. Like many people, I used these things to cope with uncomfortable or stressful situations. Of course I wasn't aware of this while I was doing it; I just thought I was having a good time. Substances like drugs or alcohol have a euphoric and/or anesthetic effect. That is, they increase pleasure and/or lessen pain.[31] This makes it easy to mistake their effects for a genuine increase in our sense of ease and well-being.

As a result, for many years, especially when I was younger, I partied my way through life. Yes, there were hangovers, missed classes and/or waking up in the wrong bed with the wrong person. But for the most part, I was able to let the good times roll. Eventually however, what had started out as a good time, morphed into something more unpleasant. It wasn't long before I stopped feeling better and started feeling worse.

This is actually true of all addictions. What used to seem to help us feel better, eventually causes us to feel worse. However, because of their habitual nature, it can take a long time to realize that the addiction is no longer working. This is usually compounded by a lot of denial, social pressure and/or physical or psychological withdrawal. Thus, it can be years before a person comes to realize the substance or behavior doesn't reduce the pain, but that it actually increases it. In particular, the body's dependency – as evidenced by withdrawal symptoms and/or physical cravings – can make it even harder to realize we have crossed over to feeling worse rather than better. When it takes years for the reality of our situation to sink in, a lot of unnecessary damage can be done to ourselves and others.

The beauty and great service of recovery programs is they help us see this reality sooner rather than later. They help drive home the fact that what we think will cause us to feel better is actually causing us to feel worse. By identifying with others who suffer from the same affliction (usually through the sharing of their stories), we get to see the true effects of our choices and

---

[31] Interestingly I learned recently *adrenaline* is one of the strongest pain-killers out there (or actually, in there). This explains why many of us deal with problems by creating drama in our lives. The drama triggers adrenaline in the body, which in turn, gives us a rush of energy while also mediating our physical and emotional pain.

behaviors more quickly than we might on our own. 12 Step programs are also known for the great support that is available to members between meetings. Regular contact with sponsors and/or program friends is very helpful in avoiding the thinking that just one more drink or toke or whatever will make us feel better. For any program of recovery or rehabilitation to work, people have to see how their old choices no longer serve them – and probably never did. They must see there is a new, more healthy way to feel better without resorting to the same compulsive behaviors.

The body as decision-maker

When speaking about addictive or compulsive behaviors, there is often an emphasis placed on the physiological effects – the bodily urges that can intensify an addiction. It's undeniable that certain substances can generate cravings. Normal hunger is a good example. Anyone who has missed a meal or two knows how powerful the desire for food can be. Yet, physical cravings and desires notwithstanding, I feel that for me at least, it is the mind and not the body that ultimately guides all my decision-making.

As I said earlier, I choose to approach this entire topic of addiction from the place that nothing and no one has the power to usurp my will. As someone who has spent a lot of time in 12 Step rooms over the past 22 years, I don't write these words lightly. I also respect and honor those who hold a different opinion. Yet I choose to look at it this way: if the body was the determining factor in our behaviors, then the body would be autonomous from the mind and we would never be able to change those behaviors. Physical cravings would rule our decision-making and we would ultimately have to succumb to those bodily urges. Yet millions of people around the world have overcome one or more substance and/or behavioral addictions. Yes, at one time they had intense urges to indulge in those behaviors; yet today they are free. Is it difficult to overcome an addiction? For many of us, yes. Is it heartbreaking to see those who have tried and failed? Indeed.

And yet for me personally, I think it's disempowering to blame cravings or "allergies" of the body for my plight. I know it often feels like the body is in charge, but I sincerely believe that the body follows the mind, and that we always have the ability to change our minds. I have met many people over the years who, in overcoming their own addictions, have described it as follows: at some point they just decided to stop – one day they knew they were done drinking or drugging or whatever. And, despite being tempted at times, they have never gone back. Some continue to work recovery programs, others don't. But the point is decisions are of the mind, not the body. Eventually the body will follow any sincere decision of the mind.

am·bi·dex·ter·i·ty

Many years ago, when I first got into recovery for codependency, I was overwhelmed at the depth and breadth of the dysfunction in my life. I thought it would be just about impossible to change all that I was beginning to identify as my codependent behaviors. As an example, I saw that I routinely relied on "people pleasing" in order to feel safe around others. One way "people pleasing" manifested for me was saying "Yes" to things I really wanted to say "No" to. I did this because I thought that's what the other person wanted to hear and thus they would like me more. But because it wasn't something I really wanted to do, I later found ways to weasel out of my agreements. Of course, because I knew nothing about taking responsibility for my actions, I would blame the other person when things didn't work out. I actually thought they should be able to read my mind and know that I didn't really want to do what I said I would do. (Yes – that's how crazy I was.)

Another thing I did on a regular basis was to become enmeshed with other people's personal or emotional problems. I tried to fix or save everyone I met, telling them all the things they needed to do to get their lives together. Ostensibly, this was my attempt to help them feel better. But looking back, I can see now that I did it so *I* could feel better. If I could solve someone else's problems or relieve their pain, I felt valuable, worthy and important. But most of all I felt *powerful*. For someone who perceives themselves as "powerless" (recall my "two problems" from Chapter Four), playing therapist and fixing other people became like a drug.

Along these same lines, I freely gave other people advice when they hadn't asked for it. I jumped in with suggestions about everything from their health to their relationships to their job situations. Then, when they declined to take my wonderful advice, I felt resentful. For me, offering others advice and suggestions was a way of showing that I cared. I wanted their lives to be better and was sure I knew how they could get there. Yet offering unsolicited suggestions or advice is actually self-indulgent and disrespectful. In addition to assuming that I know better (which is never true), it also assumes the other person can't take care of themselves. Of course, I hated when someone else did this to me – telling me all the things I needed to do to change my own life without me asking. Yet it never registered that I was doing the same thing to others. (Yes – that's how crazy I was.)

In addition, there were general codependent patterns I kept repeating in many of my relationships, such as feeling like a victim; feeling unworthy; making other people – especially women – my Higher Power; being afraid to ask for what I wanted or needed; using magical thinking to avoid hard work; and so on.

Seeing all this was quite overwhelming. Prior to learning about codependency I thought most of these behaviors were normal. Yet the more I looked, the more I could see how unhealthy I was. Codependency seemed to permeate every aspect of my life. These behaviors were so deeply ingrained that I thought it was futile to even try to change them and I ended up feeling more than a little hopeless.

Now this is where it gets a bit strange. As I was pondering the enormity and potential futility of trying to change my codependent behaviors, the thought came to mind that maybe I could experiment with something else that was also deeply ingrained in me, but wasn't the cause of so much pain in my life. I was looking for a metaphor – trying to change something that was so seemingly natural and automatic that it had to be hard-wired into my brain. My thought was if I could change something like

Be Bigger Than You Think You Are!™

that, then maybe I could change these codependent behaviors as well.

One day the idea came: "*What about being right handed?*" That seemed to be as natural, automatic and deeply ingrained as it gets. It also had the very strong element of seemingly being dictated by my physiology – the brain & body – rather than a conscious choice of the mind. So I began a journey to see if I could break the habit of being right-handed by consciously choosing to do everything with my left hand. (Told you it [I] was a bit strange.)

At first it was very, very difficult – mostly because I would forget I was doing this little experiment. I would be half-way through a meal before I realized that I was using my right hand to hold my fork instead of my left. This went on for many weeks. I would start the day determined to use my left hand as much as possible, only to have most of the day go by before I even remembered what I was trying to do.

Eventually I began to remember more and more, but then I was faced with the obvious challenge that I lacked coordination with my left hand. This made ordinary tasks quite difficult. For example, it took me more than a few days to figure out the proper way to hold a spoon with my left hand. I also remember the day I decided to try shaving left-handed. There were several anxious moments as I attempted to figure out the best way to shave both sides of my face without cutting myself. Not as frightening, but equally difficult, was learning how to brush my teeth with my left hand. I couldn't figure out how to hold the brush to get to my back teeth on that side.

I plugged along like this for a couple of months. At times it seemed impossible and at other times kind of silly. But it also felt quite profound – like I was overcoming some inherent aspect of being human – so I kept at it. I noticed from the get-go that I had to be really present and aware. This was going to require my full consciousness on a moment-by-moment basis. All the mundane things that I used to do automatically now required my undivided attention.

Still I kept at it, doing my best everyday to change this aspect of my life. Eventually, it became so "natural" for me to use my left hand, that people started to notice: "*Hey, I didn't know you were left-handed!*" they would say. "*I'm not,*" I would reply with a broad smile, "*I'm right handed but I do everything with my left hand!*" Not surprisingly those conversations were quite short and usually ended with a very confused and quizzical look on the other person's face. But I cherished those moments because I knew it meant I was making progress.

For the first few years (yes – I was at this for years), I would often revert back to the old way of doing things in times of stress. If I was overly anxious about something, halfway through the activity I would realize I was using my right hand instead of my left. We mentioned "regression" earlier. Psychologists define "regression" as a return to an earlier state in times of heightened stress. As I continued to stick with it, the length and frequency of the regressions diminished, to the point where today, I rarely regress at all. At the same time, the awkwardness I felt when I was starting out was almost completely gone. My coordination grew and I soon became very comfortable using my left hand – most days without needing to really think about it. Eventually I could accomplish many tasks almost as efficiently as I had with my right.

But the biggest change was when it began to feel *uncomfortable* to use my right hand for things. This was kind of startling at first. It was one thing to feel comfortable doing things left-handed. But it was quite another to notice it actually felt awkward – even unnatural – to use my right hand for tasks I had used it for my whole life. This is when I really began to appreciate the power of the mind vs. the proclivities and habits of the body. And in case you are wondering, I still do most things[32] with my left hand today.

The importance for me of what turned out to be this not so little experiment was that if, in fact, it's possible to change something as deeply ingrained as right or left-handedness, then it must also be possible to change behaviors and patterns of thinking that seem so natural as to define "who we think we are."

---

[32] Full disclosure - the one thing I still can't do with my left hand is write.

Eventually, I used this *"I'm right handed but do everything with my left hand"* metaphor in breaking many of my codependent habits. I could see how recovery from codependence paralleled this ambidextrous experience almost exactly.

For instance, at first I usually completely forgot I was trying to change how I interacted with others. Days would go by before I realized I had been codependent with someone. Then, when I was aware, it felt really, really awkward trying to do things differently. Saying something like, *"I'm sorry you're having trouble with your boss but you'll have to find someone else to complain to about it,"* felt really uncomfortable at first. It also required effort to do things like, not say "Yes" when I wanted to say "No", to refrain from offering other people unsolicited advice, or to not automatically assume other people were better or more important than me.

Just like switching from my right hand to my left, it took a lot of conscious awareness and hard work to begin to change my codependent behaviors. Soon I felt more and more comfortable interacting with others in healthy ways. Still, just like using my left hand, there were many times when I regressed. Something stressful would take me right back to how I used to be. Yet as I kept at it, I regressed less and less and soon it felt quite comfortable being more functional and healthy in my relationships with others.

And eventually, just like using my right hand for things, it became *uncomfortable* to interact with others the way I used to. Behaviors that were so natural and seemingly normal now felt unnatural. The discomfort when I slipped back to my old ways was often immediate – I knew instinctively I had fallen off the beam. So I'm happy to say that after many years of practice, most of the old habits have died in me. It took a lot of effort and in many cases, a moment-by-moment awareness of my choices. Yet today, in most instances, I am able to experience a new, healthier way of interacting with others.

There's no such thing as a "bad" choice or "wrong" decision

In the first chapter we talked about how "who we think we are" influences all our choices and decisions. In the second chapter we looked at the importance of taking responsibility for our lives and consciously choosing thoughts, feelings, words and actions that serve us. In the third chapter we examined the idea that power is the ability to choose and ultimately the ability to change how we respond to life. In the fourth chapter we saw how fear results from a distorted view of ourselves and directly impacts our ability to make healthy decisions. And now so far in this chapter we've examined how a desire to feel better can sometimes lead to making choices that are not in our best interests. With so much riding on our choices and decisions, there's a natural concern that comes up: *what if I make the wrong one?* The anxiety around making a wrong decision can become so acute that it stops us from making any decisions or taking any action at all.

The first thing to remember is that taking responsibility for our decisions doesn't mean beating ourselves up for the ones that don't work out. We said previously responsibility is about awareness, not blame. Thus, making ourselves wrong for *anything* is never helpful. Beating ourselves up for our mistakes does not make us better people. What we want to do is *learn* from our mistakes so we'll do better in the future.

Next, we have to ask what exactly makes a choice "bad" or "wrong"? Since we give everything all the meaning it has for us, we can interpret a situation in any way we want. We can give it a meaning that moves us forward rather than holds us back. For instance, instead of "failure", how about *"teachable moment"*, *"learning opportunity"* or *"one step closer to my goal"*?

Thus I would suggest that there's no such thing as a "bad" choice or "wrong" decision if we're willing to do two things: 1) learn from our mistakes, and 2) forgive ourselves for them. I absolutely believe there's nothing more important than forgiveness and there's nothing more important to forgive than our own mistakes. We'll never achieve anything lasting or extraordinary in life if we're constantly beating ourselves up for our shortcomings.

Listen to almost any interview with a successful person and you will hear how their biggest mistakes were often their greatest teachers. They'll say that they were able to transform some aspect of their life or business by turning a crisis into an opportunity. Every "failure" has the potential to provide us with some knowledge or information that can help us reach our goals. Thus, "bad" choices can be as helpful – if not more – than "good" ones.

The truth is, achieving anything significant in life often requires more than one try. For instance, it took Thomas Edison 10,000 attempts to invent the light bulb. In response to a critic he is said to have quipped, *"I have not failed. I've just found 10,000 ways that don't work."* I guarantee you Edison knew the value of forgiving himself for his mistakes. No one would attempt 10,000 of anything if they were still into making themselves wrong when things didn't work out. Forgiveness undoes the feelings of low self-esteem and unworthiness many of us associate with "failure." Thus, by forgiving ourselves for our poor choices and decisions, we dissolve self-recrimination and free up the energy needed to continue to move forward. Forgiving ourselves means we will be more willing to try again.

As we've also said, we can make almost any wrong decision "right" by taking responsibility for it. In those cases where we've done something harmful to another person, we've already noted that the amends process can make things right again. Taking responsibility by making restitution or doing whatever else is needed, builds our self-esteem and frees us from any guilt associated with harming someone. In my own life, taking responsibility and making an amends has almost always been a positive experience, no matter how "bad" what I initially did was.

Lastly, we also want to be conscious of who we share the results of our choices with. Surround yourself with people who will support your efforts rather than cut you down, especially when things don't work out. I realized a long time ago that I'm responsible for the people I pick to be in my life. If I share information or experiences with someone who can't or won't support me, that's on me, not them.

Beginning with the end in mind[33]

In terms of decision-making in general and taking action in particular, it's very helpful to recognize that we can decide *in advance* how we want something to go. Assigning a positive intention to an event before it occurs is a very empowered way to live. What most of us currently do is enter a situation with little or no conscious intention at all regarding the outcome. We wait for the experience to be over and then judge whether we like it or not. Doing this severely limits our power. We miss an opportunity to create the experience we desire. By deciding in advance how we want something to go, we are much more likely to think thoughts, feel feelings, speak words and take actions consistent with that goal or intention. This means we have a better chance of attaining the outcome we want.

If you recall, this was my invitation in the Preface of this book (you did read the Preface, didn't you?) I suggested that you set an intention – perhaps without even knowing what this book was about – as to what you wanted to experience as a result of reading it. I urged you to decide – in advance – what you were going to get out of my words. This is because, as you now know, you are the creator of your life. As in all things, when you take responsibility for your experience you can have whatever you decide. When you don't, you can't.

Beginning with the end in mind could be a simple as setting an intention to get a good night's sleep before you go to bed, or as complex as planning out the next 15 years of your life. Start thinking about three upcoming events and write out a positive intention for each of them. Decide – in advance – how you want to think, feel, speak and act, and what outcome you want to experience. Also – and perhaps most importantly – decide "who

---

[33] *The 7 Habits of Highly Effective People* by Stephen Covey
https://www.amazon.com/Habits-Highly-Effective-People-Powerful/dp/1476740054

you want to be" in each of those situations. Then in the weeks, days and hours leading up to the event, remind yourself of this intention often. At a minimum, entering with a new and expanded positive self-image will make the experience more enjoyable. At a maximum, it will be the beginning of a new and better you! (In case you're interested, I've included my Advance Intention for this book in the Appendix.)

Everything we do, we do for ourselves

We touched on this in Chapter Three. We said that all true decisions are made independent of what's going on around us. Our choices are at their most powerful when they are completely arbitrary *vis a vis* the external world. However, *internally* our decisions are not at all arbitrary – they are always expressions of "who we think we are" and "who we want to be" in life. In fact, the way we declare these things ("who we think we are" and "who we want to be") is by the choices and decisions we make. This is true of individuals, companies, societies and even nations.

If we make choices independent of anything external to us, then we must – by definition – be making those choices for ourselves. So for instance, as I'll show in a minute, even a decision to help someone else is really something we are doing for ourselves. This is reinforced by the fact that we have no control over how other people receive our help. We may be the most altruistic, supportive, wonderful person in the world and other people are still free to reject us. If we have no control over how our actions are received, then we must be doing whatever we're doing (and being whoever we're being) for ourselves and not for anyone else. *It has to be this way.*

An example from my own life is sponsoring people in 12 Step programs. For those who are not familiar, a Sponsor is someone who helps another member (usually someone new) navigate that particular program. They offer the Sponsee experience, strength and hope in terms of what has worked for them in their own recovery. The Sponsor provides regular contact and support to help keep the new person on track. And most importantly, they guide the Sponsee in working the 12 Steps.

Over the years, I have sponsored many people in three different programs. While it has always been a wonderful experience, I learned a long time ago that I have no control over how or if my guidance is received. I am powerless over whether the person I am sponsoring utilizes my (mostly wonderful) suggestions. The only way I know if what we're doing is working for them is if the other person keeps calling me week after week. Thus, because I can't compel anyone to follow my suggestions or do anything at all concerning their own recovery, I'm really only showing up for myself. If the other person benefits, that's great. But they're really only giving me a chance to be who I want to be in my life. Thus, even though to the outside world it may appear I am doing what I am doing for the benefit of another person, in this and every other situation, I'm doing what I'm doing for myself.

So this means when a Sponsee tells me how much I am helping them, I thank them but gently respond that they are helping themselves. I remind them there are others who I have given the exact same suggestions to, whose lives have not changed or who no longer call me. I tell them I am unwilling to take responsibility for their success because if I did so, I would also have to take responsibility for their failures and I'm not willing to do that. If what we're doing together is helpful, that's wonderful. But it doesn't change the fact that we're each doing what we're doing for ourselves, and are thus each responsible for whatever outcomes we achieve.

In fact, I would suggest this is true of everyone, all the time. Whether you're raising children, mowing your neighbor's lawn or running a nation, you are doing what you are doing for yourself. Other people may benefit and even appreciate your efforts. But that doesn't change the fact that your decision is your own and thus must be something you do for you.

I mentioned earlier the work of Dr. Joe Dispenza. In his book, *Breaking the Habit of Being Yourself*, he talks about how we have to literally become different people if we want our lives to change. We can't think the same thoughts, feel the same feelings, speak

166

the same words and take the same actions day after day and expect anything to be different.

Changing anything begins with a decision. The primary way we put that decision into effect is by taking actions consistent with that decision. Words alone – wishing or hoping things will change – are not enough. In this sense, actions do speak louder than words. I've talked about this previously with respect to my photography business. Several years ago I realized if I wanted things to be different I needed to act in a way that was consistent with my new goals and desires. It wasn't enough for me to sit on my couch eating pretzels telling people I wanted to be a professional photographer. I had to get off the couch (or at least pick up the phone while I was still on the couch) and cold call hundreds of businesses and pitch my services. I had to submit my photos to newspapers, magazines and websites week after week, month after month, and even year after year, without ever hearing back from them. I had to enter dozens of contests, shows and exhibitions where there were hundreds – or even thousands – of other photographers submitting their work, many of whom had more talent and experience than me.

The point is, it wasn't enough for me to sit around and talk about these things; I had to get up and do them. This "getting up and doing stuff" is an indicator of our true desires and intentions. We all say we want certain things in life. But are we willing to do what it takes to get them?

Life responds to our desires

A few years ago I was listening to an interview with actor/comedian Jerry Seinfeld. Seinfeld was asked what it takes to be successful in Hollywood. His response was that it's not the most talented people who end up being successful. He said the people who make it are the ones *who want it the most*. The people who succeed are the ones with the strongest desire and who do whatever it takes to reach their goals and dreams in life.[34]

---

[34] https://youtu.be/f--diHmCmhk

How much we desire something is often tempered by how possible we believe it is to achieve it. Fear of failure or disappointment can derail us before we even begin. But remember: it's our idea about ourselves – "who we think we are" – that is the greatest limiting factor in what we are able to achieve in life. Thus, how possible we believe it will be for us to achieve something is directly related to how we see ourselves in that situation.

Since page one of this book, I've emphasized the importance of consciously and deliberately choosing a "who we think we are" that serves us. The goal is to see ourselves in a way that moves us forward rather than holds us back in life. In this regard, as we discussed a few minutes ago, it may be helpful to start by deciding in advance who you want to be in connection with your goals or desires. Begin by consciously seeing yourself as someone who can achieve what you want. Tell yourself often and loudly, "*I got this! I can do this! This is entirely possible for me!*" The more you can shore up your belief that a specific result is possible, the more desire you will have for it. The more desire you have for it, the more likely you will do what it takes to get there.

In addition to Positive Affirmations, in Chapter Two we talked about using Vision Statements, Guided Visualizations, Vision Boards and Mind Movies™ to program a new powerful, positive intention around "who we think we are." These are similarly great tools to use to fan the flames of desire in one or more specific areas of our lives. We're talking about consciously creating a passion for obtaining a particular outcome or result. That passion will then become the fuel we can use to reach our goals.

In terms of setting goals, there's lots of information available about that online and elsewhere. I'll let you research that on your own. But I do want to mention one technique I have used from time-to-time. I've found it's helpful to start by setting small goals that are easily achievable. This reinforces a feeling of success rather than failure. For instance, my goal in writing this book has been to spend at least two hours each day doing it. Seeing as I wouldn't be working or travelling during that time due to my injury, it seemed like a reasonable and relatively easy goal to obtain. And in fact, that has proven to be the case. I only missed a few days during the entire six months it's taken to write this book, and most days I have well exceeded my goal. I have sometimes worked on it for as much as six, eight or even 10 hours in a given day. (I had no idea it takes this much effort to write a book!) Had I initially set my goal at eight hours, it would have created all kinds of pressure and I'm sure most days I would have come up short. This, in turn, would have created a sense of failure and disappointment – and it's quite possible that as a result I might have quit half-way through.

So my suggestion is to start small and then acknowledge yourself on a regular basis for a job well-done. The real work for many of us in realizing our goals and dreams in life is to go from being our own worst enemy to our own best friend. We want to set ourselves up for success, not failure. The idea is to catch ourselves doing something right rather than doing something wrong. (These last two sentences also apply to how we raise our kids by the way.) Fostering a feeling of success will stoke the flames of desire, which will, in turn, help us keep the forward momentum we need to achieve what we want.

Value-able

In terms of making decisions and sorting out our desires, it's very important to begin to notice what we *value* in life. We touched on this earlier in Chapter Three when we spoke about valuing happiness vs. other lesser emotions. Valuing something implies that we will feel better when we have or do that thing. Now if you want to know what you value in life, take a look at where you spend your time and where you spend your money. Both time and money are indicators of value. (I find it interesting – and not a small coincidence – that we use the word "spend" in relation to both.)

Many years ago, when I was dealing with issues related to overspending and credit card debt, it was suggested I keep a daily written record of my money – that I write down all my income and expenses for each day. I immediately saw the value in that (pun intended), and have done it pretty much every day since (more than 22 years and counting.) I use my phone and my computer to keep track of all my income and expenses and at the end of each month I organize my numbers into categories. For example, I group expenditures into categories such as spiritual, auto, travel, clothing, household, medical, meals, charity, etc. Having this kind of clarity around my finances has proven very helpful. Later, it was suggested I keep a written record of how I was spending my time each day. I did that for more than five years and it was also extremely helpful and enlightening.

The clarity around how I was spending both my time and money was quite beneficial in terms of making better choices. In addition, having a written record of both assisted me in seeing that I was valuing certain things that were not serving me. This was quite eye-opening. For instance, as I already mentioned, when I first transitioned from lawyer to photographer, I was devoting a lot of time to playing computer games. By tracking my time I could see I was spending 20 or more hours each week playing things like "Angry Birds." I also saw that I was spending another 20 hours (sometimes in tandem and sometimes separately) watching television.

Now in and of themselves, there's nothing wrong with computer games, television - or almost anything else for that matter. For many people, these are valid leisure time activities. Yet the problem was what I was using them for: I was avoiding doing what was necessary to move my life forward. The time I was spending playing games and/or in front of the TV was time I needed to get my business off the ground. More importantly, I was doing those unproductive activities mostly out of fear about doing certain things related to my business. Yet I didn't know that fear was driving my decision-making – I thought I was just having fun. Thus, another example of why it's important to look closely at the reason we do what we do in life.

Beyond that, especially on the television front, I could see the content I was filling my head with also was not serving me. Whether it was sitcoms, reality shows or cable news, my mind was not benefitting. Looking back, I find it so interesting that I would spend hours deliberating over what I put into my mouth, such as reading labels on food packaging, looking for wholesome, organic fruits and vegetables, and so on. Yet I paid little to no attention to what I was putting into my mind. I can also see now that what I fill my mind with is way more important than what I fill my mouth with. I believe for me personally, my thoughts, beliefs and emotions have a much more profound effect on my health than what I eat or drink. (I realize not everyone feels this way – just offering my own perspective as "food for thought" – once again, pun intended.)

Anyway, the end result of my little awakening as to how I was spending my time is that I haven't watched TV or played computer games in more than seven years. I pretty much went cold turkey on both and eventually cancelled my cable TV subscription. Again, I am not suggesting this is right for everyone – or actually anyone, other than me. I have no idea what's right for you. If watching TV serves you, that's great. As I said, it is certainly a valid leisure activity for many people. Yet, for me, I could see it was a way I was avoiding what I needed to do. It was "escapism" and not in a good way.

One last point on the TV and computer game thing: this is not a rant against the entertainment or news industry. Having worked in the entertainment business myself for many years, it will always hold a special place in my heart. Entertainment and leisure-time activities are important. I still have several friends in both the TV and news business and they are all really good people doing their best to help keep the rest of us informed and entertained. Yet it's also up to each of us to decide what serves us within the context of our own lives and what is the best way to fill our non-working time. Therefore, I urge you to scrutinize all your choices to make sure they are in alignment with "who you want to be."

It's not how we handle the success that matters

Back to the topic of pursuing our goals and dreams. I mentioned earlier that I really enjoy speaking publicly about my photography as well as going after what matters to us in life. When I share that I've won more than 70 awards for my photos, people's faces light up. Yet when I then tell them that for every one of those awards there have been *at least* five failures, rejections and disappointments, their smile quickly fades. No one likes to hear about failures, rejections and disappointments. Yet welcome to life. It's rare that everything goes our way the first time around – or even the fifth or sixth time around. So, as I first mentioned in Chapter Two, if we don't have a way to deal with the inevitable setbacks and disappointments, we're done.

My suggestion is to come up with a strategy that will help you to stay on track. For example, for a long time my strategy was, when I got rejected by a show or exhibition, I would automatically enter two more shows. It didn't matter why I thought I had been rejected by the first show – I didn't even think about it. I didn't lament the failure or take it personally. I just got busy with two new applications and got my photos out there. That actually worked out pretty well for me. (You can see how well on the "Awards and Exhibitions" page of my photography website www.peteralessandriaphotography.com/awards---exhibitions)

Of course, the best strategy is to be your own best friend in life. If self-recrimination creates fear, and if fear represents resistance, then we have to learn to not go there. As I keep saying, beating ourselves up for our failures doesn't make us better people. In fact, I bet self-recrimination and a general lack of kindness towards ourselves is why 50% of new businesses fail in the first five years. It's not the economy, it's not the competition, and so on. It's likely the fact that most new business owners can't forgive themselves for their mistakes. (OK – maybe I'm projecting. But I bet at least some of those failures could be turned around by a little self-love!)

So have a strategy – a plan that you turn to without having to think about it – to help you keep moving forward when something doesn't work out. Then do the other things we've discussed in this chapter, such as learning from any mistakes and forgiving yourself for them. I always say there is no guarantee of success in life, but there is one guarantee of failure: and that's if we give up. The best way that I've found to not give up, is to love the $hit out of yourself!

In this world, we have to take action to achieve our goals. Yet we probably won't be able to move in a positive direction for very long if we can't deal with disappointment or if we're beating ourselves up for our mistakes. I've done several television[35] and podcast interviews[36] the past few years and I always surprise the commentator when I say the best Business Plan[37] is to "love yourself." I'll say to you right now, if you can truly do that – love yourself – there's no way you can fail. Even if your business isn't ultimately successful, if you've truly loved yourself, you've still achieved something wonderful.

Be Bigger Than You Think You Are™
The title for this book comes from the Introduction to my first photography book, *"New York City Nights – Book 1"*[38] where I said:

> *"...[I]t's how I see myself and who I think I am that determines how far I get in life. So for the past five years, I have been on a journey to 'be bigger than I think I am'."*

Having read thus far in this book, we now know that it's pretty much impossible to act in a way, or achieve anything at all, that's inconsistent with our predominant thoughts and beliefs about ourselves. Psychologists call this "cognitive dissonance."[39] Thus, "who we think we are" (before we begin to change our self-image

---

[35] https://www.peteralessandriaphotography.com/blog/2018/12/ny1-television-interview---12-17-18
[36] https://www.peteralessandriaphotography.com/blog/2017/2/douglas-coleman-interview
[37] My Four Point Business Plan™:
1. Never give up;
2. Don't take anything personally;
3. Do at least one thing every day to move your business and your life forward;
4. Forgive yourself when you don't do 1., 2. or 3.
Point 4. Is the most important point in the plan!
[38] https://www.peteralessandriaphotography.com/blog/2017/11/-new-york-city-nights
[39] https://en.wikipedia.org/wiki/Cognitive_dissonance

for the better), is the biggest limiting factor in terms of realizing what we want in life. This means we must move beyond how we currently see ourselves if we want our lives to be different. Accordingly, I will invite you to remind yourself daily:

In order for me to achieve what I want in life, I have to be bigger than I think I am!

Then go out and do at least one thing every day that represents you "being bigger than you think you are." Taking regular action, consistent with our new idea about ourselves, is the key to overcoming the old and achieving the new that we desire.

In the next chapter we're going to look at the part of our mind which is responsible for all our dysfunctional, self-defeating thoughts and behaviors. It's the basis of all our limiting beliefs about ourselves, and keeps our lives small and filled with fear and hatred. It's the part that urges us to look outside, at everyone and everything else, as the source of our unhappiness. Or if we do look within, it directs us to use self-judgment and self-condemnation. The "ego" is the frightened, unhealed part of our minds which most of us think is "who we really are." Since it defines our sense of self quite negatively and unlovingly, it ultimately needs to be undone and healed through forgiveness if we want our lives to be different.

TAKEAWAYS:

1. Every child needs to know two things: 1) that their parents are OK, and 2) that the child matters. Both of these arise from the child's survival instincts.

2. Children often compensate for their parents' issues. For instance, a child may try to be perfect so as not to upset the parent. Or the child may learn to deny their own needs so they will be less of a burden. All such attempts to compensate

for their caregivers' dysfunction are done at the child's expense.

3. Children naturally believe what their parents tell them. If told that they are bad often enough, this idea becomes a permanent part of the child's belief system. Likewise, every time a child is yelled at, blamed, shamed or hit, their self-esteem diminishes. The message they receive is they are not worthy of being loved the way they are. Self-hatred (*"I'm bad and deserve to be punished"*) can follow.

4. The combination of fear, self-loathing and stuffed emotions inherent in the less-than-perfect upbringing many of us experience can create problems for us later in life. These include codependency, relationship and health problems, low-self esteem, depression and addictive/compulsive behaviors. Addictions, in particular, are about coping with fear, emotional trauma and stress.

5. The question *"what was my part in this*?" is a great question to ask any time there is conflict in our lives. It's a crucial inquiry in taking responsibility and thus getting our power back.

6. Making an amends for our harmful behaviors is at the heart of taking responsibility. Being willing to admit we have harmed someone is a huge and often life-changing step.

7. We are urged to clean up our side of the street and let go of what we think others have done to us. We can give that to a Greater Consciousness to work out for the good of everyone involved.

8. Self-hatred never helped anyone become a better person.

9. As long as we're alive, conscious and of a relatively sound mind, we have power over our actions and reactions. We may

currently be making terrible, harmful or even self-destructive choices, but that doesn't mean we are not choosing.

10. If there's resistance to saying, *"I do everything I do because I choose to,"* it's because of the shame most people feel when faced with their own poor choices. We're not bad or wrong for what we do – even if it's totally messed up and self destructive.

11. We all have an innate desire to feel good. However, what will feel good in any situation is relative to where we're at at the time. Thus, everything we do we do because we want to feel *better*.

12. A decision about what will feel better has to pass through the filter of "who we think we are." This means what will feel better is entirely dependent on how we see ourselves in the situation. Therefore, we may want to try changing "who we think we are" before we go out and lease that fancy convertible to help us fit in. ☺

13. Disappointment is when we're expecting something to make us feel better and it doesn't.

14. The parent that screams at their child may not feel "good" while they're doing it. But they're still doing what they do to feel better.

15. If we want to be better people and live happier lives, learning how to control our reactions is of vital importance. Planning things out in advance is one way to do this. Taking a pause and remembering the problem is always how we see ourselves is another.

16. It's true of all addictions that what seemed to help us feel better at one time, eventually causes us to feel worse. The body's dependency on a substance can make it difficult to

realize we have crossed over. As a result, it may take years for the reality to sink in during which time a lot of damage can be done to ourselves and others.

17. Recovery programs help us see the reality of addiction sooner. They drive home the fact that what we think will cause us to feel better is actually making us feel worse. 12 Step programs are also known for the great support between meetings. Regular contact with Sponsors and/or program friends is helpful to avoid the thinking that just one more drink or toke or whatever will make us feel better.

18. When speaking about addictive or compulsive behaviors, there is often an emphasis placed on bodily urges. It's undeniable that certain substances can generate cravings. Yet, physical urges and desires notwithstanding, a more empowering approach to the issue may be that it is the mind and not the body that ultimately guides all our decision-making.

19. The guy who wrote this book is right-handed – but he does everything with his left hand. WTF???

20. With so much riding on our choices and decisions, there's a natural concern about what if we make the wrong one. The anxiety around a wrong decision can become so acute that it stops us from making any decisions at all.

21. There's no such thing as a "bad" choice or "wrong" decision if we are willing to do two things: 1) learn from our mistakes, and 2) forgive ourselves for them. Bad choices can teach us what we need to do better next time, while forgiveness undoes the self-recrimination many of us associate with failure.

22. Begin with the end in mind. By deciding in advance how we want something to go, we are much more likely to think

thoughts, feel feelings, speak words and take actions consistent with that goal or intention. This makes it more likely we will attain the result we want.

23. All true choices and decisions are completely arbitrary *vis a vis* the external world. However, internally our decisions are never arbitrary – they are always expressions of "who we think we are" and "who we want to be" in life.

24. Everything we do, we do for ourselves. This is even true of a decision to help another person.

25. We put decisions into effect by taking actions consistent with those decisions. The people who succeed are the ones with the strongest desire and who use that desire to do whatever it takes to reach their goals.

26. If you want to know what you value in life, look at where you spend your time and where you spend your money. Both time and money are indicators of value. Make sure what you value is serving you.

27. It's not how we handle success that matters, but rather how we handle the failures, rejections and disappointments. It's helpful to have a strategy in place to deal with the inevitable setbacks that come with the pursuit of any worthwhile dream or desire.

28. For most of us to achieve what we want in life, *we have to be bigger than we think we are!*

EXERCISES:

1. Identify how you may have compensated for your parents' lack of OK-ness and how that affected you later in life. Describe the ways you tried to matter in your family, what roles you may have

played, and how you may have tried to care-take your caregivers. The purpose of this exercise is not to make our parents wrong – it's to shed light on why we think and act the way we do so we can begin to heal it.

2. What messages did you receive as a child about your worthiness to be loved when you made a mistake? How have you continued to give yourself the same messages as an adult and how has doing that affected your life? Again, we're not trying to make anyone wrong but rather to heal from our past experiences.

3. *"What was my part in this?"* Think of three recent conflicts you've had with others. Identify how you contributed to the problem and whether or not taking responsibility for your side of the street is warranted. Are you holding off apologizing because you feel they owe you an amends? If so, is that serving you?

4. *"I do everything I do because I choose to"* and *"Everything I do, I do for myself."* – Agree or disagree? Why?

5. Identify three different choices or decisions you made recently. For each:

   a. Write about how wanting to feel better influenced your choice to act the way you did;

   b. Describe how "who you thought you were" in each situation affected your idea of what would help you feel better; and

   c. Identify at least three different competing interests that impacted the final decision, as well as whether your solution to the problem brought the results you wanted. If you were disappointed, write about how that was related to your expectations.

6. Pick three different "bad" or "wrong" choices that you've made in your life and reframe each by identifying a) what you could

learn from the situation that would help you in the future; and b) how you could forgive yourself for your mistakes.

7. Think about three different events or situations that are up coming. Decide, in advance, the kind of experience you want to have. What outcomes do you want to achieve? Who do you want to be in each situation? Write out several paragraphs for each.

8. *"All true decisions are arbitrary vis-à-vis the external world."* Identify three choices or decisions you've made recently. For each write about whether you were influenced primarily by internal considerations, or if you made those choices in reaction to something outside of you. (Clues to the latter would be if you tried to manipulate, impress or influence someone.) Also, describe how these decisions were an expression of "who you thought you were" and/or "who you wanted to be" in each situation.

9. Taking Action and Desire:

   a. Identify three different things you'd like to accomplish in your life. Write about why you want them and what you're willing to do to achieve them. Be specific;

   b. If you haven't started taking actions towards your goal, is it because of how you see yourself? What would you have to change about "who you think you are" in order to move forward?

   c. Come up with a strategy to help you maintain your desire in the face of any failures or disappointments that may arise while you are pursuing your goals;

   d. Identify at least three small, easily achievable goals for each. Track your progress and reward your achievements.

10. Keep track of both your time and money for one week (or if you're really ambitious, for one month.) Then use the information

you've gathered to identify what you are currently valuing in your life. Look closely at whether or not those choices are serving you. Share the information with someone you trust and agree to help each other stay on track with making better choices.

11. Pick three things in your life that right now seem impossible or otherwise out of reach. What does it look like for you to be *"bigger than you think you are"* in relation to each of those things? What would you have to believe about yourself in order to achieve your goals or desires? Write out several paragraphs about being bigger than you think you are for each of them.

Chapter Six

Would You Rather Be Right Or Happy?

"Being right is massively overrated..."

-Scott Stabile

The title for this Chapter is inspired by *A Course in Miracles*.[40] According to the *Course,* our minds are essentially divided into two parts: our spiritual, or right-minded self, and our "ego" or wrong-minded self. The ego, which is the focus of much of this chapter, is the fear-based part of our mind that thrives on conflict and drama. It's always on the look-out for enemies and other dangers, and believes in victimization, justified anger and attack. It says the other person/culture/race/nation is guilty and since they are the cause of our upset, we are entitled to attack them for what they have done.

The ego sees itself as separate from other people and from all the things that make up life. This idea that we're separate allows us to believe that what we do to another has no effect on us. We can thus become indifferent to the plight and suffering of our fellow man, and we may even use this idea to feel safe in attacking them. When we are consumed by our egoic mind, we can act in ways which are inhuman and totally insane.

---

[40] The actual quote is *"Do you prefer that you be right or happy?" A Course in Miracles,* pg 616

The idea we can hurt another and not suffer any consequences is one of the basic premises of the ego. When there's conflict the ego counsels, *"Don't worry, you're stronger than they are – they can't hurt you."* But anyone who's been around this planet for a while has surely experienced that this is not the case. *"What goes around, comes around,"* is more than just a platitude. Whether it's your neighbor tossing your trash back over the fence, or a government being overthrown by the followers of a wrongfully imprisoned opposition leader, one way or another, whatever we put out there comes back to us.

The ego is also the origin of the concept that it is the world that makes us think, feel, say and do the things we do. It says that something outside us is the cause of our upset and that we have little-to-no responsibility for how our life is going. We are the innocent victim of what the world has done to us and the suffering we endure is proof that the world is evil.

Sound familiar? But wait, there's more.

Not surprisingly, as a result of this worldview the ego thrives on making everyone and everything else "wrong". It pays close attention to other people's mistakes and feels fully entitled to correct them. It continuously thinks it knows better and takes great offense when its suggestions are not welcomed. It is the part of our mind that insists on how things "should" be done. Obsessed with assigning guilt, the ego feels justified in attacking the object of that guilt. It flourishes in an environment of judgment and condemnation, and views itself as superior to everyone it meets. It longs to be seen as perfect and special, and yet is shackled with insecurity and doubt.

The ego takes everything personally. It can morph even the most neutral response into a personal attack to which it takes great umbrage. The ego seeks unfair advantage in all interactions and feels entitled to take more than its fair share whenever it has the chance. It justifies the most selfish and destructive behavior on the grounds that it is just doing what it needs to do to survive.

OK, I'm done.

Welcome to the world of the ego. It's a pretty harsh – but I think accurate – assessment of who we can be when we identify with the fearful, selfish part of the mind. "Who we think we are" when we're operating from the ego is vulnerable, threatened, and powerless, while being mired in uncertainty, fear and doubt. Seeing ourselves this way makes aggression and attacks against others seem reasonable. As *A Course in Miracles* says, the ego ranges from suspiciousness at best to viciousness at worst.[41]

Now you may be tempted to say, "*I can admit I'm a little selfish and judgmental at times, but it's been a long while since I actually attacked anyone.*" And I would agree that most of us, most of the time, keep a lid on our ego. We are usually more friendly than hostile. Yet I would submit that at least part of this is because the ego is also quite concerned with its public appearance. It has an investment in seeming to be nice and helpful rather than judgmental and attacking. The ego never wants to look bad and will go out of its way to preserve a positive and caring facade.

Yet as soon as our back is against the wall and we don't see an easy or reasonable means of escape, watch out. Whether it's with our own kids, or with a neighboring nation or race, when we feel really threatened, we attack first and ask questions later. It is in times of strife that the ego's true colors come out. Either way, we have a long history on this planet of what we can do to each other when the ego is in control of our thinking.

Even in the absence of an overt conflict between people, there's a host of ways we can attack each other. For instance, anytime we gossip about another person we are attacking them. Whenever we use sarcasm or judge or criticize them we do the same. Aggressive driving is more than just a person who's late for work. Acting with conscious disregard for the well-being of others makes us guilty of attack. Likewise, yelling at someone for how we feel – no matter how justified in our mind – is an attack. And God-forbid someone insults us or takes something we perceive as ours – we'll have some choice words for that SOB and we may even invite them to step outside to resolve our differences.

And sadly, while most of us keep a lid on our anger in public, what happens behind closed doors in our own homes with our

---

[41] *A Course in Miracles*, pg. 176

own families can be another story. Verbal attacks upon or between loved ones can often be brutal. When those attacks escalate to physical altercations, they can be fatal.

On a global scale, we appear to be less concerned with appearances. Stronger groups and nations have historically preyed upon weaker ones. Atrocities of all kinds have been justified on the grounds of "sovereign interests" or "self-defense". From slavery to war, and even genocide, nations attacking nations and groups attacking groups are historically quite common.

Now I've laid out this picture of the darkness of the ego to get your attention. Thankfully most of us don't spend the majority of our time there. We attempt to be genuinely nice and considerate of others. We want to be helpful and operate within the bounds of a civilized society. At least as long as we don't feel threatened. Yet herein lies the problem – in our modern societies where stress and anxiety are rampant, our good intentions may not be enough. As *A Course in Miracles* says:

Frightened people can be vicious.[42]

While we want to be kind and helpful, fear and the perceived need for self-preservation can sometimes impel us to act in ways that are harmful to ourselves and others.

So all this is yet another reason to pay close attention to "who we think we are" in any given situation. When we have a perception of ourselves as weak, vulnerable or unsafe, we're much more likely to put the ego in charge. Yes, as we discussed in Chapter Four, there may be the need to take certain precautions in life. And there's nothing that says we shouldn't take care of ourselves in the face of threatening or inappropriate behavior by others. Yet it's pretty obvious that our reactions are not always proportional to the actual threats that exist. And since it's often easier for us to slip back into ego-land than most of us realize, we need to be highly aware of how we see ourselves and "who we

---

[42] *A Course in Miracles*, pg. 36

think we are" in each situation. This is especially true when we feel threatened.

The projection of guilt

We said earlier that the ego thrives on making others wrong. We are constantly passing judgment on our fellows for everything from the clothes they wear to the car they drive to who they marry or divorce. Finding fault is a primary pastime of the ego. Yet according to *A Course in Miracles*, we actually see in others all that we have not forgiven in ourselves.[43] Thus, the guilt we see in them is really the guilt we believe (usually unconsciously) to be true about ourselves.

I previously mentioned *projection* – the fact that most humans deny the existence of unfavorable traits in themselves by attributing them to others. Stated more simply, all the stuff that bugs me about other people is really stuff I hate about myself. Or as they say in 12 Step programs, "*If you spot it, you got it.*"

Projection is a defense mechanism. We project out those traits which are too painful for us to look at directly. Recall that we said earlier in this book that we *dissociate* from our negative thoughts about ourselves. Psychologists will tell you projection always follows dissociation. As long as this process of dissociation and projection remains unconscious, by reacting strongly (and negatively) to what someone else is doing, I am denying that the source of my discomfort is within me. Rather, I see the source of my upset as being in the other person. Yet since I am unaware of any of this, I just think what they're doing makes them a jerk. It's only when we become aware that we're projecting our own negative traits on to others that we get a chance to heal those traits within ourselves.

Identifying when we're projecting can get a little tricky in that what I "spot", I may not actually "got" – at least not in the same way as the other person. It's not uncommon to go to the other extreme to avoid being perceived as having an unpleasant trait. For instance, if I am upset because I see someone else as a

---

[43] *A Course in Miracles*, Psychotherapy Pamphlet, P-2 VI-6.

braggart, it may be that I have gone to the opposite end of the spectrum with excessive humility. At some point I decided it was not OK to speak well of myself, and that instead, I needed to remain silent about my achievements. In this case, my upsettedness is probably more about the subconscious thought, *"Why is it OK for them to be bragging about themselves when I can't?"* than it is about the bragging itself. I'm upset because they get to act in a way which I don't allow myself.

The key to undoing our projections is to notice when and why we are upset. If the issue we're noticing in the other person isn't ours, then we won't be overly bothered by it. We may not like it, but we won't feel compelled to attack them for it. In fact, we might even want to be helpful if it's clear that what they were doing was harmful to themselves or another. It's when our reaction swings out towards left field that we need to be more aware. Judgment, moral outrage, and even just excessive irritation indicate that the problem is more about us than them.[44]

The idea that when I am upset about what someone else is doing, I am really reacting to a projection of my own unconscious guilt, is completely abhorrent to the ego. (Stop for a moment and consider how well-received this news is in your own mind right now.) Yet given all that we've been talking about so far in this book – including that we're totally responsible for our lives and that no one makes us think, feel, say or do anything – what else could explain our reaction? We've said previously that our reactions are *always* about us (based on "who we think we are") and *never* about the other person. Proof of this is found in something I've noticed in my own life: when I have forgiven myself for the same upsetting trait or habit the other person is exhibiting, I'm not upset by them doing it any more.

An example of this is "neediness" – especially in romantic relationships. I loosely define being "needy" as impulsively seeking approval and then sulking or pouting when we don't get that approval; needing constant assurance that someone else

---

[44] "You never hate your brother for his sins, but only for your own." *A Course in Miracles*, pg. 650

thinks we're OK; attempting to manipulate others to pay attention to us; and generally looking for someone else to emotionally care-take us. I often used to judge others for being needy – I was totally reactive to people who I perceived as acting this way. I saw them as weak and spineless and generally repulsive. Then one day, shortly after getting into recovery for codependence, I was working through a list of negative personality traits. When I got to "emotionally needy", I realized, *"Oh, wow – this is something I do a lot in my own relationships – and I hate myself for it."* It was quite eye-opening to see that a trait I judged so harshly in others was something I didn't like about myself.

As part of my codependence recovery work, I looked at my own negative personality traits and began to work towards forgiving myself for them. It took quite a while, but eventually I was able to forgive myself for the times I had been needy in my relationships with others. I could see this was my way of trying to overcome feelings of insecurity and anxiety about whether or not someone else would find me lovable. Eventually I began to have compassion rather than contempt for myself around this and other less than positive character traits. As a result, today I am much less reactive when I come across these traits in others. I can actually have understanding for that person rather than judgment.

Archery... the Sport of Kings!⁴⁵

We said earlier the ego feels slighted and attacked by others for any or no reason. It is the self-centered, self-absorbed, insecure part of our minds that is consumed with what it thinks other people think of us. It takes great pains to impress other people and has a huge investment in being seen as "special" and thus better than others.

Yet knowing what we now know, it should be easy to see that every time the ego takes offense, the real source of the upset lies

---

[45] I actually think fox hunting is the Sport of Kings. But I like the phrase and also imagine the foxes would have a better chance if the hunters used bows and arrows. ☺

in its own self-doubt and insecurity. As we said in Chapter Four, the only reason we are upset when someone makes a negative comment about us, is we're afraid what they're saying is true. Thus, it's our own negative thoughts and beliefs about ourselves that cause us to feel hurt or slighted. If we're secure in "who we think we are", then it doesn't matter what someone else thinks of us.

Let's see how this plays out by doing a little exercise: pick an activity you have no ability in. I'll use archery because, other than as a nine year old at sleep away camp in Upstate New York many, many years ago, I have no experience or proclivity for it. (I don't mean to offend anyone who loves archery by the way – although if you are offended you'll understand why in a minute. ☺)

The way this works is find someone you don't know and ask them to tell you that you suck at whatever activity you picked. (The preference is to do this with a stranger so you'll be less likely to try to impress them, although if you're like me and go out of your way to impress complete strangers, well then you have issues.) So for me, I would ask this person to tell me that they think I'm terrible at archery. For example they might say:

> *"You're the worst archer I know! You suck! You'll never be any good at it, so you may as well pack up your quills now. Sell your bows and arrows and get out while you can. You are a complete loser when it comes to archery!"*

And so on. Have someone do the same for you. (I'll wait.)

Now notice how you feel. In my case (other than perhaps being a little triggered by the word "loser"), I really wouldn't care about what they were saying. It might even be a little comical depending on how over the top they were. This is because I don't have an *investment* in seeing myself as good at archery. Excelling at this activity is not part of my egoic self-image.

Now moving on to part II of this little experiment, think of something you *do* have an interest or investment in. For me that might be photography. Ask that same person to tell you, in the same way, that you stink at that thing. Now how do you feel? Even though it's the same general situation – someone criticizing your abilities – you might have a very different reaction. If what they're saying hurts, it's because you have an investment in being seen in a certain way. They are threatening your self-image by attacking you in this manner. For me, I could care less if you criticize my archery skills. But God-forbid you accuse me of being a bad photographer.

Now the key point is what I mentioned earlier: the real reason we react negatively when someone criticizes us is not because of what they're saying or doing. It's because we're afraid what they're saying about us might be true. That is, how we see ourselves/"who we think we are" with regard to that thing, is secretly negative. In my case, if I am subconsciously afraid that I'm not a good photographer, I would be more apt to be upset by criticism of me in this arena. Yet I don't feel bad because of what *you've* said or done; I feel bad because of my *own* internal self-image. This is another clear example of how it's "who we think we are" that gives rise to all our feelings. Yet until I begin to grasp that my upsettedness is about me and not you, the fragility of my ego may even lead to me feeling justified in attacking you back.

Taking responsibility for our actions and reactions, as well as for how we see ourselves, means we would never be upset by what anyone else says or does. We stop giving our power away and take full responsibility for how we feel. Eventually, we have to learn to forgive ourselves – both for our shortcomings as well as for beating ourselves up for them. Forgiveness is how the ego is ultimately undone.

Self-confidence
Way back in Chapter One, I mentioned that we would be revisiting the topic of "confidence" later in this book. I said it was likely that successful people are good at what they do because they have a more positive self-image than the rest of us. They probably – consciously or unconsciously – see themselves in a way which says, "*I got this – I can handle this,*" irrespective of what may have happened in the past. But I also said there's

another type of confidence which is really important for us to have if we want to be happy in life.

When I first started working on myself many years ago, I came to the conclusion that a big part of my problem was that I lacked confidence. I thought that the anxiety I felt in most work and social situations was caused by the fact that I didn't see myself in a very positive way. So one day I went to the dictionary and looked up the definition of the word "confidence". The first one was:

"a feeling of self-assurance arising from an appreciation of one's own abilities or qualities."

I could certainly see how more self-assurance and an appreciation of my own abilities would be helpful. But it was another definition that caught my eye. It defined "a confidence" as:

"a trusting relationship."

That is, being able to trust someone to look out for your best interests and/or not attack or harm you. I extrapolated that to the issue of "self-confidence" and decided that:

Self-confidence is a trusting relationship with myself.

I mentioned in previous chapters that in the past I could be very harsh and critical towards myself, especially when I messed something up. So a trusting relationship meant I could trust myself to forgive rather than attack myself for my mistakes. It meant I could depend on myself to not abandon myself in the face of a negative comment or criticism from somebody else. In general, it meant I could count on myself to be more kind, gentle, and understanding towards myself.

We said earlier the root of almost all our emotional pain is self-hatred. Of course, it's not pleasant when someone else directs negative energy our way. Yet we now know that what other people say or do doesn't have to have a negative effect on us. On the other hand, if I can't trust myself to not attack myself when I make a mistake, then I'm kind of screwed. Being harsh with myself for messing something up is an expression of self-hatred. Thus, self-confidence is being able to trust myself to love myself when I most need it. And to forgive myself for the times that I don't.

This idea of a "trusting relationship with myself" has had profound implications for me. Throughout most of my life I feared criticism and rejection. As I mentioned, this was one of the reasons it took so long for me to put myself out there as a photographer and artist. Yet if the pain was really the result of my own lack of self-love, that meant I wasn't a potential victim of other people's unkindness – but only of my own. Once I saw this, I was more able to take steps to move forward in my career.

Like almost everything we experience as adults, I think my own lack of self-love started in how I was treated as a child. There were times when I needed to be consoled or comforted – or just allowed to be a kid and have my feelings. Unfortunately, that often was not given me. Instead, I was met with consternation, impatience and many times punishment. Not by a bad parent. Not by an unloving parent. But by someone who didn't know how else to react to me. Someone who had their hands full taking care of the family and who was just trying to do the best they could to keep it all together.

As I said earlier, the problem is as kids we don't have the necessary mental faculties and awareness to let what other people do be about them. We thus internalize everything. We also don't have any real means to take care of ourselves in our relationships with the adults or other people in our lives. So we usually just had to sit there and take it – we absorbed all the negativity and it became imprinted in the circuits of our minds.

For a long time I was very angry about what had happened to me and the way I was treated as a kid. But then it was pointed out to me that my anger was hurting me more than anyone else. I eventually realized that hating someone else wasn't being loving towards me. It was doing me more harm than good. So it became time to start looking at all this a little closer and to begin to unwind some of the hurt feelings and misunderstandings of my past.

As I began to consider some of my difficult childhood experiences a little more deeply, I could see there was another way to look at them. I realized I could tell a different story about what had happened. The new story did require seeing myself and the other people who were involved differently. It meant giving up some of my ideas about being victimized and unfairly treated. I didn't deny the pain I had experienced, but I found a new way to explain what had happened. Do I wish things had been different? Honestly, most days yes. But am I more understanding and willing to forgive the way things went down? I am, yes. Am I also more willing to accept that something much bigger than I am currently aware of might be going on? Again, yes.

This change of mind as to what happened and how I was treated as a child is helping me to treat myself less harshly as an adult. I can see that when I am beating myself up or making myself wrong for something, I am recreating what I experienced as a child. It's also true that the vast majority of the negative stuff from other people stopped a long time ago and I am no longer subjected to such treatment by them today. (In fact, I actually now receive much support and love from those same people.) So that left me with the awareness that it was my own pattern of unkindness towards myself which formed the basis of much of my anguish as an adult. Again, it's not to say we have to deny our pain or what we experienced as kids. Yet in my case at least, I can see I kept the hurt going by doing to myself what had originally been done to me by others.

Anger
Anger is the primary egoic reaction. The ego always has to be mad about something. Thus it places a high value on pain. Emotional, physical and/or psychological discomfort are the ego's justification for being upset. Anger can take many forms, including annoyance, hostility, frustration, impatience, sarcasm and rage, to name but a few. We normally react with anger when we perceive something as a threat, or as having caused us harm or

loss. "Who we think we are" when we're angry is vulnerable, attacked, powerless, etc. At its core, anger is an attempt to protect ourselves while blaming someone or something else for how we feel. It says, *"Stop – that's not OK,"* at the same time communicating, *"It's your fault that I'm upset."*

Anger may be expressed directly or indirectly. When we physically or verbally assault someone, the attack is direct. When we engage in less obvious forms of anger, such as sarcasm, gossip, character assassination or other passive-aggressive behaviors, our hostility is expressed indirectly. Resentment and grievances are two of the more common forms of indirect anger. They are usually passive in that we harbor the negative feelings within rather than outwardly expressing them. As the resentment simmers in our minds, we plan all the ways we're going to get back at the other person. Yet we usually end up doing nothing.

Consider what *A Course in Miracles* has to say about anger: it says we're never angry at a fact, but only at our own subjective interpretation of that fact.[46] This jives with what we've said a few times already – that we react to the meaning we are giving a particular situation, rather than to the situation itself. If this is true, it means our assessments are always subjective, and if our assessments are subjective, how can we be certain our interpretation is correct? How do we know that the way we see it is the way it actually is?

The Course goes further: it says, *anger is never justified.*[47] To the ego this is blasphemy of the highest order. (Once again, as an exercise in self-awareness, notice what your reaction was when you read that line.) The reason anger is never justified is because, as we just said, we're reacting to our own subjective interpretation. What's upsetting us is how we see ourselves; not what the other person is or isn't doing. We also said that our self-image is mostly made up. The result is we're getting angry based on a made-up idea about ourselves! This is all kinds of insane if you really think about it. Yet this is how most of us live our lives.

---

[46] *A Course in Miracles*, Manual for Teachers, Section 17-4
[47] *A Course in Miracles*, pg. 637

If the concept that anger is never justified is tough to swallow, it's probably because, as I mentioned above, most of us use anger as a way to protect ourselves. Thus giving up anger means potentially giving up protection. The prospect of this arouses great fear in the ego. Yet I can say for me, the more I consciously and deliberately choose to see myself as someone who can take care of himself and is thus safe in the world, the less of a call there is to anger.

Now you may say, "*If someone steals my car or hurts my kid there's not a lot of interpretation needed. I can see clearly what's going on. In such cases, I am more than entitled to react with anger.*" I would respond that, first, you are entitled to react however you'd like. This isn't an attempt to make anyone wrong for who they're being. Next, I'd remind you that nothing we're discussing here is meant to condone somebody else's inappropriate behavior. People do injurious things to themselves and to others all the time. We're not making excuses for that. So it's perfectly OK to take whatever steps are necessary to protect the safety and well-being of yourself, your loved ones and/or your possessions. Yet, I'd also say we are looking at (and if you've made it this far in the book I assume you'd agree) how we can better handle the difficult situations in our lives. We want to change "who we think we are" so we can respond in a more effective way. This means rethinking all our emotional reactions and taking our power back in whatever way we can.

It's not personal!

We've already said a few times the ego takes everything personally. This is because, not surprisingly, the ego is *egocentric*. It always makes what other people do about us. Thus, it's potentially offended by everything and anything that it doesn't interpret as praise or reverence. "*How could you/they/it do this to me?!?*" is a familiar refrain – spoken or unspoken – when the ego is in charge of our thinking. The problem is, taking things personally is a huge catalyst for anger. When we take what other people say or do personally, it's usually a short step to anger and maybe even retaliation.

196

Yet it turns out what other people do is *never* about us – it's always and only about them. We know from Chapter Three that other people have no power over us. Moreover, in the last chapter we said everyone's choices and decisions are motivated by their own internal reference of what will feel better in a given situation. This means that even if the other person attacks or intentionally tries to inflict harm upon us, their choices are about them and not about us. The end result is nothing that comes to us from another person is personal – even if it's *meant* to be personal.

Of course, once again this is blasphemy to the ego. How can someone attacking us not be personal?!? Yet we now know we always have a choice as to how we respond to life. In the next chapter, I'll describe in detail my experience of dealing with attacks against me and my photography on social media. I'll give a couple of examples of where, by not taking those attacks personally, I was able to transform the experiences from something negative into something positive.

If you think you may be taking things personally, my suggestion is to begin to notice how would you have to see yourself in order to be free of it. I know for me, not taking things personally was a huge first step in changing my life. When I stopped making what other people did about me, I was able to see both them and me in a whole new way. In fact, we can take it so far that instead of reacting with anger when people attack us, we can respond with compassion. More about all that in the next chapter.

Mad Men (and women)

As I mentioned earlier, for many of us anger is a primary way we try to take care of ourselves. It's an attempt to set a boundary when someone is acting inappropriately. But look at the dictionary definition of "anger" – it says it's a "*strong feeling of annoyance, displeasure or hostility.*" The truth is, I can say, "*Stop – that's not OK*" without feeling annoyed or hostile. I can communicate directly, even forcefully, without a hint of irritation or defensiveness. For me, this means it's possible to take care of ourselves without resorting to anger.

It is true that at certain times it may be necessary to quickly and/or forcefully grab someone else's attention. Thus, yelling or even physically engaging with that person may be required. This tends to happen with young kids since they're often distracted and/or moving around a lot. Yet what many people don't understand is that anger is about much more than just raising our voice. The communication is often laced with hatred, contempt or disdain. Anger speaks with the voice of condemnation. Thus, when we engage someone with anger, we have gone beyond just attempting to get their attention. We may actually be trying – without being consciously aware of it – to inflict harm or injury upon them. Our true intent in those situations may be to get even.

Other people feel and react to this hatred. With kids especially this can be problematic since they often don't appreciate the problem they're causing. To them, it seems like all of a sudden they're being attacked for no reason. Thus, in the face of an adult's anger, the child can be left feeling confused, afraid and powerless. If this happens often enough, these emotions become a big part of who the child thinks they are. They may also eventually take on their parents' rage or anger to the point that it becomes a part of the child's own personality.

Keeping our cool extends beyond our peers or children. For instance, many of us feel some level of threat or vulnerability with anyone we perceive as having power over us. For this reason, lots of people resent authority figures such as the government or police. We said earlier to react to anything with anger, we would have to perceive ourselves as weak, threatened, vulnerable, etc. By changing how we see ourselves when dealing with authority figures or anyone else for that matter, we can lessen the possibility of overreacting.

Now again, this stuff is relatively simple but it's definitely not easy. I'm personally still a long way off – at times at least – when it comes to reacting without anger. I've been conditioned to reach for the anger pill when I feel frustrated or threatened for so long that it is a difficult habit to break. Thus I'll be the first to admit that keeping cool in the face of another person's transgressions can be very difficult. I can still lose my temper in certain situations and with certain people. In particular, I find I am sometimes really challenged by the kids in my life. They are wonderful and adorable and I am blessed to be part of their family. And there are times I just lose it. I feel so threatened and powerless that all I can do is react. But I am more conscious than ever when I do that. And I also try to forgive myself, and then apologize to them when I can.

If you're like me, my suggestion is to go easy on yourself. For many of us, overcoming anger is one of the steepest hills we will have to climb, right after overcoming fear and self-hatred. Yet if our goal is to stop giving our power away and to become more effective in how we deal with people, then we're going to have to try as much as possible to respond rather than react. We must take responsibility for our thoughts, feelings, words and actions with *all* people and in *all* situations. I can also say that, little by little, as I have begun to see myself differently, I feel less threatened by the world. I don't need to rely so heavily on anger to take care of myself these days. And the roads and highways of New Jersey are a safer place as a result!

But there's a second part to this puzzle: once we begin to change "who we think we are" and stop relying on anger as a means of protection, we need to find another way to take care of ourselves. In our relationships with other people, the best way I know how to do this is by having *healthy boundaries*. We'll spend a lot of time discussing "boundaries" in the next chapter. But I will mention here, healthy boundaries are about taking responsibility for what we think, feel, say and do and then exercising our true power in a way that protects us without harming others.

The desire to feel better

In the last chapter we said everything we do, including reacting with anger, is motivated by a desire to feel better. For example, lashing out in rage can be seen as an attempt to feel powerful (i.e., better) in a situation where we feel powerless. Recall my definition of "fear" from Chapter Four: we said it's "*an emotional response to a perception of ourselves as powerless... in a given situation.*" Thus, anger, like fear, is born out of a perception of ourselves as *powerless*. This is a really important connection since it means that if we're lashing out in anger, we're really lashing out because we're *afraid*. This is so significant I'm going to say it again:

If we're lashing out in anger, we're really lashing out because we're afraid

Which brings us to another important point:

Fear always precedes anger

This means that underlying all feelings of anger are actually feelings of fear. Why is this so significant? If the problem when I feel angry is I'm really afraid, I am probably better served to look at the source of my fear rather than why I think I'm angry. Anger usually keeps the focus on the other person and what they are doing to us. Fear is usually more introspective, inviting us to look inward for the source of our discomfort. It's more likely I'll see the truth if I'm looking within myself rather than directing my attention out on to the situation or another person.

Of greater importance is that expressing fear is more conducive to opening lines of communication between people than is expressing anger. As I mentioned in Chapter Four, defensiveness begets defensiveness. The same is true of anger. If anger is about blaming someone else for how we feel, the natural response of the other person is to shut down. Expressing fear, on the other hand, can be much less threatening. When we communicate that we're afraid, we're usually not blaming or accusing the other person. Their defenses don't get triggered so they're more likely to listen. Thus, there's a better chance to come together and find a peaceful solution.

As an example, let's say your teenage daughter has an accident while using the family car on her way home from a party. Like any parent, the news of an accident involving one of your children is bound to be quite upsetting. Your initial response is one of concern (fear) regarding the well-being of your daughter. While she may be shaken up by the event, it's likely your daughter won't feel threatened or attacked by you showing concern. She may actually interpret your response as an expression of your love for her.

Yet once you find out she's OK and learn that it was her carelessness that caused the accident, you may end up having a different reaction. At some point, it's quite possible that your anger about her carelessness would supersede your concern. You may even yell or scream at her for being so stupid. Now your daughter shuts down, feeling like she's being attacked. Frustrated with your child's lack of response, you unleash more anger and threaten punishment in the form of grounding and/or loss of driving privileges.

Over the next few days you calm down. Because you're reading this damn book, you realize that maybe you could have handled things better. You now understand that when you're lashing out in anger, you're really lashing out because you're afraid. You understand that the cause of your anger was that you were actually terrified your daughter might have been injured or killed, and it would break your heart to lose her. Thus, you can see that it was your fear which was the cause of your anger; not what your child did or did not do.

So you talk it over with your spouse and she urges you to have another conversation with your daughter. Your wife implores you to tell the truth about what was so upsetting to you – the fact that you were afraid of losing someone you loved – rather than dancing around the issue by repeating – albeit in a nicer tone – how important it is to pay attention while driving. You set up a time to discuss things with your daughter. She is understandably reluctant to meet, still feeling guilty about the problems she caused. Also, given your past track record in situations like this, she expects another tongue lashing for her misdeeds.

When you finally sit down together, your initial instinct is to lecture her further on why it's important to pay attention while driving. Yet out of the corner of your eye you see your wife watching you. Brought back to the purpose of your talk by your wife's look, you hesitate, not sure what to say. Your daughter, head hung low, briefly brings her eyes up to meet your own. She's somewhat confused as you're uncharacteristically at a loss for words.

Eventually you start speaking. *"Listen honey. I'm sorry about the way I reacted the other night."* Your daughter, continuing to look down, listens. *"I was, eh, worried."* You glance quickly at your spouse and then rephrase it: *"I mean afraid. I was afraid something awful had happened."* A moment passes. Your daughter lifts her head. Your eyes meet. There's a longer pause and a tear wells up in your right eye. You continue with a somewhat unsteady voice: *"I thought maybe..., maybe you had been hurt, or maybe even..."* Your voice trails off, you can't finish the sentence. Your daughter stares at you intently. You let out a small sob, but no more words come. Suddenly you break down, crying. Your daughter stares, transfixed. She's never seen this side of you before. Eventually, choking back the sobs you say: *"I don't know what I would do if something bad had happened to you. I'm so sorry for yelling."*

At this point, your daughter's surprise gives way to her own tears. She apologizes for being so careless. You hold your finger to your lips indicating she doesn't need to say anything else. You reach forward and embrace her. She falls into your arms. You both weep together. Years of tension, hurt feelings and misunderstandings are suddenly released. Eventually, a sense of peace descends upon you both. Over her shoulder you can see your spouse is also crying. It's a healing moment for all three of you.

That little story illustrates the difference between approaching a conflict with the truth about being afraid vs. hiding our fear behind anger. Which approach do you think is more effective? And which was closer to the truth?

If you're reading this book and have had a similar experience with someone in your own life, I urge you to revisit what was behind your angry reactions. If it turns out it was fear, I promise you it's never too late to go back and admit the truth. Having a discussion like this with someone you love can heal wounds and mend relationships that have seemingly been lost for years.

Judgment

A close first cousin of both fear and anger is *judgment* (as I am using it here, the term is a negative closely related to "condemnation.") We said the ego thrives on assigning guilt and judgment makes guilt specific. It is a subjective determination that someone or something is "bad" (and not in a Michael Jackson kind of way. RIP MJ. ☹) Because they're bad, they are unworthy of our love. Judgment is also a way we feel superior to others. We evaluate some aspect of their lives and condemn them for it. The belief that we are better than someone else allows us to feel justified in all kinds of negative behavior towards them.

Judging another as unworthy give us license to keep our distance from them. Accordingly, judgment fosters separation (a key egoic belief), and like defensiveness, it is a coping mechanism. It's a way we keep ourselves safe by being separate from others. The conscious belief is, *"I'm better than you so I don't have to hang out with you."* But the subconscious belief is, *"If I don't get close to you, you can't hurt me."*

Like anger, judgment is a reaction by the ego to feeling threatened. It's about making someone or something else wrong so we can feel like we're in control. As such, it's a form of attack. This may be a silent attack in our own minds, or we may make our judgment known by sharing it with others. When we share a negative judgment, we're usually looking for allies to help support our belief that we're better than the person we judge. In this respect, the ego – like misery – loves company.

The problem is, we're usually not aware that we feel threatened by another person when we judge them – we just think they're a jerk. The ego jumps straight to the idea that they're unworthy, skipping over the fact that it feels threatened in some way. It's not obvious we're reacting to a threat in this situation because the threat is not to our physical self; rather, it's to our egoic self. The ego lives by comparisons and is inherently insecure. It's almost always afraid other people are better. Not wanting to feel less-than, the ego quickly turns around and judges the other person first.

But because the ego's position is so tenuous, it will latch on to any – or no – reason at all to judge another person. Think of all the shallow and inherently trivial reasons that we judge others: the car they drive, the street they live on, the clothes they wear, etc. The ego is so insecure that it strives to convince itself that even the most superficial things make it better than anyone else.

Judgment is another good example of why it's important to be aware of "who we think we are" in each moment. When we judge someone based on something as trivial as the clothes they're wearing, we must really see ourselves as less-than. Yet we usually have no idea that we're reacting to our own sense of inadequacy when we judge someone else.

We also react negatively to someone who reminds us of an unhealed part of ourselves. I mentioned earlier I used to react very strongly to people who exhibited "neediness" in their relationships (especially when those relationships were with me!) I judged them very harshly, completely unaware that I was really reacting to something I didn't like about myself. Thus, judgment can also be an indicator that we have more work to do in terms of healing a particular aspect of our own personalities.

Once again, this is a massive call to consciousness. We have to become so aware of "who we think we are" in each moment, that our old programmed habits won't pass by unnoticed. As we said in Chapter One, sometimes we're not aware that there's a problem until after the fact. We have to work backwards, unpacking our reactions and asking, "*How must I have seen myself in that situation to have acted that way.*" Judgment, in particular, is so habitual and seemingly natural that it passes by without being questioned by us. Now we know better. Judgment is never about the other person or the situation. It's always about how we see ourselves. Use that bit of knowledge to begin to undo the do-do that you've been doing for so long. The people in your life will thank you for it. And you will thank yourself.

"Won't you be my neighbor"
Judgment is a good lead-in to the next little anecdote from my own life. During the past 30 years or so I've been on a sort of

journey of self-discovery. At a certain point in that journey, I became aware that the same types of problems and issues were recurring in my life. There was always someone or something outside of me making things difficult. While the particular people or places might be different, the form of the problems were almost always the same.

One particular issue that's plagued me over the past 15 years or so has to do with living with neighbors. Whether it's loud TV's or music, noisy parties or family events, blocking my parking spaces, or – my favorite – cooking odors, I always seemed to be challenged by the people who lived in close proximity to me. I'll describe the specifics of these conflicts in a minute, but let me say upfront that none of what I experienced was anyone else's fault. While they may or may not have had a part in what transpired, my reactions were always about me and had their origins within my own mind. Thus, how I experienced what they were doing was on me.

We said earlier the ego thrives on feeling victimized. Well that's a good way to characterize how I felt for the better part of the past 15 years when it comes to my living situations. I saw myself as the innocent victim of other people's inconsideration. They just did what they did without considering me or my needs. Now right off the bat you might see a problem. I wasn't living in the same space with any of these people nor did I have any kind of prior relationship or even acquaintance with them. (These were all adjoining living situations – either apartments or duplex/subdivided single family homes.) Yet I was assuming – at some level – that they were supposed to be considerate of me and my needs. That's how out to lunch I was.

I justified this by thinking I could point out all the ways I was so thoughtful and considerate of them. For instance, I always turned down my TV at night, I never had parties or gatherings that would potentially disturb them, and I never cooked smelly food. They, on the other hand, were the inconsiderate monsters who ruined my life – sometimes on a daily basis – with their noise and disgusting cooking habits! Thus in my mind at least, they should be considerate of me because I was so considerate of them.

Mind you they never asked me to do any of those things. I did them of my own accord and expected my neighbors to read my mind and then reciprocate.

Yes – that's how crazy I was.

Without going into all the gory details, the problems spanned three different living situations in two different states with at least six different sets of neighbors. Over the years my attempts to resolve the issues included everything from *"let's sit down and work this out"* meetings, to shouting matches in the driveway, to calling the police in the middle of the night, to contacting the local housing authority to try to get them evicted, to hiring realtors to help me find a new place, and so on. In fact, I tried everything short of a full blown lawsuit to resolve the issues, but nothing seemed to work.

Seeing myself as powerless in this ongoing drama created a lot of stress in my life. Recall we said stress is when we focus on something we have no control over. In each case, I became obsessed with my neighbors' habits and behaviors. For example, I knew their work schedules, their kids' school schedules, what time they usually ate, when they woke up, when they went to bed, etc. In fact, in a few cases, I was so obsessively over-focused on them I could tell you – based solely by the sound of their car – when they were driving down the street! (One day one of them got an electric car and that really messed me up!) So as you can see, I was totally focused on them, their habits and their behaviors – three things I had absolutely no control over.

Now I may be insane but I'm not crazy. I thought I needed to know all this stuff to protect myself. In many cases, because of the nature of the living situation, their actions often had a detrimental effect on me. For instance, as I mentioned earlier, in one case, whenever they used their shower or toilet, I lost all my water pressure and temperature. (Yes – I spoke to the landlord about it and they claimed there was nothing they could do.) Now low water pressure may not seem like a big deal. But when it happens often enough that you regularly get out of the shower with shampoo or conditioner stuck in your hair, you start to pay attention to these things. And it did get worse – in more than a couple of instances, things like yelling, screaming and even domestic violence between them occurred. So I needed to know as much as I could to take care of myself.

Yet since I had no control over these things, the result was my feeling stressed. It affected my psychological, emotional and even physical health. It was so bad at times that I got really ill over the whole thing. I think most people who know me would consider me a fairly level-headed person (well after reading the last few paragraphs maybe they actually wouldn't.) Yet when it came to dealing with neighbors, many days I was completely out of my mind. On more than one occasion, I honestly felt like I was going insane.

While it was true I had no control over their behaviors, it was entirely *untrue* that I had no control over how I reacted to them. At a certain point I realized I was giving my power away and that this was the genesis of a big part of my distress. Thus, I began to look at the whole situation differently – not because I'm such a nice guy or good hearted person (I am actually both those things ☺). But because my health and sanity depended on it!

The first thing I had to look at was that I thought everything they were doing was personal. I mentioned earlier that the ego takes everything personally. In most of these situations with my neighbors, my mind constantly went there: *"These inconsiderate people are infringing on* my *life."* *"I'm the innocent party here."* *"They are deliberately attacking* my *peace and tranquility."* *"My landlord doesn't care about* me,*"* and so on. As I mentioned, at times my frustration and despair were overwhelming. Yet as I now know, the problem was not with how they were acting; it was with how I saw myself. Seeing myself as helpless, a victim, unimportant, powerless, etc., led me to give the situation a correspondingly disempowering meaning: *"I'm screwed. I can't do anything about what's happening. I'll never get out of here. Now I just have to suffer. No one cares about me."* And so on.

Today I can see that in large degree, my neighbors actions had absolutely nothing to do with me. None of what they were doing was personal. They were just living their lives in a way that felt right to them. Yet at the time I took everything personally and so felt justified in attacking them back (remember – the ego always feels justified in attacking those it deems as guilty.) Thus, at a certain point, out of sheer frustration, I started acting negatively towards them.

It started out small. For instance, at times when we passed each other I would pretend I didn't see them, or I would not return their greeting. As my retaliation progressed, once or twice (or maybe 10 times – I can't really remember ☺), when their mail was erroneously placed in my mail box, I kinda tossed it in the garbage. (Before you call the Postal Police, it was always junk mail – well, almost always.) At times, I would also sit around thinking of ways I could get back at them for making so much noise or cooking stinky food. Once I Googled how to make a stink bomb so the next time they cooked I could unleash my own noxious fumes upon their inconsiderate noses. (I never actually made the stink bomb of course.)

At other times I was more aggressive. From complaining to the landlord, to banging incessantly on the floor or walls when they were making too much noise, to the aforementioned calling the police or Housing Department, I wasn't shy in letting them know of my displeasure. I even went so far once as to buy a mini, home-theater surround sound system. I placed it against the common wall and tried to blast them out in the middle of the night. (I say "tried" because I turned the volume so high it blew up within 20 seconds and was thereafter useless. I felt like a fool – but luckily the store gave me my money back the next day.)

A particularly dark incident occurred when I confronted them about blocking my driveway. Now I'm not a confrontational person, yet never in a million years could I imagine being so inconsiderate as to block someone else's parking space. When I saw what they had done, my rage boiled over and the situation quickly escalated. We almost came to blows. (I can see now how people kill each other over parking spaces at Walmart.)

Needless to say, my ego and its associated negative thinking definitely got the best of me at these times. Of course, I had no idea the problem was with *me*. I was certain *they* were the cause of all my woes. Looking back too I can see I really felt crazy when I was doing some of the things I described. It was like I had become someone else. That's a good way to know when we're operating via the ego – we lose our sense of self. That is, if we can pull out of it long enough to notice what we're doing and who we're being.

Now speaking of insanity, there was something else that happened several times which completely surprised and shocked me. When I confronted them about their misdeeds, instead of being met with an apology and regret for having disturbed me, I was met with an equal or greater dose of their anger. They were as hostile towards me as I was towards them! We said earlier defensiveness begets defensiveness and anger begets anger. I was so certain I was right and they were wrong that I expected a contrite and remorseful response from them. When they replied with their own rage, it blew my mind. I simply couldn't believe they could be upset with me. Wasn't it obvious that *I* was the victim here? How could they possibly feel victimized by me? And yet it turns out that's exactly how they felt.

This is a perfect example of how the ego, self-centered to the extreme, is completely void of empathy for others. It discounts their experiences and places no value or credence on their perspective. When we're identifying with our ego, we have no ability to see someone else's point of view. This is why I said at the beginning of this chapter, when taken to the limit, it is possible to do barbaric and inhumane things to other people when we're run by our ego.

As I mentioned above, at a certain point I realized I had to look at myself. The faces and places were different. Yet the problems were always the same. After a while it was difficult to deny that the common denominator was me. Once I was willing to at least consider that part of the problem was with how I was reacting, I began to look for a solution. That solution eventually came through applying the principles we've been discussing in this book: taking responsibility, exercising my True Power, owning my fears, and then tying it all together with forgiveness.

With respect to the last point, I'll say to the extent I am willing to forgive myself and others, the more things change for the better in my life. Issues that never got resolved through confrontation or aggression (or passive aggression – hey! it was only a few pieces of junk mail!), seem to take care of themselves when I apply forgiveness. The result is I'm not hyper-focused on what other people are doing or not doing and I'm rarely upset with anyone anymore, including my neighbors. It's been a long, long time since I've had an angry confrontation with anyone. (Just don't block my driveway – don't ever do that...)

Now as we'll see in the next chapter, the thing that's so important about forgiveness is –perhaps not surprisingly – I have to see myself differently to do it. To truly forgive someone, I can no longer see myself as powerless or a victim. This is one reason why forgiveness is so good for us – we have to change our self-image for the better to do it.

The final thing I'll say about the neighbor situation is that for the longest time I resisted getting to know any of them personally. I was keen on maintaining that sense of separation that is the lifeblood of the ego. Even when I had opportunities to put my grievances on hold, and for instance, socialize with them, I didn't. I was adamant that I was better than they were and thus they didn't deserve my time. This distance and separation allowed me to continue to hate and blame them for my unhappiness. In hindsight, that's probably exactly what I wanted. I didn't really want a solution to my problems – I wanted to be able to continue to blame and point the finger at someone else for my suffering.

Whether with neighbors or anyone else in our life, it's clear that it's harder to hate them when we get to know them personally. Keeping someone at arm's distance is the ego's way of keeping the conflict going. So in my case, with my current neighbors, I've made an effort to do things differently. I have taken the time to get to know them, at least a little. I always say "hello" and have inquired about their lives. I've even offered to be helpful a few times. They have reciprocated and things between us are decidedly different than they would have been in the past.

The biggest thing I've found is that my neighbors are normal people living their lives in a way that feels right to them. They're pretty nice and are actually willing to go out of their way (at least a little) to accommodate me. Instead of yelling and screaming and banging on walls, all I had to do was ask them nicely. Who knew?!? It's not all perfect. But it's way better than it's ever been. I see we have much more in common than I would have thought. They're simply trying to take care of themselves as best they can and do what they need to do to survive – just like me.

"*Just like me*" – that's something the ego would never say.

Would you rather be right or happy?

So this brings us back to the title of this chapter. I'll ask you now, "*Would you rather be right or happy?*" Earlier in Chapter Three, we looked at what it means to be "happy". For the remainder of this chapter we'll consider what it means to be "right."

The first thing to notice is that the way the question is phrased, it implies that "right" or "happy" are mutually exclusive – i.e., you can be one or the other, but not both. Like many people, I used to think being right *made* me happy. There was a sense of satisfaction when my version of reality triumphed over someone else's. I would even enjoy gloating at times over my opponents' defeat, feeling vindicated that I knew better. Yet as we'll see in a minute, being right, at least as the ego defines it, doesn't leave room for True Happiness.

The dictionary defines "to gloat" as "*dwelling on one's own success or another's misfortune with smugness or malignant pleasure.*" So hopefully the problem with being right (and with especially gloating over it) is coming into view. But we need to dig a little deeper to see why being right is actually antithetical to our happiness.

The short answer is, "being right" is an ego thing. Most of us most of the time are certain that we're right and everyone else is wrong. This is especially true whenever we feel resentful or victimized because of what someone else has done to us. In my example of my conflicts with my neighbors, I never once doubted I was right and they were wrong. Even when it turned out that they were just as unhappy with me as I was with them, I was still convinced I knew better and that they were out of their minds. Yet they were just as sure that they were right and I was wrong.

When there's such a discrepancy, how can anyone know who or what is actually right?

The problem is we all see "right" and "wrong" from our own perspectives. Like everything else, we decide these things based on our own subjective interpretation of the situation. Thus, we're at least one step removed from any kind of objective assessment of "right" or "wrong" (if such a thing were even possible.) Even worse, the ego always and only sees things from its own point of view. It does this while simultaneously discounting everyone else's perspective. Thus while we're in our egoic mind, it's very difficult to see things as other people see them. Moreover, what's "right" or "wrong" is constantly changing. Even if we could identify a set of norms which everyone agrees upon as "good" or "right," overtime, as the society or group changes, those norms must change too. Therefore, what's right today for a person, group or society may be wrong tomorrow.

But by far the biggest problem with "being right" is what it means we must do to the other person or group of people. In a world dominated by the ego (and if you don't believe that that's what this world is, reread the first seven paragraphs of this chapter), someone must be wrong if someone else is to be right. Thus,

In order to be right we have to make someone else wrong

Making someone else wrong never makes us truly happy. Of course, the ego would have us believe otherwise. The ego loves being right because it's another way the ego gets to see itself as "better." If I'm right and you're wrong, I must, in at least one or more respects, be superior to you. Seeing itself as better is a cornerstone of the ego's existence. Yet at what cost do we do this?

Earlier in this book, we discussed the effects of making ourselves wrong. We said self-hatred is one of the most debilitating things we can do. I'll mention now making others wrong is just as bad. Hatred – whether of ourselves or another – weakens us mentally, emotionally and even physically. Anger and hatred deny our own or someone else's goodness. As such they are, metaphorically speaking at least, "soul-killing." If the basis of life is love and we practice love's opposite all day long, well maybe you can see the problem.

You may be saying, *"I don't hate them. I just think they're wrong."* Yet thinking someone else is wrong clearly isn't loving them. (Despite what the ego would tell you, "sympathy" or "pity" isn't love.) Therefore, making someone else wrong so you can be right is a form of attack, and attack is always rooted in hatred. Think about it this way: Spirit is never worried about being right and thus never makes anyone or anything wrong. This is because Spirit is always about Love and Love worries not about who's right and who's wrong.

And even if you don't believe making someone else wrong has negative effects from within you, consider the potential negative effects from outside you. No one likes to be made wrong. We will often go to extremes to prove we're right when confronted with someone else's pronouncement that we're wrong. Another person, group or religion, therefore, may seek to assert that they are right through revenge, retaliation, etc., and that's never good for us. This is why a simple disagreement can deteriorate into physical violence. One person feels slighted or like their integrity has been questioned and now their ego kicks in. Defending their honor means taking the conflict to the next level. Thus any "solution" that relies on making others wrong cannot produce long term peace – whether in the boardroom, bedroom or international meeting room.

What if after all that it turns out the other person really is wrong – i.e., incorrect in their interpretation of things? We must learn to correct others without making them wrong. Just like we don't need to be angry to protect ourselves, we don't need to attack others to prove we're right. This is especially true of children. Children often lack the information and/or life experience needed to see certain things correctly. If we attack them for their lack of knowledge often enough, we can destroy their self-esteem. Instead, we want to communicate non-violently and non-judgmentally at first, and listen to the other person's reply with an open mind. Then we can offer correction with love, understanding and compassion.

The last thing I'll say about making others wrong is that, without knowing it, we treat ourselves the way we treat others. So if we condemn other people for their sins, chances are pretty good we will condemn ourselves for ours. We can't judge others as being wrong and then expect to be free of self-judgment and/or self-condemnation.

In the next and final chapter of this book, we'll address this and related issues head-on. "Forgiveness" embodies everything we just said and much more. It invites us to refrain from making others wrong and instead meet them with kindness, understanding and compassion. It suggests we let go of our incessant need to be right and extend to others the mercy we would want to receive when we mess things up ourselves. Forgiveness urges us to choose love rather than fear when correcting someone else's mistakes. We'll explore all this and more in the next chapter.

TAKEAWAYS:

1. The ego is that part of our mind that believes in victimization, attack and justified anger. It's always on the look-out for enemies. The ego is also the origin of the concept that the world makes us think, feel, say and do the things we do.

2. The ego thrives on judgment and is obsessed with making others "wrong". It pays close attention to their mistakes and feels fully entitled to correct them. The ego thinks it knows better – and therefore *is* better – than everyone else.

3. The ego is the part of us that sees itself as separate from other people and from all the things that make up life. It's convinced we can hurt another and not suffer any consequences. We can thus become indifferent to the plight

and suffering of others and may even act in ways which are inhuman and ultimately insane.

4. The ego seeks unfair advantage in all interactions. It feels entitled to take more than its share and justifies the most selfish behavior on the grounds that it is just doing what it needs to do to survive. The ego never wants to look bad and will go out of its way to preserve a positive and caring facade.

5. We see in others all that we have not forgiven in ourselves. "Projection" is the unconscious process whereby we deny the existence of our unfavorable traits by attributing them to others. All the things that upset us about other people are usually things we hate about ourselves.

6. The key in becoming aware of projection is to notice when and why we are upset. If the issue we're reacting to in another person isn't ours, we won't feel compelled to attack them for it. When our reaction swings out towards left field we know the problem is about us and not them.

7. Every time we feel insulted or offended the real source of the upset lies in our own self-doubt and insecurity. It's these things – not what someone else is saying or doing – that cause us to feel hurt or slighted.

8. Most of us suck at archery. And that's OK.

9. "Self-confidence" is a trusting relationship with ourselves: we trust ourselves to forgive rather than attack us for our shortcomings. It means we can trust ourselves to be more kind, gentle, and compassionate towards ourselves no matter what we say or do.

10. Anger is the primary egoic reaction: the ego always needs to be mad about something. It thus places a high value on pain. Anger is an attempt to protect ourselves while making

someone else feel guilty for how we feel. It says, *"Stop – that's not OK!"* while also saying *"I'm upset and it's your fault."*

11. Anger may be expressed directly or indirectly. When we physically or verbally assault someone, the attack is direct. When we engage in sarcasm, gossip, character assassination or other passive-aggressive behaviors, the anger is expressed indirectly. Resentment and grievances are two of the more common forms of indirect anger.

12. We are never angry at a fact; but only at our subjective interpretation of that fact. Since we're reacting to the meaning we've given to the situation, we cannot be sure our interpretation is correct. For this reason anger is never justified.

13. For many people, anger is a primary way we try to take care of ourselves. Yet, the key is to understand we can protect ourselves without feeling annoyed or hostile. We can communicate directly, even forcefully, without irritation or defensiveness, or without trying to hurt the other person back.

14. Anger is more than just raising our voice. It is a communication laced with hatred, contempt and/or disdain.

15. Lashing out in anger is often an attempt to "feel better" in a situation where we feel powerless. This means that if we are lashing out in anger, we're really lashing out because we're afraid. Underlying all feelings of anger are feelings of fear.

16. Anger is an attempt to make someone else feel guilty and the natural response of the other person is to shut down. When we communicate we're afraid, we're usually not blaming the other person so their defenses don't get triggered and there's a better chance to reach a peaceful solution.

17. It's not personal! The ego takes everything personally. It's potentially offended by everything and anything. Yet what anyone does is always about them and never about others. We all make choices based on our own internal decision-making process. This means nothing anyone ever does is personal – even if it's meant to be personal.

18. Judgment is our subjective determination that someone or something is unworthy of our love. Judgment is also a way we keep ourselves separate and thus safe from others. The need to see ourselves as better than others is born out of the ego's insecurity and fear that it is not good enough.

19. I love my neighbors (most of the time ☺).

20. It is harder to hate people when we get to know them. *"They're just like me,"* is something the ego would never say.

21. Being "right" or "happy" are mutually exclusive. We all see "right" and "wrong" from our own perspectives and decide these things based on our subjective interpretation of a situation.

22. Being "right" usually means making someone else wrong. Any "solution" that relies on making wrong cannot produce long term peace.

23. We often go to extremes to prove we're right when confronted with someone else's pronouncement that we're wrong. Another person, group or nation may seek to assert that they're right through revenge, retaliation, etc., and that's never good for us.

24. Hatred – whether of ourselves or another – weakens us mentally, emotionally and even physically. Making someone else wrong so we can be right is a form of attack, and attack is always rooted in hatred

25. We treat ourselves the way we treat others. If we condemn another for their sins, we will eventually have to condemn ourselves for our own. We can't judge others and expect to be free of self-judgment.

EXERCISES:

1. Review the first seven paragraphs of this chapter and then think about three recent situations where you identified with your ego (any conflict with another person is usually a good place to start). Go through the different characteristics of the ego described in those paragraphs and write about how they apply to you in those situations.

2. Write about at least one situation where you did something negative to someone else and it came back around to hurt you.

3. *"If you spot it, you got it."* Identify at least three personality traits or behaviors that upset you when you see them in other people. Explore whether you judge yourself for having those same traits (or their opposites). If you do, write about how this affects your reactions when you see those traits in others.

4. Think about a time when you were upset by someone else's criticism of you. How did you see yourself with respect to the thing they were criticizing you for? Did you have an investment in being seen differently? Were you afraid the other person was right?

5. Do the "Archery" process we discussed earlier in this chapter with another person.

6. Write about a "trusting relationship with yourself." Describe what it would look like and how it would change your life.

7. Recall the last time you got angry and lashed out at someone. See if you can differentiate between your subjective interpretation of what was happening vs. the actual facts. Looking back, was anger really justified?

8. Referring to the incident you identified in #7, would it have been possible to take care of yourself without resorting to anger? Could you have responded peacefully and achieved the same or a better result?

9. Referring again to the incident you identified in #7, explain how fear preceded your anger. Note how things might have gone differently if you admitted to yourself and/or the other person you were actually afraid (concerned, worried) rather than angry.

10. Write about the last time you took something personally. Reflect upon whether what other people do could ever really be about us. Describe how the situation might have been different if you hadn't taken things personally.

11. Most coping mechanisms (like judgment) are attempts to take care of ourselves when we don't know a better way. Review the section on "Judgment" and write about how you have used it as a way to stay separate and thus safe. Notice if it creates more harm than good in your life. Identify any costs of engaging in judgment in terms of your relationship with yourself and others.

12. Is judging yourself as better than others really a cover for your own insecurities? If yes, describe how you can overcome this.

13. It's harder to hate people once we get to know them. Identify three people in your life who you only know casually and with whom you have strained relations. Make a commitment to get to know each one of them better over the next 30 days. Identify how that changes your perception of (i) yourself, (ii) the other people, and (iii) of the relationship.

14. Would you rather be right or happy? Identify three past situations where you were certain you were right. How did you make someone else wrong as a result? Indicate how it affected your relationship with the other person and with yourself. How "right" do you feel today now that some time has passed? Could there have been a better way to approach the situation than you were right and they were wrong? If so, describe.

Chapter Seven
Forgiveness

"Holding on to resentment is like drinking poison and expecting the other person to die." [48]

Forgiveness is a key ingredient in happiness and good health. It's a way to heal all wounds and mend all relationships. It can restore an individual's sanity or world peace. And it's the last thing most of us want to do on any given day. Go figure.

The dictionary defines "to forgive" as:

> *to stop feeling anger toward someone or something;*
> *to stop blaming;*
> *to give up resentment;*
> *to grant relief or to pardon*

In the last chapter we spoke at length about the ego. Everything the ego represents is essentially the opposite of forgiveness. For instance, we said the ego thrives on conflict and drama. Forgiveness has as its essence, peace. The ego loves to make others wrong and believes in judgment, separation and justified anger. Forgiveness stands for innocence, compassion and oneness, and promotes fairness and equity amongst all people. The ego blames everyone else for how it feels and freely

---

[48] Many people attribute this saying to the Buddha, but it appears it may have actually originated in the Alcoholics Anonymous program.

condemns all who don't agree with it. Forgiveness encourages taking responsibility, praising others and seeing only the best in us and them.

I think many people, in theory at least, agree it's good to forgive. So how could it be the last thing most of us want to do on any given day? I believe this is because as we move beyond the theory to its practical application, forgiveness gets a little more complicated. For instance, how many of us are really ready to let our enemies off the hook? How willing are we to see those who have hurt us as innocent? Can we really give up resentment, judgment and condemnation once and for all? Are we prepared to see the best in others no matter what? And are any of us really down with giving up attack?

Forgiveness encourages – even requires – all of this. Letting go is the price we have to pay to be free of the ego. If you're like me, anger, resentment and judgment can be a way of life. It's almost impossible for me to go to anywhere without judging someone for something. And now I'm saying we gotta give all this up?

Yup, I'm saying exactly that – we gotta give it all up.

But only if we want joy, connection, prosperity and health. Only if we want our family, friends and co-workers to feel safe and loved in our presence. Only if we want nations to peacefully coexist with nations, and races to peacefully coexist with races.

But it gets worse.... Take a look at this definition of forgiveness:

> "A *conscious, deliberate decision to release feelings of resentment or vengeance toward a person or group who has harmed you, regardless of whether they actually deserve your forgiveness.*"[49]

Are you kidding? Really? Who lives this way?!?
You and I. (Or at least we're invited to.)

---

[49] "*What is Forgiveness*", Greater Good Magazine
https://greatergood.berkeley.edu/topic/forgiveness/definition

The Big Lie
The ego tells us we can love a little and hate a little. We can attack sometimes and heal at other times. We can be angry today and forgiving tomorrow. But the reality is, this is an all-or-nothing proposition. We either love unconditionally – or we're not loving at all. Love and judgment, peace and anger, innocence and guilt, acceptance and condemnation, may appear to coexist for a short time. But they're actually all mutually exclusive. Eventually one always undoes the other.

As we've already said, for many of us anger is our attempt to protect ourselves when we feel threatened. Likewise, judgment, resentment and blame are also ways we try to feel safe and in control. So if forgiveness means giving all these things up, and if we rely on them for protection, well – you can see the problem. Most of us don't know how to feel safe without anger or in control without judgment. We don't know who we would be without resentment or blame. So to ask us to surrender those things in the name of forgiveness is a big deal.

Thus, we're talking about a pretty radical shift in how we live. When we spoke previously of unconditional love, we said it means loving someone when we least like who they're being. Forgiveness means the same thing – except now with the added twist that the ones were loving may have actually caused us harm. Thus, while we may pay lip service to the idea that it's better to forgive than attack, for many this is a 180-degree reversal of how we're currently living. And even if as individuals we're able to forgive certain people at certain times, consider this on a national or global scale: are we really ready to forgive those nations or peoples who have hurt us or who mean us harm?

OK, now that I've got your attention, let's back things up a bit.

Forgiveness is something we do for ourselves
I think the first major obstacle to forgiveness for most people (after they realize it means giving up their anger, blame, and judgment) is that they see it as something they're doing for someone else. There's an idea they're letting another person (or nation) off the hook, scot-free, and that the other person (or

nation) doesn't deserve such clemency. As we'll find out shortly, we can forgive and still defend ourselves and/or hold others accountable for their actions. Yet what most of us don't get is that forgiveness is something we do for *ourselves*. For instance, letting go of resentment frees *us* from the negative consequences that come with hating someone. At the most rudimentary level, being preoccupied with negative thoughts about what someone else did to us reinforces our own victim mentality and distracts us from more productive thinking. Most people have no idea how much energy they consume every day being angry or annoyed. Ruminating over another person's bad behavior does nothing to them – but it can easily ruin *our* day. Also, there's mounting evidence that persistent negative emotional states like anger, hatred and resentment, can adversely affect our health.[50] So it's quite possible we are actually *harming ourselves* by hating someone else.

At the next level, if, instead of forgiving the other person, we act on our negative emotions, such as by seeking revenge, this almost always makes things worse. While I'm sure some people feel differently, in my own life revenge tends to escalate the conflict rather than resolve it. We said in the last chapter everyone thinks their perspective is the correct one. Thus whatever the other person did that may have harmed us, they did because they thought it was the right thing for them to do. In fact, they may have thought they had no other choice but to do it. So when we seek revenge, instead of them rolling over and agreeing to our point of view, now they feel attacked and in their mind further retaliation is warranted. At a certain point it doesn't matter who started it (both will claim the other did anyway.) As each side feels justified in seeking retaliation and revenge, the conflict escalates and both sides end up losing.

To the ego, forgiveness feels like giving up. Yet as my story with my neighbors shows, we gain a lot more than we lose when we extend forgiveness. In most cases what we're gaining is peace.

---

[50] https://www.webmd.com/balance/stress-management/features/how-anger-hurts-your-heart

This is no small thing. As long as we deal with conflict by using force, especially when that force is driven by anger, there can be no peace. We will live in constant fear of retaliation from the other side. The fact that we may have more or bigger weapons does not promise an end to conflict. At best, it buys time between attacks. Yet until we truly forgive, there will always be the possibility of more strife. The ego will see to it.

One of the biggest benefits to us from forgiveness, which we'll discuss in more detail later, is that when we truly forgive we change how we see ourselves. We stop giving our power away and no longer see ourselves as victims. I said in Chapter Three, no one has the power to hurt us unless we give them that power. Thus, when we truly forgive, "who we think we are" becomes someone who can't be hurt by others. We may in fact have suffered loss or damage, but as we'll see later, "hurt" is a subjective determination that is made separately from actual harm or loss. This is a pretty radical shift in thinking for most people. Yet, when we embrace it, it changes "who we think we are" and opens up many new possibilities.

The first step to forgiveness and thus to lasting peace is the recognition that we all do what we do because we believe it's what we need to do to survive. All people share this motivation. (While there are different levels of "survival", this fits squarely with what we said in Chapter Five about doing what we do to feel better. Nothing feels better than surviving!) The reason this is important is, the more we can identify with others, the more potential there is for peaceful resolution of our differences. When we see our opponents as having the same impulses as we do, we can begin to see the problem in a new way. And when we see the problem differently, we'll have a better chance to work things out.

Know thy neighbor as thy self...

As in my example with my own neighbors, the more we get to know other people the harder it is to hate them. Therefore, it would behoove us to become well acquainted with anyone who's actions may affect us (especially if we consider those people potential adversaries.) We can actually get to know other people so well, and have such clear lines of communication with them, that we can diffuse potential problems *before* they happen.

But again, this is all very difficult to do when we're locked into the ego. The egoic mind is paranoid – it's always on the lookout for enemies. It's also egocentric – it takes everything personally and never gives anyone the benefit of the doubt. It prefers attack to peace and is entirely unwilling to see someone else's perspective, especially if it feels vulnerable or threatened. This is why the ego is an all or nothing proposition. We truly can't love a little and attack a little. This will never work if we want lasting peace.

As I mentioned a moment ago, forgiveness is not about letting the "bad guys" off the hook. We're not releasing someone from the consequences of their actions. We also don't have to give up our right to defend ourselves. We can still hold others accountable and use force if necessary to protect our interests. Yet force must be a last, last, last resort. Diplomacy, dialog, and a commitment to peace must come first. Actually, what must come first is seeing ourselves differently. When we see ourselves differently, we'll see others differently, and it's then that we'll finally have a real chance at peace.

I've often thought about what would happen if we, as a species, were confronted with a threat from outside our solar system. Imagine this alien force was significantly more advanced and it was clear it would take everyone on Earth working together to overcome this adversary. Do you think as human beings we'd have any problem putting our differences aside to get this done? If the future of the planet were at stake, would we care about what some other country did to us last week, last month – or last century? Of course not. The only thing that's stopping us from coming together like that right now is our ego. Obviously I hope it never comes down to something like an alien threat to bring the nations of the Earth together. But maybe that wouldn't be such a bad thing...?

Boundaries

I alluded to this in the last chapter: if we're going to leave our anger behind as a means of taking care of ourselves, we'll need to replace it with something else. Whether as individuals or as nations, we can replace our anger with *healthy boundaries*. I'll share some of the things I've learned about this over the years below, but for anyone who's interested in a more in-depth discussion of this topic I highly recommend the book *Facing Codependence* by Pia Mellody.[51]

OK, so to start, let's look at what boundaries are. Boundaries are dividing lines between ourselves and others. Some people visualize them as fences or barriers. I prefer to think of them more as guidelines or rules as to what is acceptable to and from me when interacting with others. Boundaries are the primary way we take care of ourselves in our relationships. They can reduce stress, promote harmony, foster intimacy and avoid violent confrontations between people. Thus, they can make a huge difference in the quality of our relationships, and ultimately, in the quality of our lives.

There are five main types of boundaries that I have used in my own life (other people may prefer less or more). They are: physical boundaries, temporal (time) boundaries, verbal boundaries, mental boundaries, and emotional boundaries. There's a lot of overlap between these five types and there's no right or wrong when it comes to which type you use. The rule in terms of choosing a boundary is what is needed in order to see ourselves as safe and/or comfortable in specific situations or with specific people. I'll give some examples of each in a minute.

While our boundaries may change over time, it's important to keep in mind that when we modify things it could be a source of confusion and/or tension with others. This is because, as we'll discuss below, we teach others how it's OK to treat us. So we need to be prepared to deal with what may happen when we change the rules. That said, just like all our other choices and decisions in

---

[51] https://www.amazon.com/Facing-Codependence-Where-Comes-Sabotages/dp/0062505890

life, we don't have to explain, defend or justify our boundaries to anyone if we choose not to. Taking care of ourselves in all situations and with all people is our responsibility. While we can negotiate with others about what might work for both people in a given situation, ultimately we have to choose boundaries that work for us. This is a big part of taking our power back in our relationships and as we'll discuss later, when we fail to do this, resentment (or worse) is bound to follow.

Here are a few examples of boundaries I've used over the years in my own life:

1. Physical – *physical contact limited to handshakes with strangers; open hugs and maybe kissing on the cheek with family or friends; no lip kissing with non-intimate partners. Avoid certain types of people (e.g., heavy drinkers, drug users) and/or places (e.g., loud, smoke-filled bars or restaurants); I only eat certain types of foods (no meat); I don't lend money, clothing or camera equipment to others, etc.*

2. Temporal – *Visits with certain people are limited to a certain number of hours (I may alter this if it's a special occasion and other people are there with me); Phone calls limited to a certain number of minutes with certain people; no professional work for free; bill for all time (including travel expenses) when working for clients; etc. I don't have to respond to texts or emails immediately – depending on the tone/content, I may wait to respond to allow things to cool down.*

3. Verbal – *no unnecessary yelling, screaming, name-calling; no sarcastic, blaming, shaming remarks. I will leave the conversation and/or room if these rules are broken. No gossip or tattling on others.*

4. Mental – *I will not feel compelled to explain or defend my decisions to anyone unless I choose to; I will ask for clarity about things I don't understand; I never make decisions or sign*

agreements under duress; I don't have to accept another person's idea of who I am.

5. Emotional – *No driving with someone when they are under the influence of drugs or alcohol, or if they are angry or emotionally volatile; if someone has violent or emotional outbursts such as slamming doors or cabinets, or breaking things, I will leave the premises; I am accountable for my own behaviors but will not take responsibility for someone else's feelings. I will be empathetic but will not enmesh with or emotionally care-take another adult.*

It should be obvious that boundaries primarily serve to protect us. But as Pia Mellody points out, they can also serve to contain us – they keep us from infringing on another's physical, temporal, emotional, verbal or mental space. For example, I always try to be cognizant of how much of someone else's time I am taking when I meet with them in person or on the phone. I usually try to be conscious of my emotional and/or verbal temperament when I drive with others in my vehicle. And so on. It's difficult – and probably pretty unreasonable – to expect others to contain themselves with us when we don't contain ourselves with them.

Many people think of boundaries as walls: rigid and impermeable. They can be, depending on the situation, but for me, healthy boundaries are usually both flexible and permeable. For instance, if I have a time boundary with respect to the length of a phone call with a particular person, I don't have to hang up at the end of so many minutes. I may choose to either extend or curtail that time depending on the tone and content of the call. With respect to all my boundaries, I'm responsible for monitoring the situation to make sure that continued interaction with the other person is both safe and healthy.

In terms of permeability, healthy boundaries let information pass in and out. When the information comes in, we use our mental faculties to assess whether it's true or safe for us. For instance, let's say you have a personal boundary that says you don't gossip about others. One day your boss calls you into his office to discuss your latest expense report (he ended up sending you back to Vegas after all.) During the conversation, he gives you important information about a potential job opening in another division. But he also gossips about a female co-worker. You thank him for the division job info but also let him know that you don't feel comfortable talking about others when they are not present. In that situation, you assessed all the incoming data from your conversation and accepted what was safe and relevant and rejected what was not. You respected your own boundary (more about that in a minute) and you also respected your boss by speaking calmly and professionally about what was OK and not OK for you. At the end of the day, it's always our responsibility to decide what we let into our bodies, hearts and minds.

In some cases, we may want to have a bottom line in terms of what's acceptable behavior in our interactions with others. A bottom line means, despite being flexible and open-minded, there are certain things that are just not OK. An example might be that we will not allow smoking or drug use by our teenager while they are living at home. We don't compromise on this no matter what. Having a trusting relationship with ourselves means keeping true to all our boundaries, including any bottom lines. It also means not abandoning ourselves or selling ourselves short when people challenge us.

Of course, we have to be prepared to follow through on our bottom lines or boundaries when people cross them. Teenagers are particularly good at calling our bluff. Having a plan in advance is especially helpful in this regard. For instance, you can formulate your plan by talking to a friend about what you intend to do if your teenager violates a bottom line. This may go a long way in helping you be better prepared and can also avoid the emotional outbursts and volatility that can accompany such a conflict. Also, sharing in advance with the other person, in a non-threatening, non-confrontational way, the ramifications of transgressing one of your boundaries may also be very helpful. Some people use written contracts, even within a family setting, to make sure everyone is on the same page.

Something else to keep in mind is that our boundaries should be consistent. While this is especially important with children, all our relationships will run smoother if we're not randomly enforcing/not enforcing the rules. We said earlier it's OK to be flexible and even change our boundaries from time-to-time. But if we're constantly moving the goal posts, other people will lose interest in the game. They may either ignore the rules (*"he's just crying wolf again"*) or they may become defiant or resentful. Thus, if we expect our boundaries to be effective, it's important we have consistency, especially in terms of enforcement.

In his book, *Pulling Your Own Strings*[52], Wayne Dyer says we teach other people how it's OK to treat us. That is, we let them know what is acceptable and what is not in terms of their behavior towards us. So for instance, if we allow our boss to constantly be disrespectful of us in front of other people, we're sending her a message that that's OK. It may not be appropriate to interrupt her mid-stream (although it might be depending on the nature of her comments), but certainly afterwards we would want to raise the issue. Ultimately, if this behavior continues, it would be up to us to take whatever steps are necessary to take care of ourselves. Taking responsibility for our lives means being conscious of the messages we send to others regarding what will be tolerated or not in the relationship.

In my own life I've found that the closer I am to someone, the more I need to have healthy boundaries with them. Boundaries with strangers or acquaintances are usually much simpler compared to boundaries with friends, family and lovers. Strong emotional attachments – positive or negative – can make it difficult to set healthy dividing lines between people. Yet this is exactly why we need them. Failing to take care of ourselves in our family and other close, personal relationships can be detrimental – to us and to them. Moreover, emotional enmeshment, such as minding other people's business, feeling overly responsible for their emotional well-being, having a history of rescuing, saving

---

[52] https://www.amazon.com/Wayne-W-Dyer-Pulling-Techniques/dp/B00HTK2X8G/

and enabling them, etc., can all make setting healthy boundaries difficult, if not impossible. We want to be close to the people we love without becoming overly enmeshed with their lives. This is especially true of adults with other adults. Having healthy boundaries promotes genuine love and intimacy whereas enmeshment erodes those things.

Also, with close relations, a long history of interactions usually means certain patterns and expectations are already firmly established. Thus, as we mentioned a moment ago, not everyone may be happy when we try to change the rules. In fact, they may not be happy even when we're only changing ourselves. People tend to prefer that the same person they know shows up day after day, year after year. Unhealthy people don't like change – either in themselves or others.

"Better Living Through Boundaries"™

Back in the day, when I first began exploring the idea of having better boundaries, I just assumed other people would automatically respect those boundaries. I went out of my way to let them know what I considered OK or not OK in the relationship, often being quite detailed and specific. I was trying to impress upon them how fair and thoughtful I was being about all this. The responses I got were as follows: Sometimes the other person was emphatic in their agreement, claiming they fully understood. Other times they were less understanding and even a little skeptical. And in several cases the other person just kind of stared at me blankly, eventually wandering off shaking their heads in disbelief (that should have been a clue for me). Yet regardless of how explicit I was in stating my boundary, or how emphatic the other person was in their agreement, *in every case my boundaries were transgressed and eventually ignored or discarded entirely by the other person.*

As you might imagine, this was quite frustrating – and not a little confusing. I tried so hard to be clear as to what I thought the new rules should be. And when someone agreed, didn't that mean they were obligated to play by those rules? Yet all my boundaries ended up being ignored. I was perplexed. Then one day I realized these were all my rules, not the other person's. They had no investment in seeing things my way. Moreover, even if they said yes, once they figured out my way was not so good for them, the game was over. But even worse, I got to see what was really going on: I was trying to use my boundaries to control somebody else's behavior. Because I was using a fancy word like "boundaries" I thought it was OK. But trying to control another person is trying to control another person, no matter what you call it. Thus, eventually, when they finally caught on, they lost interest – or worse.

So then I thought, *"What the heck good is it to have boundaries if the other person isn't going to listen, and if I'm really just trying to control them anyway? What could possibly be the point?"* Then it hit me:

My boundaries are for me; they're not for other people.

In their purest form, boundaries set limits on *my* behaviors – not the other person's. They are guidelines I establish for *myself* – what I am willing to accept or not accept regardless of how the other person sees them. This also means it's up to me to enforce my boundaries – *with myself*, not with another person! This is the most important thing I've learned about boundaries – and the toughest thing for most other people to understand. So let me give an example from my own life.

The story of Stan

This is a story about a former legal client of mine – let's call him "Stan". For many years when I was practicing law, I worked from home. Stan was – and I'm sure still is – a super nice guy. He's also what most people would call an "idea man" – lots of big ideas on how to make things better for everyone. Shortly after I started working with him, Stan also referred another client to me – an out-of-state company that soon became my biggest client (this is the company I mentioned in the Introduction.) Thus Stan was responsible, directly or indirectly, for probably 90% of my monthly income at the time.

Now I was very grateful for this – but I was also very codependent. This played out in many ways in our relationship, including me finding it very difficult to say "No" to him. It could also be seen in the fact that I was afraid of doing anything that I thought might disappoint or upset him. (This was not unique to Stan by the way – I had similar issues with other relationships – both business and personal.)

Now Stan was a bit of a night owl. His work day often extended well past normal business hours. Knowing that I worked from home, he didn't hesitate to call me even relatively late at night. For a while this was kind of OK, but eventually our pay structure changed making these late night calls less lucrative for me. Beyond that, however, and as I'll describe in more detail in a minute, I was beginning to feel the pressure of having poor emotional and psychological boundaries with him. Getting these late-night calls only made that worse.

Before we go any further, I want to be clear that everything I am about to describe was in no way Stan's fault – it was completely on me. I wanted to be empathetic. I wanted to be helpful. And I wanted my clients to get good results. But I didn't know anything about separating my work life from my personal life. It was also around this time that I started learning about codependency. As such, I was faced with a growing – and often uneasy – awareness that I might be codependent in all my relationships, including the one I had with Stan. The end result was it became increasingly difficult to take his late night phone calls.

Even before learning about codependency, I knew these calls were not serving me. I could feel in my gut something was off. On top of that, they often weren't really even necessary. There was usually nothing so pressing that it couldn't wait until the next day during normal business hours. As my angst grew, I realized I had to set a boundary with respect to these calls. So I resolved to bring it up the next time we spoke.

This proved to be more difficult than I thought. As I mentioned earlier, I was reticent about doing anything I thought might upset or disappoint him (and he was responsible for most of my income after all). Yet finally – mostly out of desperation – I mustered the courage. At the end of one of our daytime calls I explained to him, in a very calm and even tone, that while I certainly valued his business and our relationship, I was trying to establish more normal working hours for myself. This meant that even though I worked from home, it would be better for me if he called before 7PM. (I felt like this was a reasonable compromise – as opposed to 5PM – given his propensity to work at night.) When I shared all this with him he seemed to understand and he even appeared to acquiesce.

However, I soon found out my boundaries didn't mean squat to him.

For the first couple of weeks, everything was fine – we spoke during the day and stuff got done. But then one night around 9PM the phone rang. Now this was so long ago that it was before we had Caller ID on our phones. This meant I had no way of knowing who was calling unless I actually answered. But having had that wonderful conversation with him about my boundaries a couple of weeks earlier, I convinced myself it couldn't be him calling. Except when I answered, it was.

He immediately started the conversation by saying, "*I know I'm not supposed to call after seven, but this is really important.*" Despite my initial shock and confusion, and perhaps because I was feeling guilty that I had requested the boundary in the first place (I can *still*, 25 years later, feel guilty when I put my needs ahead of someone else's), I acquiesced and proceeded to let him ramble on for 45 minutes about something which it turned out was not at all important. When we finally hung up, I felt terrible – it was a mix of anger, rage and disgust, all aimed at myself for allowing this to happen.

All was quiet for another week or so. Then one night the phone rang. It was 9:15PM. I immediately had a sinking feeling. I considered letting it switch over to voicemail, but something compelled me to answer. He started by saying the same thing – "*I know I'm not supposed to call after seven but...*" My blood began to boil. I felt hot with rage all over. I couldn't focus on what he was saying I was so mad. Yet I didn't know what to say or do. This wasn't in the book I had read on setting boundaries. I just assumed people would automatically respect my wishes once they knew about them. My mind and body were in turmoil. I ended up saying nothing, but after listening for 30 minutes, I was livid. When we finally hung up my mind was still racing: *"What the f was going on! Why does he keep calling me at night after I told him not to?!?"*

Looking back I can see this relationship was Codependency 101. I had no idea how enmeshed I was with him. We knew a lot about each other's personal lives but it was more the emotional caretaking I was doing with him that was creating all my problems. I thought it was my job to make him feel OK. For instance, if he had a business problem that was troubling him, it was up to me to resolve it. That may not seem so abnormal in the context of an attorney-client relationship. But without going into all the details, the way in which the problems kept coming, and the way I was handling them, went beyond a normal working relationship. In addition, I was also a devoted "people-pleaser" and couldn't grasp that it was alright for me to say "No" if something wasn't working for me. Thus, the problems kept coming... and coming... and coming. Despite the lighthearted tone with which I am writing some of this, this was quickly turning into a very dark and painful experience for me.

I remember not sleeping well the night of that second call. The next day when I awoke, I realized it was up to me to somehow enforce my boundaries with him. But I had no idea what that meant or how to do it.

Now in Stan's defense, I had trained him in how it was OK to treat me. We had a long history during which I had proved over and over that I was willing to drop everything to attend to his needs. We had an unspoken agreement that he always came first and I would just take whatever he gave me. And to his credit, for a while at least, he was willing to pay for this kind of service. But as I said, the monetary arrangement had changed, and now, money or not, this kind of interaction was no longer working for me. It soon became clear to me that I had created this monster (no offense Stan!) and now I had to find a way to deal with it.

Over the next couple of days I pondered all this: do I drop him as a client? Do I not answer my phone after 7PM? Do I talk to him again about my boundaries? No clue what to do. Then (as I mentioned in the previous section) it hit me: *my boundaries were for me, not other people*. This meant that if he called again after 7PM it was my job to nip the conversation in the bud and get off the phone. I shuttered at the thought of prematurely ending our conversation like that, but what other choice did I have?

I wouldn't have to wait long to find out...

A couple of nights later the phone rang. It was 9:30PM. I immediately knew it was Stan. For a moment I hesitated – yet I also knew I couldn't go on like this. I had to face my demons. So I took a deep breath and answered the phone:

> Peter: "*Hello?*"
> Stan: "*Peter, it's Stan. Hey, sorry to call so late but...*"
> I cut him off.
> Peter: "*Stan, hang on a minute.*"

I was aware my body was trembling. He stopped, probably more out of surprise than anything else.

> Peter: (In a warm but direct tone) "*You know I've asked you not to call after 7PM. I told you I want to have a personal life.*"

I paused but he said nothing so I continued,

> Peter: "*You said you understood, yet here you are calling me again late at night.*"

Another small pause, and again he said nothing – I'm guessing he was too dumbfounded to speak since this was very unlike me. All of a sudden I became aware my heart was pounding in my chest, but I continued:

> Peter: "*Now if this is truly an emergency I suggest you call 911.* (I have no idea where that came from.) *Otherwise, I am going to ask you to call me back tomorrow during my regular business hours and we can discuss whatever you need to then.*"

I stopped. My hands were shaking and my heart was now pounding up in my throat. There was a long silence during which I thought I might actually die. Then I heard him say,

> Stan: "*OK, I'll give you a call tomorrow. Have a good night.*"

And he hung up.

I was in shock – total disbelief actually. I held the phone in my hand for a few moments. I think I was afraid to hang up in case he might still be there. There was also probably a body reflex that says a phone call with Stan can't be this short.

After a few more moments, I finally put the phone down. Everything was quiet. Even the voice in my head had stopped. Then it hit me – I had done it! I had faced my fears and actually stood up for myself! I was so happy I thought I might cry.

What followed over the next few hours and days were continually alternating waves of relief followed by waves of guilt and remorse. I was relieved to have finally stood up for myself. Yet I feared I had alienated my star client. And as I said, Stan was a genuinely nice person. This made it even more difficult for me to set a boundary with him and take care of myself. But I could also see that if I felt guilty when I put my needs ahead of someone else's, I had more work to do. A little voice in my head said I should never feel guilty for taking care of myself.

Stan never called again after 7PM. Our professional relationship continued for another year or so, but something definitely changed that night. I began to view myself and all my relationships differently. When Stan and I eventually called it quits, I was most grateful for my time with him. It had been the perfect opportunity to see that I was the one who was responsible for my own unhappiness. I did it by consistently letting all the things I didn't like slip by. I was also the one who taught him how it was OK to treat me – and I paid a huge price for that. Yet to this day, I still have great appreciation for what I learned during my time with Stan and I certainly wish him all the best.

Resentment, revisited

We discussed "resentment" in Chapter Six. We said it is a passive form of anger where we harbor negative feelings within rather than outwardly expressing them. It's based on a perception of ourselves as the victims of someone else's wrongdoing. (Pia Mellody says resentment is *"victim anger"* while the *Big Book* of

Alcoholics Anonymous refers to resentment as the "'number one' offender."[53]) We may plan in our own heads all the things we're going to do to get even, but we usually end up doing nothing. Or if we do, it's most likely a passive-aggressive response. But like almost everything else we've discussed so far, resentment has something to teach us about ourselves. It's related to whether or not I'm looking out for my own best interests and taking responsibility for my life. I have learned that for me, "resentment" means:

I have not done what I needed to do to take care of myself in a given situation and now I'm blaming someone else for that. And the anger I think I feel towards them is really misdirected anger that I feel towards myself.

Now this can be a little confusing. Other people's behavior can definitely have an impact on us. Yet if no one makes us feel anything, and if we're responsible for taking care of ourselves in all our relationships, then when we react with any form of anger (including resentment) we must be really angry at ourselves. My relationship with Stan is a perfect example. If I had set some healthy boundaries sooner, I would have never felt the upset and turmoil I did. And prior to the moment that I realized my boundaries were for me and not for other people, I was convinced it was all his fault. It was only after I took responsibility for my part in the situation that things changed.

Stan is also a good reminder that we don't need anger to take care of ourselves. Recall my actual telephone conversations with him. I didn't lash out or even blame him for anything. Each time we spoke, my voice was calm and friendly. Even when I actually confronted him and finally set the boundary, despite being scared out of my mind, I spoke calmly but directly. I recounted our prior discussion on the topic and reminded him that at the time he said he understood. Then I offered a solution that would work for me going forward. I did all this without attacking him or hurling

---

[53] *Alcoholics Anonymous* pg. 64

angry accusations his way. In each conversation I did my best to be clear and forceful without invoking any negative emotions.

To overlook or look past

A Course in Miracles says to forgive is to "overlook or look past."[54] It suggests we make a decision to *overlook* the things that we think upset us. In terms of the other people in our lives, this means we *look past* their harmful or inappropriate behavior and strive to see the good in them – no matter what they've done. When we withdraw our attention from their wrongdoing, we are able to see them in a new way.

It can be quite difficult to overlook someone else's mistakes when we are identified with our ego. The ego's main purpose is to find fault and then attack based on that fault – not forgive. Also, as I mentioned earlier, the ego is both paranoid and egocentric. This is a deadly combination that removes any hope we can count on it for true forgiveness. Being paranoid, it sees enemies and danger everywhere. Being egocentric, it makes everything everyone else does about us. Therefore, it's hard to look past someone's mistakes and let them off the hook when we have such a profound lack of trust in our own safety. This is not to make anyone wrong for not forgiving. But it does serve to illustrate what we're up against when we are identified with our ego.

Generally speaking, it's helpful for us to overlook whatever is bothering us in life. There's a metaphysical principle that says, *"attention = intention."* That is, whatever we give our attention to, we activate in our lives. You may have also heard it said that *"what we resist, persists,"* or *"if you don't feed it, it won't grow."* These ideas all stand for the proposition that we play a role in what comes to us in life. Thus, by overlooking what we don't want (forgiveness) and paying positive attention to what we do, we can begin to shape who and what we attract into our lives. Of course, this is what we do when we consciously and deliberately choose

---

[54] *A Course in Miracles* also says forgiveness is a "selective remembering". That is, we deliberately focus on memories from the past that are positive and loving about the other person, rather than focusing on what they did wrong, then or now.

thoughts, feelings, words and actions that serve us. We increase attraction for what we do want and decrease attraction for what we don't. On the other hand, living life on autopilot and reacting rather than responding, we end up with a lot more of what we don't want.

Along these same lines, I realized some time ago that whatever I say "Yes" to I am going to get more of in my life. For instance, if I continue to work with difficult clients, more difficult clients will show up in my life. I also notice that complaining about those clients doesn't help. As long as I continue to work with them, I am saying "Yes" to that situation. While it may seem counterintuitive, complaining about, or fighting with, something is the same as saying "yes" to it. Anything we give our time, focus or mental energy to – no matter how much we think we don't want it – will expand in our awareness and thus manifest in our experience. For those familiar with "Law of Attraction"[55] it says something similar: "*We get what we think about whether we want it or not.*" The very short answer is, focus on what you do want and don't think about what you don't. Overlook or look past all the negative stuff in your life. In terms of what we've been talking about in this book, we always attract the people and situations into our lives that match our predominant thoughts and beliefs about ourselves – i.e., "who we think we are." Thus, when we forgive rather than fight new things can come our way.

"Good" vs. "bad", "right" vs. "wrong"

We often justify our lack of forgiveness on the basis that we're "good" or "right", and the other person (or nation) is "bad" or "wrong." We talked extensively about the effect of seeing ourselves as right and others as wrong at the end of the last chapter. We also looked at how we use "judgment" to proclaim someone or something as "bad" and thus unworthy of our love. Those discussions can be applied here as well. But what I want to draw your attention to now is being aware of how we use these words as labels. Calling things "good" or "bad" or "right" or

---

[55] https://www.abraham-hicks.com/

"wrong" is simply our attempt to justify how we feel. If you look closely, I'll bet you'll see that "right" is always something you agree with while "good" are things that please you. "Wrong" or "bad" are the opposites. As such, these words are just made up labels with no objective or absolute meaning.

The reason this is pertinent to our discussion of forgiveness is, to the ego, if someone is "bad" or "wrong" they deserve to be controlled or punished – and maybe even annihilated – but definitely not forgiven. This may seem trivial – the words we use to label someone or something shouldn't really matter. Yet our words have meaning and can convey intent to others. For me, at a minimum, we want to eliminate the terms "bad" and "wrong" from our vocabulary if we want to truly forgive. We need only turn to history to see how races and nations have used their subjective assessments of "bad" or "wrong" to justify oppression, war and even genocide. There is no hope for peace – whether on the world stage or in our own homes – if we continue to employ this dualistic mode of thinking.

But wait – there's more: The idea that bad people deserve to be punished carries over into our subconscious evaluations of ourselves. If "who we think we are" is bad, unlovable, evil or guilty, then we subconsciously assume that we deserve to be punished. This eventually boils over to our conscious minds where we brand ourselves or others as "sinners," "evil," "bad-seed", etc. We can create entire theologies based on the notion that we're bad people who deserve to be punished. This can be expressed by seeing the difficult or unpleasant things that happen to us in life – illnesses, financial setbacks, loss of a loved one and so on – as a form of punishment. The fact is, it's difficult to forgive others when we believe God is punishing us for our sins. Actually, it's not difficult; it's impossible.

"Forgive them Father, for they know not what they do"
Speaking of God, in this well known quote from the Bible, Jesus is asking for forgiveness for his persecutors. Hanging from a cross, presumably in great pain and suffering, he is beseeching his Father to show these people mercy. The implication is they are

innocent because they lack awareness of the nature and/or magnitude of their actions.

I personally believe this is the ultimate message of Jesus' life: all of us are innocent and thus worthy of forgiveness no matter what we've done. I would suggest that most of us, certainly on a spiritual level, lack conscious awareness of the effects of much of what we're doing all day long. This is especially so when it comes to our interactions with others. Something unexpected or frightening occurs and we feel overwhelmed and panicked. We react without thinking and do something harmful to ourselves or another. The point is, when we're caught up in intense emotions, or maybe even just distracted by life, we can do things that cause harm or damage. In those moments it can be said we have no idea what we're doing. Forgiving those who are unmindful is merciful. Withholding forgiveness because they "should have known better" is a lost opportunity to love others when they probably least like themselves.

Some will say a mistake is one thing; deliberately trying to hurt another person is something else. I'll say again, we're not condoning violence or making excuses for harmful behavior. Yet I believe, in our normal, healthy state as human beings, it's not in our nature to knowingly want to harm another person. Rather, all anti-social behavior can be traced to something that happened to that person in the past. In 12 Step programs they say, *"Hurt people, hurt people"* – that is, we only harm another when we ourselves are hurting. For me, even a "normal" childhood can create reactive personalities. Add physical or emotional abuse, or being raised in an environment dominated by addiction, mental illness or religious indoctrination, and even seemingly normal, well-intentioned people can do crazy things to themselves and others. This is all my way of saying that when we hurt or injure anyone, we are usually not in our right mind. Again, this doesn't mean we let people walk away scot-free. There are still consequences for their actions. But approaching it from this place has the potential to inject a greater measure of compassion and understanding into the discussion.

Like most everything else we've covered so far in this book, the extent to which we can forgive another is determined largely by "who we think we are". We'll discuss this in more detail in a few pages but I want to mention here that as long as we see ourselves as vulnerable, threatened or in danger, it will be very tough to forgive. In fact, if that's who we really are in that situation, it probably wouldn't make any sense to forgive. We'd only be setting ourselves up for more potential harm with that person.

Of course, we've already talked about how we can begin to change how we see ourselves in any situation. And I have mentioned in passing that as we change how we see ourselves, this can also change how we see others. Now I am going to suggest explicitly that an important component of forgiveness is just that: changing how we see others. In the last few paragraphs, I've tried to suggest that those who have harmed us are not necessarily bad or evil. They may be living with the effects of a difficult or even traumatic upbringing. Or they may be suffering with an undiagnosed mental or emotional condition. They may be relatively normal and of sound mind, yet something extraordinary may have happened in the moment which leaves them in a reactive, overly anxious state. Or they may just be having a bad day. For example, think about the last time you were aggravated by something at work and became unduly aggressive on the drive home.[56]

Seeing another person as struggling or frightened or confused, and then in some measure giving them the benefit of the doubt, opens the door to forgiveness. Greek philosopher Plato is said to have said, "*Be kind, for everyone you meet is fighting (the same) hard battle.*" Most of us do experience life as a battle, and a losing one at that. We are often so stressed, it's easy to do things which may negatively affect ourselves and others.

---

[56] The AAA Foundation for Traffic Safety reported that during a recent four-year period, more than 100,000 fatal crashes involved drivers who committed one or more aggressive driving actions. http://www.adtsea.org/Resources%20PDF%27s/AAA%202009%20Aggressive%20Driving%20Research%20Update.pdf

In his book *Tomorrow's God* (a part of the *Conversations with God* series of books), Neale Donald Walsch suggests asking this question of another person when they have harmed us: *"What hurts you so much that you feel you have to hurt me to heal it?"* [57] For me, this is a wonderfully powerful question. First, we're not reacting defensively or dropping down to their level by retaliating against them. Then we're inquiring if something negative (perhaps even truly devastating) has taken place in their life which is causing them to act this way. This makes it a compassionate rather than attacking response which has the potential to awaken them to the fact that what they're doing is inappropriate. Instead of giving our power away, we maintain a position of strength and respond with empathy and compassion.

In my own life I've thought of something similar. With regard to the people who have done or would do us harm: if we saw the world the way they saw the world – and specifically for this book I would add, if we saw ourselves the way they saw themselves – then we would probably be doing the exact same thing they're doing. And that makes us the same as them. This acknowledges that we all behave in accordance with our own subjective perception of the world, and the beliefs about what is best for us and our loved ones that flow from that perception. In this regard, while we may be insane, we're not crazy. Our points of reference and/or perceptions of the world may be totally off-base. But within the confines of those perceptions, each of us is doing exactly what makes sense in order for us to survive.

Again, this doesn't mean we have to condone someone else's irresponsible or harmful behavior. We can respond as necessary to take care of ourselves. Yet looking at the situation this way changes the equation. Rather than taking their actions personally, we can have empathy. We can understand their craziness, as opposed to feeling victimized and shaking our heads in disbelief that they could do such a thing to us.

---

[57] *"Conversations with God: Tomorrow's God"*, pg. 143.

A Call for Love

A Course in Miracles says all attacks are a call for love.[58] I made the point a moment ago that when someone attacks us, chances are pretty good they are not in their right mind. Sane, healthy, secure people don't attack others – they find peaceful ways to settle their disputes. Now what's true of other people is also true of us: when we attack another (even by doing something as seemingly innocuous as gossiping about them), we are not in our right minds. Think about a time in your own life when you felt great – when you were free of worry and feeling good about yourself. Were you judging or bad-mouthing other people? Were you consumed with resentment and thoughts of getting even? Did you want to harm anyone for any reason? I would submit that when we engage in any form of attack, we are not in our right minds. We're not bad for doing any of this. But we may need help to get back to sanity.

In Chapter Four we spoke about unconditional love. We said it's easy to love people when they're doing what we want them to do. The truer measure of our love is how we treat them when we don't like what they're doing or who they're being. Most of us are still consumed with our egoic minds. We're nice individuals, compassionate and deeply caring at times. But eventually we draw a line. There are certain people who just don't deserve our love. We all have our reasons. And there are probably many others who would agree that our reasons are sound. Yet for love to be love it must be unconditional. This is why I said earlier we cannot love a little and attack a little. One tiny gap in the fabric of our love and eventually the entire cloth will come undone.

Punishment, condemnation, judgment and attack are all decisions to withhold love, and as such are expressions of fear. We think that by withholding love we will be protecting ourselves. Yet if fear is the absence of love as we said in Chapter Four, you can see how we create our own fear by condemning others. Every time we attack another, justified or not, we create, both in our minds and in reality, the potential for more enemies.

---

[58] *A Course in Miracles*, pg 216.

More enemies create more fear and the cycle continues. Forgiveness, on the other hand, breaks the cycle. The decision to overlook whatever we think is threatening us and extend love instead creates allies not enemies. Forgiveness is thus an expression of love that ultimately undoes fear.

At this point (or maybe many, many pages ago), you may be thinking that I'm off in fantasyland. That my solutions would never work in the real world. I'll acknowledge that much of what I am suggesting is new, or at least out of step with the current view on things. But I would also suggest that the status quo is not working. We have not solved the problem of conflicts within our own neighborhoods or cities, much less our conflicts with other nations. Business as usual is not sustainable. Ultimately, what I'm suggesting may not be the total answer. But I do feel we have to move in a new direction if we want a better future. We must move towards oneness rather than separation, towards similarities rather than differences. Peace begins not with government policies or race relations; peace begins with you and me in our own hearts and minds. Seeing ourselves differently and then seeing all others differently (so we actually see them more like us), is the way home.

Haters gonna hate

Forgiveness means we don't get upset by what other people do to us. We don't lose our cool or give away our power. As we discussed in the last chapter, we don't take anything personally – *even if it's meant to be personal!*

I've already mentioned that part of *"being bigger than I think I am"* has been to regularly post my photos on social media. (I use Facebook[59], Instagram[60] and YouTube.[61]) Of course, the downside of social media is the possibility of running into folks who may not think you're as cool as you do. I've actually experienced very little negativity on social media. The vast majority of people are

---

[59] https://www.facebook.com/PeterAlessandriaPhotography/
[60] https://www.instagram.com/peteralessandria/
[61] https://www.youtube.com/user/alessandriaphoto

great – they love all my photos and openly acknowledge my talent. But there have been a few instances where people went after me publicly concerning my photography. They seem to think that some of my photos are too good to be true. The usual claim is that they are faked, as in being Photoshopped. So these people take it upon themselves to attack me for those shots.

I will say I am not alone in this – several of my photographer friends who post similar photos are also often met with non-believers. These days I kind of see this as a good thing: if our photos weren't something special, no one would be commenting on them. The fact that some people see them as too good to be true means we've done a great job! Having haters means we've arrived!

Whenever someone makes a negative comment on one of my photos, I do my best to not react defensively. If I choose to respond to their comments,[62] I do so via direct/private messages. I have learned to never engage in a public discussion with these people for two reasons: first, there's no upside to me in defending myself publicly. I know the photos are genuine so defending myself in a situation like this would only mean I was afraid what the other person was saying about me was true (recall the Archery example in the last chapter.) Second, people are less defensive/confrontational if the discussion is private. As you'll see in a moment, by keeping the discussions just between me and the other person, there's no ego-need to defend their position publicly. In my experience, even if I can prove without a doubt that my photos are real, the other person will never acknowledge that publicly. This is because when they feel like other people are watching, the ego's need to save face is too great to ever admit they were wrong. (Before I learned my lesson about never debating these things publicly, on more than one occasion I was absolutely astounded to see people clinging to their original position despite a wall of evidence to the contrary. Even when neutral third parties chimed in on my behalf with similar photos

---

[62] Sometimes I don't respond at all – I just delete or hide their comments and block the person if they are a repeat offender.

from other professional, well-regarded photographers, the hater would still not let go of their position. Instead, they would claim that other picture was Photoshopped too. To me this was living proof the ego would rather die than admit it is wrong.)

Anyway, in terms of the private messages, I always keep the tone light and positive. I usually start by thanking them for taking the time to comment on my photo. I try to find some reason to appreciate what they said and acknowledge them for it. This in and of itself, usually disarms them, at least a little. And even if they continue their attacks in private, I make sure to never lower myself to their level of commentary.

Now there are two instances where people were voicing negativity towards me, that I feel may be helpful to our discussion of forgiveness. In both cases, using some of the principles I am outlining in this book, I was able to turn the situations around into something positive.

In the first instance, the person thought one of my New York City skyline photos was fake. He accused me of altering the image because he didn't believe the lineup of landmarks in the picture was possible.[63] He was relying on the fact that he lives in New York and had never seen such arrangement of NYC's iconic buildings. As I dug a little deeper, I discovered that he was an artist and photographer who sold his own photos. To make them more attractive to tourists, he sometimes altered his pictures. Since my photo was similar to one of his altered images, he assumed I had modified mine too.

I reached out to him after reading his comments on a Facebook group of which we were both members. At first, his messages were as hostile as his public comments. I used this as an opportunity to practice deflecting his accusations to a more neutral subject. As I insisted on engaging with him in a positive, non-defensive manner, over the course of several conversations he eventually became less accusatory. (Remember: defensiveness

---

63

https://www.peteralessandriaphotography.com/nyc_winter_2018/ec0f1849d

begets defensiveness and anger begets anger – by me not responding with either, he eventually let his guard down.)

At a certain point, I offered to take him to the spot where I took my photo so he could see for himself it wasn't a fake. As locations are often a well-guarded secret for photographers, I think that went a long way in gaining his trust. I also sent him a Friend Request (which he accepted) and we became friends on Facebook. I publicly "Liked" and commented on some of his photos and he eventually did the same with me. We continued our private conversations and the more I got to know him, the more I liked him. He was an artist and entrepreneur as well as being an immigrant (English was his second language). I really respected what he had been able to accomplish for his art and photography business.

Now here's the really cool part: he eventually ended up becoming a customer of mine. I was able to shift the tone of our interactions so much that he licensed one of my photos for his business. Even cooler is he introduced me to the owner of a larger company in the same line of work. While I didn't end up working with that company, I learned a great deal about the business from them. I then took what I learned and went to an even larger, national company in the same field. I eventually did a very lucrative five-figure deal with that second company for the use of several of my photos. It turned out to be my single largest licensing deal ever. And it all came as the result of my forgiving someone's attacks on me on social media.

In terms of our discussion of forgiveness, this is a good example of the power of not taking things personally. It turns out this person who initially attacked me publicly was just a really nice guy who, for whatever reason, was having a difficult time of it. What he said online was never about me – it was always and only about him. By deliberately putting my ego on-hold and choosing to overlook his negative public remarks, I was able to practice dealing with conflict and seeing myself in a new way. Plus, I made some good money to boot!

The only way I could do any of this was by changing "who I thought I was" in that situation. I have to admit when I first read his comments, my face flushed with anger and I wanted to attack him back. But then I realized that was not who I wanted to be anymore in my life. There had been a few other instances before him where I went the old way and things turned out badly. So I took this as an opportunity to practice doing things differently. And in case you're wondering, we're still friendly to this day.

With the second person, things were a little different. He accused me of bragging on Facebook about some of my successes. I had won a bunch of awards for my photos and was eager to share the news. So eager, that in addition to my own Facebook pages, I posted on a closed group of which we were both members. In hindsight, I think he may have actually been right about me sharing my private successes beyond my own Facebook pages. I was probably a little too enthusiastic about sharing the news.

When I saw his comments, I again didn't respond publicly. I reached out privately via Messenger and again did my best to maintain a positive, non-defensive tone. It turned out we had actually met once previously in person so I suggested we get together again to try to work things out. (I thought it would be good practice for me to learn how to apply these principles in person.)

I suggested a public place for our mutual comfort and safety. Despite our first meeting being quite amicable, this time I had to endure several emotional outbursts and disparaging comments. He accused me of being a braggart and also attacked my integrity. He was really upset and our interaction got pretty heated at one point. More than once I wondered if I had bit off more than I could chew.

Despite several unpleasant moments, eventually the tone calmed down enough for me to dig deeper. I sensed he was reacting to something personal, rather than just to my postings on my awards. As we talked more, it became clear that he felt slighted by something I had done several months earlier. It hadn't registered with me at the time, but I could see now how he ended up taking what I had done personally.

When I finally realized what was going on, a little light bulb went off inside my head. I know the power of making an amends, so I did just that. I acknowledged my part in the previous misunderstanding and sincerely apologized to him for it. This seemed to be what was needed to fully diffuse the current situation, and we ended up having a pleasant conversation for the remainder of the meeting. We parted friends and are now on good terms. He happens to be a really good photographer and as a result I didn't hesitate to refer some business his way recently. I genuinely respect his work and see him as a talented professional and a nice guy. There have been no more issues between us.

In both these situations, I realized I had a choice as to how I was going to respond. I did my best to apply some of the principles we've been discussing and both cases provided me with powerful learning opportunities. For instance, with the second gentleman, I was able to practice having permeable boundaries. His feedback about the closed group not being the best place to toot my own horn was actually well-founded. What I didn't have to take in were the disparaging, negative tone and commentary that accompanied that information. In general in both situations, I learned the importance of not taking what other people say or do personally. I also learned the value of not being defensive in how I respond. I got to experience what it means to be understanding of the way someone else sees the world, and how, if I had been in their shoes, I might have seen things the same way. And in both cases, I learned the power of forgiveness by consciously seeing myself differently than I might have in the past. If I saw either of those two people as having power over me, it wouldn't have made sense to forgive them. I would have been potentially setting myself up for more harm. Yet by changing "who I thought I was" in those situations, I was able to bring about a different – and much more positive – result.

To Thine Own Self Be True

Now, again – and just to be really clear – acting in the spirit of love and forgiveness doesn't mean we put ourselves in harm's way. Loving another doesn't mean we stop loving ourselves. It's our responsibility to stay safe in all situations and with all people. In both the cases I mentioned above, I did what I needed to do to take care of myself before, during, and after each interaction. I reviewed my intentions and began with the end in mind. Even in the case where I met with the person face-to-face, I made sure not to put myself in harm's way – I picked a public place and had a clear exit strategy. I was also mindful not to become a receptacle for any inappropriate behavior. Then, after making sure I was OK, I tried my best to engage with the other person from a place of compassion, understanding and forgiveness.

Now you may say, *"Dealing with people on Facebook is one thing; it's quite another when people are threatening your home or family."* And I would agree the magnitude and scope of the two problems are different. I would also say my heart goes out to anyone living under the specter of such a threat. I do acknowledge the problems we face on a societal or global scale may be quite complex and also go far beyond my own personal understandings or experience. Yet, I can't help but wonder if there aren't also some important similarities. For instance, in both the case of my new friends on social media and acts of violence between races or nations, the problem is still how we see ourselves. "Who we think we are" will determine every response. And it is those responses that will invite further attack or make way for peace.

As I mentioned earlier, getting to know our adversaries goes a long way in diffusing potential conflicts. Dismissing others as "zealots," "fanatics," etc., does not serve us. We're all crazy in one way or another – yet we also said that everything everyone does makes sense within the context of how they see themselves and how they see the world. Thus, no matter how extreme an individual or group may seem, they are mostly rational actors within this context.

We also said it's in our best interests to look for the common links between us and others. For example, the idea we're all doing what we think we need to do to survive. We can extend this to say everyone wants some measure of safety, security and peace in their lives. While we don't have to agree with their positions about the best ways to achieve these things, understanding *why* they think, feel, speak and act the way they do can pave the way for non-violent resolution of our differences.

Lastly, again as I mentioned earlier, when we change our perception of ourselves, our perception of other people also changes. For instance, I used to see myself as a victim in many of my relationships. This meant I had to see the other people as victimizers. I often felt like they had power over me and so I acted and reacted accordingly. Today, since I don't see myself as a victim as much, I also don't see other people as victimizers. Because I trust myself more and more to take care of myself, I am less defensive. If other people do act inappropriately, I know how to set a boundary. I can also see them as regular people who sometimes have a bad day – just like me. Thus, I can have compassion and maybe even be helpful when someone does something harmful. Do you think this might have the potential to improve the quality of our relationships as well as the quality of our lives? I believe we can see ourselves in a new way, whether as individuals or as nations, and when we do, the results will be the same – more peace and better relationships.

True Forgiveness

If you want to question everything in your life, write a book like this! I've spent a lot of time the past few months thinking about all the things I'm saying here. I'm constantly testing whether or not they are true, and examining how much I actually apply them in my own life. I mentioned once and I'll mention again, I am a work in progress. I don't do any of this perfectly – especially when it comes to forgiveness. Yet, I'll say to you what I've been saying to myself: the fact that I'm not doing it perfectly doesn't mean I shouldn't continue to try. As I referenced earlier, in my opinion the status quo is not serving us, either individually or as society as a whole. Making the effort to move beyond what is common place is the only way to realize an extraordinary life.

The other thing about writing a book like this is that I find I am constantly thinking about all this stuff – even when I'm not writing. For instance, tonight while doing the dishes this thought popped into my head:

True forgiveness is when the other person is wrong and/or has harmed us – and we forgive them anyway.

This may be obvious to you. And now that I look at it, it seems obvious to me. Yet before tonight I guess I was still thinking of forgiveness as something like, "*If you make a mistake, that's fine; I can forgive you. But if what you did hurt me or someone I love, there's no way I'm letting you off the hook.*" Obviously, that's not forgiveness. For those who read the Bible, forgiving those who have harmed us is what I believe is meant by "turning the other cheek." Instead of resisting evil, we acknowledge it has no power over us by responding thusly.

I said it at the beginning of this chapter and I'll say it again: this forgiveness stuff is rad! For many, it's a call to live life in an entirely different way. I'm not saying we have to be saints. Nor do we have to apply forgiveness perfectly. But I do think we have to try. And even if we're just being more forgiving of ourselves, that's a great start. Being more forgiving of myself has changed my life in numerous ways and I bet it could do the same for you.

Another thought that popped into my head tonight was:

I'm not angry because of what they did;
I'm angry because I'm afraid;
and I'm afraid because of how I see myself.

We've touched on this several times before. For me, this as a powerful reminder that ultimately it's "who we think we are" that determines our response to everything. It places the cause of our experience back in our own hands. It also places the power to change our experiences there as well. In addition, this thought serves as an important reminder of the relationship between fear and anger. In the last chapter we said fear always precedes anger. This means, as my thought above states, that when we're angry, we're really afraid. Thus, by addressing the fear that's behind the anger, we can become more effective in terms of how we respond to life.

"What was my part in this?"

We touched on this briefly in Chapter Two when we spoke about taking responsibility. In all those situations where we experience conflict or negative emotions towards others, it's important to ask the question, *"What was my part in this?"* The first time I did this I was shocked to see that in almost every case where I felt angry, hurt or resentful, I had contributed (often significantly) to the problems between myself and the other person. While the specifics varied, there were six general ways I did this:

1. I ignored warning signs;
2. I had unreasonable expectations;
3. I failed to speak up for myself;
4. I was dishonest;
5. I didn't respect my own boundaries.

The sum total of 1. through 5. is that I wasn't doing what was needed to take care of myself in the relationship. Then when things didn't work out, I blamed them. (Notice this is the definition of "resentment" I mentioned earlier.) With regard to 4. and 5. in particular, for much of my life, fear of disapproval made it very difficult for me to say "No" or otherwise set boundaries with other people. (My story about Stan from earlier is a real-life example of this.) By ignoring my truth, I was creating my own distress and unmanageability. In particular, saying "Yes" when I really want to say "No" is a form of dishonesty, and dishonesty always leads to problems in relationships. Thus, part of taking responsibility for my life means being honest and acting with integrity. However, this can mean risking disapproval or upsetting the other person. Thus, in order to act with honesty, I have to see myself as someone who can tell the truth and still be OK in life.

I didn't always see myself this way. Many years ago when I was a young lawyer, I was struggling with money. As a result I wasn't entirely honest in certain financial dealings. The amounts were relatively small, but I thought I had to bend the rules to get by in life. Looking back, I can see this was such a disempowering way to live. "Who I thought I was" was someone who didn't have what it took to succeed in life without being dishonest. And it turns out this belief about myself went way beyond my finances. Today I have replaced that old belief with a new one: "*I can play by the rules and still win; I am someone who can be honest and still get what I want or need from life.*"

In terms of saying "Yes" when I wanted to say "No", for me I am very careful about what I say "Yes" to these days. I now more deeply understand the ramifications of agreeing to something without really meaning it. Oddly enough, today I also love when people say "No" to me. This is because I know it means they are being honest. It also serves as a reminder that I have the right to say "No" when something isn't working for me. So while of course I also love when people say "Yes" to me, the next time you see me feel free to say "No" about something if that's how you really feel!

"Hurt" vs. "Harm"

In terms of both forgiveness and taking responsibility, it's helpful to make a distinction between "hurt" and "harm". I define harm as "*the unjust diminishment of someone's life experience.*" It has an objective, quantitative analysis to it. For instance, if I steal from you, or break an agreement with you, or attack you physically, I have diminished your life experience. Hurt, on the other hand, is a subjective determination. If I feel hurt by something, it's because of the meaning I am giving the situation. While there may or may not be actual harm accompanying my hurt feelings, hurt is always the result of me seeing myself in a certain way, usually as unworthy or less-than others. Since my decision to see myself this way is about me, the other person is not responsible for my feelings or reactions.

My five year old niece recently started telling everyone that they hurt her feelings when they say or do something she doesn't like. Now in her mind, that's true. The other person says or does something and she feels bad. Since she wasn't feeling bad before they said or did that, it must be their fault. (It's interesting to note how few of us as adults have progressed beyond this type of five-year-old thinking.) Anyway, me being who I am, the next time she said that I turned to her and said, *"Sweetheart, I understand you're not happy about what so and so did. But no one can make you feel anything. If you feel hurt it's because you are choosing to feel that way."* She took a long pause, looked at me like I was crazy – and then went back to fighting with her brother. Oh well – maybe she'll read this book when she gets older!

(Don't) Say you're sorry!

Most of my life I apologized compulsively. When I sensed something I was saying or doing was not pleasing to another person, my kneejerk response was to say I was sorry. Because I thought I was responsible for everyone else's happiness and emotional well-being, I was usually quick to jump in with an apology.

I can see now compulsively apologizing is a coping mechanism. It's a way I tried to feel safe by controlling someone else's reactions. My subconscious thought was that if I apologized they wouldn't be upset and therefore I would feel safe. It also stemmed from my negative core belief that I was bad or wrong. This meant it was probably my fault that they were upset, so I had better apologize. Saying we're sorry to feel safe or because we think we're bad are not appropriate reasons to apologize. This is typical of highly codependent thinking and over the years created a lot of unmanageability in my life.

Rather, we only want to apologize or make amends for actual harms done. Earlier we defined "harm" as the unjust diminishment of someone's life experience. Thus, we only apologize when what we've done has caused another person's experience to be lessened in an objective way. In that case, we can be willing to be accountable for our behavior and offer an apology or an amends to set things right. The corollary of this is we don't apologize or make amends to another person for their "hurt" feelings. As we said earlier, someone else feeling hurt is a subjective interpretation they make in their own minds. The hurt they think they feel may or may not be objectively considered harm. For instance, someone may claim we hurt their feelings by not showing up at their kid's dance recital. It may in fact be true that their feelings were hurt. However, those hurt feelings are the result of their own subjective interpretations of our actions. This is shown by the fact that someone else may not have cared at all that we weren't able to make it. The second person doesn't project anything on to our actions and thus is not upset.

Unless we broke an explicit promise to attend the recital, or unless we did something like gossip or badmouth the parent or child to others, we probably don't need to apologize or make an amends for not attending. It's only when we do something that meets the "harm" standard that we take responsibility for our part.

Admittedly, this isn't always black and white. It may take some deep thinking on our part to discern if what we did was harmful or not. The main point is, the fact that someone else thinks we hurt their feelings is usually not enough to determine that we owe them an apology. Similarly, the fact that they don't complain may not be enough to determine that we don't. Even if they don't feel hurt, it's still possible what we said or did was harmful. Thus, we want to look at the situation closely to consider whether what we did resulted in harm, and whether, as a result, we should offer to set things right. They may reject any offer we make – but the fact that we attempt to take responsibility and make an amends is what's important.

Likewise, thinking we were justified in what we said or did doesn't mean we don't owe an apology. The ego always thinks it's right. Thus, the determining factor is the unjust diminishment of someone else's life experience; not whether we think we were right about doing it. We have to look at whether what we did was "just" (i.e., fair and/or appropriate) rather than "justified." An example of a "just" diminishment of someone's life experience might be injuring them while defending ourselves.

Again, it's not always black and white. But if there was a way we could do what we needed to do without causing harm to others, or if they didn't bring the harmful results upon themselves, then an apology is probably in order. Even if we had no other choice but to do what we did, it may still be helpful for the relationship to offer an explanation. Not because we have to explain ourselves to others (remember: we never have to explain, defend or justify ourselves to anyone). But because it is a gesture of good-will when we communicate with others what was actually going on with us when we did what we did. This alone may be enough to diffuse a tense situation and prevent retaliation. The trick is to learn how to take care of ourselves without, to the greatest extent possible, harming other people. And then if we do inadvertently cause someone harm, to take responsibility or at least offer an explanation for our part in that.

When actually making an apology or amends, keep the focus on your offending behavior (words or actions) and the direct effect that behavior had on the other person. Do this as opposed to focusing on how the other person might be feeling as a result. For instance, you can say something like, *"I'm sorry for interrupting you during dinner last night. I'll try my best not to do that again."* As opposed to, *"I'm sorry if I embarrassed you in front of all those people and hurt your feelings when I interrupted you at dinner."* While the second apology is probably better than no apology at all, the truth is, we don't know how someone else experiences what we say or do. For instance, in the dinner example, they may or may not feel hurt or embarrassed by our actions. So keeping the focus on what we said or did is better than jumping into the subjective world of their internal thoughts or feelings. One more time, none of this is black or white. And a sincere attempt at apologizing for what we did is probably better than nothing at all. But keep in mind projecting on to them what we think constitutes their feelings may be just as, or even more, harmful in certain situations as what we did to begin with.

We also don't apologize for thinking bad thoughts or holding negative feelings about someone. We make amends for our words and actions only. This is because our thoughts and feelings cannot harm another person – unless we act on them. So, for instance, if I feel angry or resentful of you, that alone is not grounds for me to apologize. But again, a deeper look might be warranted. If I harbor negative feelings towards you and if we spend any amount of time together, then chances are good that those negative feelings will at some point seep into my interactions with you. The anger or resentment may taint, or at least temper, how I treat you. In those cases, I will probably have to pay extra attention to what I say and do to see if those negative feelings tip over into actual harm.

"You don't have to apologize for that!"

Another thought on the topic of making an apology or amends is how it is received by the other person. In my experience, I usually get one of three responses:

1. *"Thanks so much – I really appreciate that!"*
2. *"Oh, you don't have to apologize – that was nothing"* (or *"I don't even remember that!"*); or
3. *"Go F yourself, I'm not interested in your apologies."*

The main thing to keep in mind is that not everyone is going to appreciate or acknowledge an apology. As my experience shows, our amends may not be considered warranted or even welcomed by the other person. Moreover, the varied nature of these responses produces a curious and somewhat counter-intuitive result. As a practical matter:

We make amends for ourselves and not for the other person.

As I mentioned in Chapter Six, everything we do, we do for ourselves. It turns out apologizing or making an amends is no exception. The primary reason for this is, as I just laid out above, we have absolutely no control over how our amends or apology is received. We'll talk about the case where it's actually unwelcomed in a moment. But even in the case of #2, the other person may not value our attempts to apologize. Thus, it must be something we do for ourselves since they have not asked for it. Rather, to whom and for what we apologize becomes a statement of "who we think we are" or "who we want to be" in that situation.

I mentioned earlier that taking responsibility can free us from the feelings of guilt we often experience when we've harmed someone. I also mentioned how not taking responsibility can exacerbate our negative feelings about ourselves and actually lessen our self-esteem. Thus another reason making an amends is something we do for ourselves is that it has the potential to free us from our guilt. (Recall that in Chapter Two we said that "guilt" is just another word for self-hatred.) Yet we can't do it for that reason alone. It has to be a genuine attempt to right a wrong we have committed. Otherwise, we may end up inflicting even more harm upon the other person. For instance, we can't try to force an apology on someone who may not want it just so we can feel better. The minute it becomes clear our amends is unwelcomed, we need to abandon any further attempts or action associated with it. Likewise, apologizing to impress someone or because we want them to like us, is to use the amends process selfishly. And selfishness almost always produces more harm than good.

Finally, as people familiar with the 12 Steps know, Step Nine suggests we make a direct amends to the people we have harmed *"except when to do so would injure them or others."* Thus as I mentioned a moment ago, making an unwelcomed or unwanted amends should be avoided as potentially injuring that person. We should also be cognizant of the effects our responsibility taking will have on other people. A common example might be admitting infidelity within the scope of a marriage or other intimate relationship. This admission to your own spouse or partner could eventually come back to harm the person you were having the affair with and/or their family. In these types of situations it's always helpful to seek counsel from others before taking it upon yourself to apologize or make an amends.

Forgiveness as a decision

Forgiveness is a conscious choice to not take things personally, to let go of anger, rage and resentments, to accept rather than judge, and so on. We decide to overlook someone else's (or our own) mistakes and imperfections. If they've actually harmed us, we have to make the admittedly tougher decision about whether or not to "turn the other cheek."

As we've already discussed, all true decisions are *arbitrary* vis-à-vis the external world. They are made irrespective of outer circumstances or conditions and are not dependent on what another person (or persons) is doing or not doing. Yet we also said all true decisions are not at all arbitrary when it comes to our internal world. They are an expression of "who we think we are" and of "who we want to be" in our lives. With respect to a decision to forgive, we choose to see ourselves in a way that says no one and nothing has the power to hurt us. "Who we think we are" is someone who is able to take care of themselves. We stop seeing ourselves as victims and other people as victimizers. True forgiveness can also be an expression of "who we want to be" as kind, compassionate and merciful. We may choose to hold other people accountable for their harmful actions, but we do it without anger or vengeance.

As we stated in the last chapter, our goal is to undo the ego. Forgiveness is the best way to do that. The ego never turns the other cheek or lets anyone off the hook. It knows nothing of compassion and is addicted to vengeance, retaliation and justified anger. We overcome the ego by consciously and deliberately choosing to release our perpetrators and love our enemies – all while continuing to take care of ourselves without rage, resentment or undue harm to others. We intentionally foster a self-image of strength, peace and compassion irrespective of what's happening outside us. Each such decision is a conscious choice to express love rather than fear.

Booooring!
The choice to forgive, especially in close personal relationships, can present challenges. The following three things may undermine our efforts to change our relationship for the better and could eventually make the situation worse.

1. *No more drama.* The end result of both taking responsibility and forgiving others is that life has the potential to become a lot

more *boring*. Much of the drama we experience on a daily basis is eliminated when we stop blaming others for how we feel. If I truly forgive you, the emotional charge that accompanies the horror, anger, and utter disbelief you could treat me this way, is gone. For many people, conflict and drama are primary ways they interact with others. This drama has an addictive quality and its loss can act as an impediment to sticking with our decision. We may let them off the hook for a while, but eventually the unconscious craving for the emotional high of anger and victimization may send us back to our old ways of interacting with that person.

2. *The loss of our sense of identity*. We talked about this in Chapter Four. Practicing forgiveness requires us to give up our anger, resentments, judgments, taking things personally, and so on. This can result in a very strong – and often unconscious – discomfort around losing a part of our personal identity. For example, if you've been someone who has used anger for the last 40 years to get your way with other people, when you give that up in the name of forgiveness you could find yourself in a bit of a bind. You've not only lost an identity which says, "*I'm an angry person*," but now you also need to figure out a new way to relate to people. A loss of a sense of identity is so terrifying to the ego that there may be a strong and immediate pull to revert back to your old ways. Thus, you'll need to figure out how to fill the void that's left by letting go of your anger, lest you slip back to "who you used to be."

3. *Expecting others to change now that you've forgiven them*. I'm as guilty of this as anyone. I think because I've let someone off the hook, they should now be different. The truth is, they may continue to do things that harm or annoy us. Moreover, as I'll mention below, in most cases, the person we're forgiving doesn't even know they've been forgiven. Thus, it's kind of crazy to think that by forgiving them they are now going to magically change who they are. If someone continues to act in harmful or inappropriate ways, it's up to us to take care of ourselves. This may include removing ourselves from the situation – or them

from our lives. Yet if we're expecting other people to change just because we think we have forgiven them, we may be in for an unpleasant surprise.

Forgiveness processes

OK, so now let's take a look at some of the specific ways we can practice forgiveness. This is obviously not meant to be an exhaustive list. I'm including some methods that have worked for me but you're encouraged to look for other methods that resonate with you – or even make up your own. Also, it's not about doing the processes perfectly. The intention to forgive matters much more than the particular words or method you use.

Something else to keep in mind is *forgiveness is something we do by ourselves, for ourselves*. The other person's participation is not required and may in fact be counter-productive. This means none of these (or any other) methods require the involvement or knowledge of the other person. We said previously that making an amends is something we do for ourselves. This is so because we have no control over how our amends are received. The same is true of forgiveness – other people may not want our forgiveness or even think they need it. Thus, forgiveness is something we do for ourselves. Yet unlike making an apology or amends to another person, forgiveness is always done within the confines of our own heart and mind.

In terms of sharing with someone else that you're forgiving them, keep in mind what we said in Chapter Six: everyone thinks they're right. This means the other person may not agree with your assessment that what they've done is wrong and thus deserves forgiveness. Therefore, it may be presumptive – even arrogant – to tell somebody you're forgiving them. (A possible exception is when they've acknowledged their wrong-doing and have asked to be forgiven. But that happens a lot less often than our ego would have us believe.) Accordingly, you're urged to use discretion in announcing that you are letting another person off the hook – especially if they weren't aware they were on the hook in the first place!

The first method I am including is suggested by Gary Renard.[64] Gary has written several wonderful books related to *A Course in Miracles*. His first book, *Disappearance of the Universe*, is a great introduction to the principles found in the *Course*, while two of his other books, *Your Immortal Reality*, and *Love Has Forgotten No One* are equally wonderful.

Gary's forgiveness process is quite simple. Holding the person's image in your mind, say to yourself:

> **"You [name of person] are Spirit, pure and innocent, all is forgiven and released."**

Repeat this phrase to yourself several times until you begin to notice any feelings of upset dissipate. This is very simple and straightforward – but it can also be very effective. When we go from seeing the other person as bad or wrong to seeing them as "Spirit, pure and innocent", we have experienced a shift in "who we think they are." As our animosity fades there is more room for peace. A side benefit of seeing them as innocent is we will begin to see ourselves as innocent as well. *A Course in Miracles* says, "*As you see another you will see yourself.*"[65] So for instance, as long as I see others as bad or evil, chances are I will harbor similar thoughts about myself. It may not be in the exact same way or in the exact same situations. But continuing negative thoughts about others will continue to feed negative thoughts about ourselves. Of course, once again, keep in mind the other person shouldn't even know we're doing this – that is, except when they experience our new, beneficent attitude towards them. ☺

The second forgiveness process I use is adapted from *A Course in Miracles*, Lesson 161, from the *Workbook for Students*. I've changed it around a bit but the gist is the same. The *Course* suggests that in response to the temptation to be upset by someone else's behavior, say the following:

---

[64] http://www.garyrenard.com/
[65] *A Course in Miracles*, pg. 141

"Give me your blessing Holy Child of God, that I may look upon you through the eyes of Christ, and in You, see my own innocence."[66]

(I have actually created my own, much longer version of this process, which is included in the Appendix.)

First, notice we are asking them to give us *their* blessing. This is because if we are upset we have lost our peace and so we are in need of a blessing. Losing our peace hurts us and may then result in us hurting others. Notice also we're acknowledging them as a "Holy Child of God." It's hard to hate someone when we truly see them this way. Finally, this process is also an acknowledgment that as I see another person I will see myself. Here, by seeing them the way Christ would see them, we see their innocence and thus our own.

The third forgiveness process is my take on a healing prayer originally taught by Morrnah Nalamaku Simeona from Hawaii, known as the *Ho'oponopono.*[67] Start by getting quiet for a few minutes. Then pull up an image of the person you want to heal with in your mind. When you're ready say to yourself:

"[name]: I am sorry; please forgive me;
I forgive you; we are at peace; we are One;
I love you; thank you."

Repeat this several times until you feel any blocks to your forgiveness of that person slip away. You can use this prayer many times during the day. Keep repeating it until you notice a shift in your thoughts about them. It may take numerous times over several days to get a full release depending on how deep the hurt is.

---

[66] *A Course in Miracles*, Lesson 161
[67] https://www.hooponopono.org/

Now you may ask, "*Why am I apologizing to them, and also asking for their forgiveness, if they're the ones who have harmed me.*" Remember: unless you're a saint (like me – "Saint Peter", get it? ☺), your initial reaction to being harmed by them was probably judgment, anger, resentment and so on. By apologizing and asking their forgiveness first, we are acknowledging any negative reactions and showing a level of humility commensurate with true forgiveness.

The fourth method is a prayer that I came across recently, known as the Buddhist Prayer of Forgiveness.

Buddhist Prayer of Forgiveness
If I have harmed anyone in any way either knowingly or unknowingly
through my own confusions, I ask their forgiveness.
If anyone has harmed me in any way either knowingly or unknowingly
through their own confusions, I forgive them.
And if there is a situation I am not yet ready to forgive, I forgive myself for that.
For all the ways that I harm myself, or negate, doubt, belittle myself, or that I
judge or am unkind to myself through my own confusions,
I forgive myself.

I like this last prayer a lot, especially because it suggests we can forgive ourselves for not forgiving. I have to admit there are still some days I would rather just be angry than forgive – not many, but still a few. So forgiving myself for not being ready to forgive is actually huge. Equally (and perhaps even more) important is being willing to forgive myself for all the ways I can harm myself. As the prayer implies, every time I negate, doubt, belittle, judge or am otherwise unkind to myself, I am harming myself. So forgiving myself for all these and any other ways I visit harm upon me is really important. Finally, notice that, if I can forgive myself for not forgiving myself, I am still doing forgiveness – and that's the whole point!

Photographic memory

As I was finishing the first draft of this chapter, I came up with another forgiveness technique that I'd like to share. I've never seen it before and it came to me spontaneously as I was dealing with a very difficult situation in my own life.

You'll need a photograph of the person you'd like to forgive as a young child. Obviously this is easier with family and close friends. But if you're one of those people who holds grievances against certain public figures (like politicians ☺), those photos may be available online.

Take the photo with you into your meditation. Look at the person's image in the photo and imagine what they were like as a young child. If you knew them personally, recall any positive feelings you had about them. Did you love being with them? If you didn't know them personally, see if you can sense the innocence and beauty that all children have. Be with those thoughts and feelings for a little while. Then remind yourself that the little kid in the photo is still present inside the adult who you are now trying to forgive.

If you want to take it a step further, begin to have a dialog with that child. To start off, you can ask them stuff you'd normally ask a kid, such as what's their favorite food or color, or whether they like school. Then once you sense they feel comfortable with you, ask the child (in your mind) what had happened that caused them to act the way they were acting as an adult. In my particular case, I got that it was a combination of fear and overwhelm that had morphed into the anger that I had recently witnessed. I thought about it and then I understood in my heart how they could be affected in this way. Then, slowly, as I continued to quietly look at the photo, I felt a sense of release – my own feelings of fear and anger were dissipating.

It turns out this was a powerful healing experience for me, one that I don't know I could have achieved in any other way. Instead of being angry about what had happened, I asked in my heart how

I could be of help – what I could do to assist the healing for them and the other people involved in the situation.

I did have to repeat the process a few times since I was quite upset about what had happened. When I finished my first meditation with the photo and then got on with my day, my egoic mind came roaring back. I kept having flashes of all the good reasons I had for being angry. I replayed the initial scenario over and over in my head, and then was sure the only rational response was to attack them back. It was very interesting to see the ego trying to reassert itself as the controller of my mind.

I mention this for two reasons: first, for any forgiveness process, be aware it may take more than one time to fully forgive someone. Repetition is often necessary to begin to see things differently. Second, be on the lookout for the ego's attempts to re-commandeer your thinking. The ego will take advantage of any opportunity (such as when you're feeling stressed or afraid) to reassert itself in your decision-making process. You'll know this because the idea of forgiveness will slip away being replaced with the notion that retaliation and attack are the only appropriate responses.

Reclaiming your inner child

This photo forgiveness process reminds me of another process I used to do when I first got into recovery for codependence many years ago. I found a photo of myself as a young child. It was a school picture either from Kindergarten or First Grade. I would take the photo with me into my meditation and place it opposite me on a table. Then, after centering myself with a series of deep breaths, I would look at the photo and concentrate on getting in touch with what it was like to be that little kid. At a certain point, I would begin to dialog with him. I asked "Little Peter" some of the questions I mentioned earlier (e.g., how do you like school, etc.) This process of reuniting with our childhood self is similar to the

Inner Child work described by John Bradshaw[68] and other authors.

Lots of feelings came up as I did this process: my feelings for him, his feelings for me, and both our feelings for life in general. For instance, I could see at first he really didn't trust me. He was like, "*Dude, where have you been? I needed you to protect me but I could never depend on you.*" This kind of surprised me. But even more surprising was when I realized I blamed him for being so emotional or needy at times. Whenever I was angry at myself for trying to get other people to like me, I could see I was also angry at him. Then we both also shared certain feelings about certain situations. For instance, we would both get really anxious when there was a lot of yelling and screaming – especially parents yelling at their kids. Even as an adult, I could be out someplace, such as the grocery store, and hearing an adult scold or shame a child would just really trigger me. Same for him.

Over the course of a few months, I established a new relationship with Little Peter and thus with myself. I acknowledged I could have done more to protect him and promised to try harder in the future. I also stopped blaming him for some of my emotional issues and agreed to check in with him every now and then to see how he was feeling. Eventually, I felt like I had arrived at a place of peace with this part of myself. It was actually a pretty awesome feeling and I highly recommend this process, or other similar Inner Child processes, for anyone who is curious.

Change of heart, change of mind

I offer these forgiveness processes as a way to help you get started. But remember, as I said earlier, there's no magic in these or any other words. What brings about change in our lives is our intention. You can say these words over and over, but if you don't mean them they can't help. You can also say nothing yet hold a firm intention to release another person and you can be healed.

---

[68] https://www.amazon.com/Homecoming-Reclaiming-Championing-Inner-Child/dp/0553353896/

The other thing to remember is we need to act in accordance with our intentions. True forgiveness means our words and actions are consistent with releasing the other person. We can't say we forgive someone and then a week later attack them for leaving the cap off the toothpaste or the lights on in the kitchen all night. True forgiveness means changing our thoughts, feelings, words and actions to coincide with forgiveness. This results in a change in "who we think we are" as well as how we see the other person.

In my own life I've noticed that when I choose to forgive someone, there is often a shift in the relationship. This happens even though the only change that has taken place is within my own heart and mind. I've had the experience several times now where, after I forgive, there is less tension and conflict. In fact, in some cases there is even voluntary cooperation from a previously uncooperative person. We've already said forgiveness changes how we see ourselves as well as how we see the other person. But what's really interesting is when I change how I see the other person, they often change to meet my expectations. It doesn't always go that way, and I can't do forgiveness for that reason. But it has happened enough that I believe it is possible for me to shift the entire tenor of a relationship simply by changing my mind about it.

Forgiveness is the key to happiness

As we bring this chapter to a close, I want to share a couple of thoughts on the relationship between forgiveness and happiness. I started this chapter by saying:

> Forgiveness is a key ingredient in happiness and good health. It's a way to heal all wounds and mend all relationships. It can restore an individual's sanity or world peace. And it's the last thing most of us want to do on any given day.

Starting with the last part first, hopefully now, having nearly completed this chapter and this book, you are a little more likely to choose forgiveness than you were before. I know it can still seem like a tall order, especially if we or someone we love has been harmed by another person. But I've tried to lay out the benefits in such a way that it makes forgiveness a more attractive option than seeing ourselves as victims and judging, holding a grudge, or trying to get even.

For many of us, forgiveness is a radical way of living, previously the exclusive dominion of saints and prophets. We've all read about the power of forgiveness in our spiritual and religious texts. But few, if any of us, seem to be able to apply it regularly in our daily lives. As I said before, I've had to look closely at my own life while I was writing this book and ask myself how willing am I to take my own advice. I have to admit I'm not entirely there yet – in fact, some days I'm not even close. But more and more I am at least willing to consider forgiveness as an alternative way of dealing with my problems.

I want to stress again that in order for forgiveness to stick, we must *want* to see ourselves differently. As long as we hold on to our old ideas about ourselves, such as that we are weak or vulnerable or threatened in some way, forgiveness is well nigh impossible. We said earlier that if that's who we really were (weak, vulnerable, threatened, etc.), it wouldn't make any sense to forgive. We'd only be setting ourselves up for more potential harm. The key is in our desire to change "who we think we are" in life.

I've also mentioned that for many of us (myself included) there is still a payoff at times to seeing ourselves as victims in one or more areas of our lives. Being a victim is very attractive to the ego and can be difficult to give up. It fuels all the ego's other characteristics, such as judgment, blame, revenge and justified anger. Thus, we need to let go of this love affair with seeing ourselves as victims before we attempt to forgive. Taking full responsibility for everything that happens in our lives is a necessary first step in making true forgiveness a viable and lasting option.

Finally, in case you haven't figured this out yet, when we change how we see ourselves, *it changes who we actually are in life*. Everything we think, feel, say and do realigns with our primary notions about ourselves. Now the reason the saints and prophets were so good at forgiving is they knew Who They Really Were. There was no question as to their own innocence, divinity and goodness. Once we know and fully embrace the truth about ourselves, forgiveness will be easy. For now, note that, like the saints and prophets, you too are innocent, divine and really, really good. Your True Self is wholly adorable and totally lovable. Moreover, no one and nothing can harm your True Self in any way. Imagine how our lives would be different if we all walked around knowing that!

With regard to being happy now, it should be obvious that if we're mired in anger or resentment or if we see ourselves as victims, the odds we'll have a happy day are not so good. After reading this book, you now know that you can consciously and deliberately choose happy thoughts, no matter what is going on around you. And like being happy for no good reason, we want to forgive for no good reason. When we forgive, we free ourselves from anger, fear, resentment, judgment, and so on. Letting these go are the first steps to experiencing more joy.

Yet, actually, now that I think about it, letting these things go is a good reason to forgive, meaning instead of forgiving for no good reason, we're forgiving *for a really good reason*! ☺

Goodbye for now...

I hope you have enjoyed this little journey into the land of responsibility, power and forgiveness. Hopefully you realize that these and the other principles contained in this book are your path to a whole new life. If you've made it this far, I guarantee your outlook has already changed. Going forward, use as much or as little of what I've said as is helpful, and make it a springboard to discover more of your own truth.

Finally, I also want to say that while I may not know you personally, I do know that Who You Really Are is a wonderful, spectacular, amazing person who has sensational gifts to bestow upon the world. Loving and forgiving yourself and others is the fast track to realizing those gifts and having the life you want!

Until next time, all my love!

TAKEAWAYS:

1. Forgiveness is a key ingredient in happiness and good health. It's a way to heal all wounds and mend all relationships. It can restore an individual's sanity or world peace. And it's the last thing most of us want to do on any given day.

2. Forgiveness encourages us to let our enemies off the hook, see the people as innocent, and give up resentment, judgment, anger and revenge. This is the price we have to pay to be free of the ego.

3. The ego tells us we can love a little and judge a little. We can attack sometimes and heal at other times. We can be angry today and forgiving tomorrow. But the reality is, love is an all-or-nothing proposition. We either love unconditionally – or we're not loving at all.

4. Most of us don't know how to feel safe without anger or in control without judgment. We don't know who we would be without resentment or blame.

5. Forgiveness of others is something we do for ourselves. Negative thoughts about what another person did to us reinforces our own victim mentality. Ruminating over another person's bad behavior does nothing to them – but it can easily ruin our day.

6. Everyone thinks their perspective is the correct one. Thus whatever the other person did, they did because they thought it was the right thing to do. As each side feels justified in seeking retaliation, the conflict escalates and both end up losing.

7. We all do what we do because we believe it's what we need to do to survive. This can be the starting point for seeing ourselves as the same as others.

8. It would behoove us to get to know everyone who's actions affect us. We can actually get to know other people so well, that we can diffuse potential problems *before* they happen.

9. Boundaries are physical, temporal (time), verbal, mental and/or emotional dividing lines between ourselves and others. They are the primary way we take care of ourselves in our relationships.

10. Our boundaries are for us, they're not for other people. They set limits on *our* behaviors. Other people may not automatically – or ever – respect our boundaries.

11. We teach other people how it's OK to treat us. We let them know what is and is not acceptable in terms of their behavior towards us.

12. "Resentment" means we have not done what we needed to do to take care of ourselves and now we're blaming someone else for that. The anger that we think we feel towards them is really misdirected anger that we feel towards ourselves.

13. To forgive is to "overlook or look past." This suggests we deliberately overlook the things that upset us and look past another person's inappropriate behavior.

14. "Attention = Intention." Anything we give our time, focus and energy to will expand in our experience. This means fighting against something is the same as saying "Yes" to it.

15. We often justify our lack of forgiveness on the basis that we're "good" or "right", and the other person is "bad" or "wrong." Calling things good or bad or right or wrong is

simply our attempt to justify how we feel. These words are just made up labels with no objective meaning.

16. *"Forgive them for they know not what they do."* We have all acted insanely at one time or another in our lives. Forgiving those who are unmindful is merciful. Withholding forgiveness because they "should have known better" is a lost opportunity to love others when they probably least like themselves.

17. *"Hurt people hurt people." "All attacks are a call for love."* When someone attacks us, chances are they're not in their right mind. Sane, healthy people don't attack other people – they seek peaceful ways to settle their disputes.

18. *"What hurts you so much that you feel you have to hurt me to heal it?"* With regard to those who would do us harm, if we saw the world the way they saw the world, and if we saw ourselves the way they see themselves, then we would probably be doing the exact same thing they're doing – and that makes us the same as them.

19. To truly forgive another, we must first see ourselves differently. We must have changed our idea about ourselves. This is another reason practicing forgiveness is good for us.

20. True forgiveness is when the other person is wrong and/or has harmed us – and we forgive them anyway.

21. We're not angry because of what they did; We're angry because we're afraid; and we're afraid because of how we see ourselves.

22. *"What was my part in this?"* When we look at the situations where we have conflict in our lives and ask this question, the healing process begins. Our part may fall into one or more of these or other categories:

a) We ignored warning signs;
b) We had unreasonable expectations;
c) We failed to speak up for ourselves;
d) We were dishonest;
6) We didn't respect our own boundaries.

23. There's a difference between "hurt" and "harm". "Harm" is *"the unjust diminishment of someone's life experience."* It has an objective, quantitative analysis to it. "Hurt" is a subjective determination. If you feel hurt by something someone else did, it's because of how you see yourself and the meaning you've given the situation

24. I'm sorry but don't compulsively apologize. (Oh, sorry – oops ☺)

25. Not everyone is going to welcome our apologies. This means we make amends for ourselves and not for the other person. We do it as a statement of "who we think we are" and "who we want to be."

26. Forgiveness is a decision. It's a conscious choice not to take things personally, to let go of anger, rage and resentment, to proceed with compassion rather than vengeance, to accept rather than judge, and so on. We decide to overlook someone's mistakes, and see only the good in them.

27. The end result of both taking responsibility and forgiving others is that life has the potential to become a lot more boring. Much of the drama is eliminated when we stop blaming others for how we feel. This drama has an addictive quality and can actually be an impediment to our truly forgiving another.

28. Forgiveness can result in discomfort around the loss of our personal identity. A loss of a sense of identity is terrifying to

the ego and thus there may be a strong pull to revert back to our old ways of being.

29. Forgiving someone doesn't mean they are going to be any different. If they continue to act in inappropriate ways, it's up to us to take care of ourselves. This may include removing ourselves from the situation – or them from our lives.

30. Forgiveness is something we do by ourselves for ourselves. The other person's participation is not required and may even be counter-productive. The person we're forgiving may not think they've done anything wrong.

31. Forgiveness is a key ingredient to our happiness. If we're mired in anger or resentment, or if we see ourselves as victims, it will be very difficult to have a happy day. Like being happy for no good reason, we want to forgive for no good reason.

32. The reason the saints and prophets were so good at forgiving is they knew Who They Really Were. Like the saints and prophets, we too are divine and good. Our True Self is wholly innocent and totally lovable. Moreover, no one and nothing can harm our True Self in any way. Imagine how our lives would be different if we all walked around knowing that!

EXERCISES:

1. For many of us, forgiveness is a 180 degree reversal from how we now live. Think about your own life – are you really ready to forgive? Can you let your enemies off the hook? Are you ready to give up anger, resentment, and judgment? Are you prepared to see the best in others no matter what they've done? Can you fathom no longer feeling justified in your anger? And are you down with giving up any form of attack? Discuss.

2. Choose three situations where you haven't forgiven someone and write about:

  a. What negative emotions you would have to give up if you were to truly forgive them;
  b. How you can take care of yourself in a healthy, positive way without those negative emotions; and
  c. How a. and b. above result in you changing how you see yourself in those situations.

3. Identify at least one situation where you were pre-occupied with negative thoughts about another person. How did ruminating over what they did affect you? How did it affect the other person?

4. *"Forgiveness is something we do for ourselves."* Pick three situations or people you haven't forgiven yet (different than those you picked in #2 above.) Write about how practicing forgiveness in each of those situations would benefit you. How would your health, attitude and general level of happiness be different if you forgave those people or situations? What would you have to change about yourself in order to forgive them? What has kept you from forgiving them up until now?

5. Identify at least one person you are currently in conflict with. Look closely at who you think *they* are. Write about how getting to know them better would change how you see them and transform the conflict. Then write about how you and this other person are similar. Can you see that you both did what you did because you thought it was the right thing to do? Does that make you the same?

6. Look at three on-going relationships with other people in your life where there is conflict or tension. For each relationship, write about how you taught them how it was OK to treat you. Identify what changes you would have to make in yourself in order to

have more harmony and less tension in each of those relationships.

7. *"My boundaries are for me, not for other people."* What does this mean to you? Give specific examples of physical, temporal, verbal, emotional and mental boundaries that would be of benefit to you with at least three different people in your life. Then write about how it is up to you to respect your boundaries; not the other person.

8. There's no such thing as "good" or "bad", or "right" or "wrong". Instead of emailing me about how I'm wrong about that ☺, write your thoughts here. Will adopting this understanding serve you in any areas of your life?

9. *"Forgive them for they know not what they do."* Identify at least three situations where you acted without thinking, or where you intentionally harmed someone else, and the effect it had on you and the other people who were involved. Now turn it around and identify three situations where other people acted this way towards you. Can you see how you were not in your right mind when you did what you did? Can you see how maybe the other person was out of their right mind too?

10. *"We're not angry because of what they did; We're angry because we're afraid; and we're afraid because of how we see ourselves."* Discuss how this is true in your own life. Give examples.

11. Choose three situations where you hold resentments or grievances. Write about your part in each of those situations. Did you fail to do what you needed to do to take care of yourself? Indicate if one or more of the following apply:
  a) ignored warning signs;
  b) had unreasonable expectations;
  c) failed to speak up for yourself;
  d) were dishonest;

e) you didn't respect your own boundaries;
f) other.

12. "Attention = Intention;"
"You get what you think about whether you want it or not."
"Whatever you say 'yes' to you're going to get more of."

Write about at least three different situations where your attention to a problem served to hold it in place and/or to attract more of the same into your life. What are you currently saying "Yes" to – and thus keeping in your life – by complaining about it

13. *"Hurt people hurt people."*
"Frightened people can be vicious."
"All attacks are a call for love."
"What hurts you so much that you feel you have to hurt me to heal it?"

Write about what each statement means to you. Feel free to give actual examples from your own life.

14. Discuss the difference between "hurt" and "harm". In particular, identify one or more situations where you feel someone "hurt" you. Then run that incident through the objective test of "harm" – i.e., an unjust diminishment of your life experience. Notice any difference?

15. What does it mean to you "to turn the other cheek" and "resist not evil"?

16. Booooring! – how would the dynamics of your relationships change if you no longer used anger, judgment, blame or victimization to relate to other people? Give at least three specific examples.

17. Practice one or more of the forgiveness processes outline in this chapter at least twice per day on a specific person or situation

for one week. Then send me an email and let me know how it has changed 1) you and 2) the relationship.

18. Can you hate someone and be truly happy? Can you resent anyone and feel joy in your life? Can you judge yourself or another and feel good inside? Explain your answers.

19. Write at least three paragraphs on how you are a wonderful, spectacular, amazing person who has sensational gifts to bestow upon the world, and how by forgiving yourself and others, you can fully realize the life you've always wanted to have.

EPILOGUE

It's been nearly 25 weeks since I injured my leg and started writing this book. Man, what a ride!

I made it back to New Jersey as originally scheduled. Despite my calf muscle being swollen and painful, I somehow managed to drive myself from Yosemite to San Francisco. It's a three and a half hour drive, the first quarter of which takes you through tight, twisting mountain roads. While I normally enjoy the challenge of driving on such roads, having a torn right calf muscle and using my left foot for the brake made for a little too much challenge this time. Heavy rain plus more than an hour of stop and go traffic in San Francisco didn't help much either.

I called ahead to the airline and requested wheel chair assistance at both S.F.O. and Newark. United Airlines was great – someone met me at both airports and wheeled me around (maneuvering with all my bags while using crutches would have been a nightmare.) So thank you United! I managed the flight itself OK and overall the return trip wasn't too bad.

The first two and a half months of my recuperation were relatively uneventful. I knew I wasn't going to be able to drive or work, so I devoted myself to healing my leg – and writing this book. As I mentioned in Chapter Five, my goal was at least two hours of writing per day and I pretty much met or exceeded that. Setting a small, easily attainable goal was very helpful. And in fact, I only missed a few days writing during the past 25 weeks.

EPILOGUE

At around the 11 week point I decided to print out what I had written. Up until then, I had only viewed my drafts on the computer. When I printed it out I noticed a big problem: it didn't read very well. In fact, it was almost unreadable. I had been doing "stream of consciousness" writing and while there were some great ideas and concepts in there, there was a real lack of continuity or flow. There was also a general lack of structure and a lot of unnecessary repetition of ideas.

To be honest, this kind of freaked me out. I had spent nearly three months doing what I thought was exceptionally good writing. I figured another couple of weeks and I'd be done. Instead, now I was faced with a page-one rewrite. To say I was bummed was an understatement. On top of that, I had been working in a complete vacuum. I had no idea if what I was saying would make sense to anyone else. While I had discussed some of these ideas with other people over the years, I was going way deeper now. Doubts about whether these concepts would be helpful or meaningful to a broader audience filled my mind.

It was also around this time that the reality of my health situation hit home. Despite steady improvement in my calf-muscle, being off my feet for so long had aggravated a genetic neurological issue I have with my legs and feet. This is a life-long condition and the worst thing for it is extended periods of inactivity. So even though the calf was getting better, because of this other issue, I was still having a lot of trouble walking.

But it gets worse: not being able to walk or drive also meant not being able to work. The financial pressures of not having income for almost three months were mounting and I had no idea when – or if – I would be able to return to my career. I had to turn down several gigs because of my health and my savings were dwindling. This all was wreaking havoc with my brain.

Then around the 13 week mark, my dad passed away. He had been ill for a long time and the whole ordeal was quite awful for everyone. His condition was particularly wearing on my step mother. Because I was still having trouble walking or driving, I couldn't be much help. Even when I finally started driving again, my leg would quickly swell up after any extended period of time in the car. This made the two hour plus drive from New Jersey to where he was on Long Island excruciating at times.

When he finally made his transition, despite all the mental preparation, I was overwhelmed with sadness and grief. I loved my father very much. Looking back over our lives together, I can say he was one of my heroes. He overcame a lot of challenges in his own life, and he did most of it with a smile and positive attitude. Nothing was more important to him than his family and he always made time for his wife, children and grandchildren. He wasn't perfect, but no one is. Yet he always tried his best and did whatever he could do with an open heart. So I will miss him dearly.

I do want to acknowledge my step-mother for really being there for him throughout his life, and especially at the end. She had to endure some very, very difficult stuff over the last two years and really rose to the occasion. She helped make his transition as comfortable and dignified as possible. I am eternally grateful to her for that.

So... here I was, more than three months since my injury with persistent health problems, no income and no clear path back to work, a book that was looking quite iffy, and the loss of my dad. Needless to say I was not a happy camper. On more than one occasion I considered abandoning this book – and everything else. I don't mean to be overly dramatic, but this was probably the lowest point in my life.

I soon realized that I was depressed. Depression is a very profound thing for me as I'm sure it is for a lot of people. I had only had it one other time – that was when a relationship ended when I was around 33. Thankfully, it only lasted a few weeks and I was able to pull myself out of it. I remember it wasn't so much a feeling of sadness that one would expect at the loss of a relationship. Rather, it was a profound sense of hopelessness and the gut wrenching feeling that *nothing in my life mattered*. All the things I had previously enjoyed or found value in, I no longer cared about. A kind of small example of that was, at the time I was really interested in computers. This was when personal computers were just hitting the scene and I always looked forward to receiving my monthly computer magazines to read up on all the latest and greatest news. Well for around three or four weeks after the break-up, when the magazines came, I didn't even open them. I just didn't care. As I said, nothing was important. I was aware enough to notice it was a very, very strange feeling and my heart goes out to anyone who has to live with this on a regular basis. I eventually rebounded from the depression and hadn't experienced anything like it since then.

Now, 24 years later, right after my dad died, I was experiencing something similar. Everything seemed so meaningless to me. I was overwhelmed by feelings of hopelessness and saw very little to look forward to in my life. Despite how bad I felt, I did realize it was more than a little ironic that I was writing a book about being happy for no reason and becoming the powerful creator of my life. Yet, even with this awareness, for the first couple of weeks after he passed, I couldn't do anything to change how I was feeling. I was unable to pull myself out of it. I also realize now maybe it wasn't so ironic. Maybe this experience was exactly what I needed to practice what I was preaching. *A Course in Miracles* says we teach what we need to learn. I couldn't argue with that – I definitely needed to learn everything I was trying to teach in this book!

Eventually, I took a hard look at "who I thought I was" in this situation. I recognized that how I was seeing myself was really, really negative. I was focused on all my problems and ailments and was certain they were insurmountable. Then I thought, *"How would I have to see myself to experience this situation differently?"* I began to consider the idea that maybe my life wasn't over. I thought even if my health condition worsened and I couldn't continue to work as a photographer, I would still find a way to be creative and serve others with my talents and abilities. I also realized my father's life was his own and I didn't have to repeat his mistakes. And I also recognized that I had to put all my fears and doubts and self-pity aside. I had to end the love affair with seeing myself as a victim!

From that point, I tried to consciously and deliberately change my idea about myself. Whenever I noticed the negative thoughts and feelings, I would try to repeat hopeful, positive things in my mind like, *"I got this," "I can handle whatever life sends my way," "I'm not alone," "No matter how things go, I'll be OK,"* and so on. I will admit it wasn't always easy, but when I did it I felt things shift.

I also stepped up my meditation practice and continued listening to a bunch of different spiritual and personal growth literature. While no one specific thing turned it all around, eventually the sum total of everything I was doing caused the feelings of depression and hopelessness to lift. I also decided that finishing this book was going to be my full time job. So I stepped up my writing to as much as six to ten hours per day, while also continuing to work on my attitude and outlook. Some days were better than others, but I soon found I was in a much more hopeful place.

At about 15 weeks I finally finished a new first draft. That was really important. A month earlier I was seriously considering giving up. Yet somehow, no matter how bad I felt emotionally or physically, I managed to continue writing. We spoke in Chapter Four about how action is the antidote to fear – and in my case, also hopelessness. Writing almost every day, even in some cases only for 15 or 20 minutes, while I was feeling so down proved to be enough to keep me going.

Technically what I'm finishing now is a first final draft. I will be sharing it with a few select people that I trust to give me their feedback. Once I get their notes, there'll probably be one more rewrite. Then, since I am self-publishing, I will have to do the actual layout for publication. I'll have to reformat it for a trade-sized commercial book. Once it's ready for publication, I need to do a bunch of short 1 to 2 minute videos presenting different core ideas for Social Media, as well as a series of longer 30 to 60 minute video lessons as part of the online courses I am planning. I also have to setup my new website and eventually will record the audio book in my own voice. That could easily take another 3 or 4 weeks. So while I am still almost three months away from everything being finished, for today at least, I feel like I have accomplished what I set out to do 25 weeks ago.

EPILOGUE

Six months may not seem like a long time to write a book. But as I said in the Introduction, it's actually taken me nearly 30 years to get to where I am today. All the self-help and personal growth stuff I started doing back then was leading me to this point in my life. And now, having almost completed it, I get why: I really wouldn't have been able to say – or even understand – most of what I've written (at least not at this level) before today.

I also mentioned in the Introduction that I had made two or three false starts on writing this book over the last six years or so. Yet when I planned my trip to California, it was the last thing on my mind. It had actually been many months since I had even thought about it. Likewise, while I was there, I was completely focused on getting my client work done in Los Angeles, and then fulfilling my artistic dream of photographing Yosemite.

Now the reason I am telling you all this is because I am going to reveal something I haven't publicly shared before now. I mentioned at the beginning that injuring my leg in the way I did was a total shock – it came completely out of left field. Basically, all I did was get out of my rent-a-car after the long drive from Los Angeles to Northern California. Within a few steps I stumbled on a hidden curb. I didn't actually fall but was instantly overwhelmed with the searing pain of having torn my calf-muscle. It immediately rendered me lame and I couldn't put any weight on my right leg.

Now here's what I haven't shared before: literally within the first 10 or 15 seconds of hurting my leg – despite the intense shock and physical pain – a very clear thought popped into my head:

"Now you can write your book."

I was like, *"What the hell???"* As I said, the book hadn't even entered my mind for months. The thought went as quickly as it came, and nothing like it has come back since. But from that point on, I knew what I had to do. I'm also absolutely certain I would have never written this book if I hadn't hurt my leg. I was too busy being super-photographer. For more than six years I was consumed with doing everything I could to move my business and career forward. All the things I talked about in this book – from the cold calling to the awards and publications to the public speaking – were consuming me. I was out in the middle of the night in all kinds of weather (including the dead of Winter), trying to capture unique and compelling images of New York City and other places.

Looking back I can see now I was really, really pushing myself. Probably too much. I was ignoring my health, and in general, trying too hard to make things happen. I also see I was caught up in the excitement of social media. While I enjoyed going above and beyond to get amazing photos, I was also overly focused on how many "Likes' and Followers I got, especially compared to other photographers I knew. While it was great to excel at doing something I loved, there was at least a part of me that was motivated by approval-seeking and/or out-doing others.

Not being able to shoot for the past six months has given me a whole new perspective. While I have maintained my social media by posting older photos, I am less concerned about it. Don't get me wrong: social media has been wonderful for me. I have met dozens and dozens of amazing people – both fellow photographers and followers – who have all enhanced my life in many great and wonderful ways. I've also gotten a fair amount of business through social media. But I can see that going back to what I was doing before probably won't serve me.

Social media wasn't the problem; rather the problem was how I was using it. So instead of abandoning it entirely, I have gone back to something that was really helpful for me when I first started: supporting other people. I've gone out of my way to Like and Comment on other people's photos who's work I really enjoy. I try to support many of the people who have been supporting me and it feels great.

I am also picking up on another concept which I have applied at various times in my career: *if you want to be successful, help someone else be successful*. So, for instance, for the photography client work I haven't been able to do because of my leg, I have been recommending or referring other good photographers who I want to help. I am also trying to encourage certain photographers, who I think are really talented but who have been slow to put their work out there, to start pursuing shows and exhibitions. Sharing what I've learned with them and re-affirming how talented I think these other people are also feels really good to me.

So after the past six months, I am definitely feeling a shift in my priorities. So much so, that I am actually thinking of no longer working full-time as a photographer. The whole experience of writing this book has aroused another passion in me: a passion for being an author, speaker and teacher. Of course, we'll have to see what the future holds, but right now I have big plans for myself and this book. I can envision online classes, public speaking engagements, workshops, seminars, and so on. I have a vision of helping people around the globe to be *"bigger than they thing they are."*™

I will admit I've had big plans in the past that didn't always work out. So what I'd like to do differently this time is hold the vision – but also allow things to unfold on their own. I'm open to the Universe doing some of the heavy lifting for me. If it is meant to be, I'm sure a path will be made clear for me to follow. (To see more of my big ideas for this book and my new life, I refer you to the Appendix where I have included my Advance Intention [Begin with the End in Mind] as we discussed in Chapter Five.)

As I close, I want to thank you again for investing your time and energy in this book. Please visit my website www.bebiggertoday.com for more info on any upcoming online classes or live workshops or lectures in your area. Also, please let me know what you think about the book. I especially look forward to hearing actual stories of how you were able to apply these principles in your own life. And of course if you do find value in what I'm doing, please tell your friends about it. This book will make a great gift for someone you know. I will also have gift certificates available on my website to help you share this work with others.

I'm honored that you took this little journey with me and I hope to see you online or at a live event real soon! And remember:

Be bigger than you think you are – today and everyday!

Peter Alessandria
New Jersey
August 2019

APPENDIX

Notes:

APPENDIX

(Blank worksheet from Chapter One, Exercise 1.)

Situation	How do I describe the situation	What are my internal thoughts and feelings about it	Who do I think I am

Vision Statement
by Peter Alessandria

I am an award winning, internationally acclaimed author, speaker and photographer. My work and life positively impact millions of people each year. I carry the messages of self-love and self-forgiveness, and assist others in seeing themselves in new and empowered ways. I inspire everyone I meet to *be bigger than they think they are!*

I am confident, energized and focused. I see myself as lovable and powerful in all situations and with all people. I am kind and compassionate, and quickly forgive my own and others' mistakes. I take great care of myself physically, emotionally and mentally. I enjoy radiant health and have all the energy and vitality I need to do all the things that I want. My body feels great and supports me in all my intentions.

I have wonderful, joyful relationships with family, friends and lovers. I travel in comfort and luxury and get enough rest and personal time to keep me at my best. I have a strong connection with my Higher Power and set aside time each day to commune with Spirit. I have deeply profound mystical experiences and move ever closer to my True Self.

My books are read by millions of people around the world. They make the New York Times Bestseller list, as well as all the best recommended reading lists. I receive top dollar as an author, teacher and speaker. My lectures and workshops are sold out months in advance and I am invited to give multiple TED Talks on the subject of "Being Bigger Than We Think We Are." I regularly speak at commencement ceremonies, corporate events and to philanthropic organizations.

My staff and I lead dynamic and life-changing workshops, seminars and retreats, many of which are held in beautiful resort destinations. We assist individuals and businesses in transforming their lives and bring a powerful, positive message of hope to all those we touch. Our students have amazing experiences of emotional healing, personal empowerment, and spiritual growth.

Everyone I work with values my talents and abilities and I am not afraid to ask for what I am worth. My businesses earn me an abundant eight figure income each year and my investments grow by a minimum of 20% each year. After I retire, I enjoy an abundant stream of passive royalty income from my past work.

I am Truly Happy, excited, and inspired no matter what happens, and I behold myself and others in loving kindness as our journeys unfold. I am immensely grateful for the out-pouring of love and encouragement I receive as well as for the material and financial abundance my business provides.

I see the light of God in myself and in every one I meet.

A Forgiveness Process by Peter Alessandria

Dear [name of person]:

Please forgive me for judging you, please forgive me for hating you, please forgive me for blaming you for how I feel [wishing you were dead ☺].
I give you my blessings and look upon you through the eyes of Love that I may see my innocence within you.
I'm responsible for how I feel, I put the meaning in everything,
I choose the sensations I experience.
I decide upon the outcomes I would achieve.
And everything that seemed to happen to me I asked for and received as I had asked.
I forgive you for all you haven't really done.
The Secret of Salvation is but this: *I am doing all of this to myself.*

Higher Power/Holy Spirit/God:
Please help me see [name of person] the way you see them.
Please help me overlook, look past and forgive all the things I think they've done that are upsetting me. Help me see they and I are united forever as one in God's Love and that that is Our Will.
Help me see that all the things I think they've done that are upsetting me, I put there because I value pain [I value guilt]. It's a vain attempt to see outside myself all the guilt I think I would see if I looked within. Help me see there is no guilt within.
Help me see I am as pure and innocent as the moment God created me and nothing I think I've done has had any effect whatsoever.
Heal my thinking, correct my perception, show me a new way of being in this World that I may play my part in God's plan for Salvation.

[Name of person], We are at peace, we are one, I love you, Thank you.

APPENDIX

Advance Intention
"Be Bigger Than You Think You Are!"

My INTENTION with respect to this book is that it is a HUGE SUCCESS. It inspires MILLIONS of people around the globe to see themselves in a new and empowered way. It awakens people to the possibility of consciously and deliberately CREATING their lives and seeing themselves as LOVABLE, VALUABLE, WORTHY and POWERFUL. My READERS deeply comprehend the concepts contained in the book and it helps ACCELERATE the evolution of consciousness on the planet to new and astounding heights.

The messages of RESPONSIBILITY, POWER and FORGIVENESS are fully embraced by people AROUND THE WORLD. Many of the ideas in this book make their way into mainstream media and entertainment programming enabling the book's message to go far beyond those who actually read it. People INTUITIVELY grasp the concepts and use them in creative and innovative ways to IMPROVE life for themselves and others.

The result is the UPLIFTMENT of millions of people to a new and JOYFUL awareness of their personal POWER and inherent SELF-WORTH.

July 2019

RECOMMENDED READING
Some of these books may be available online

A Course in Miracles	
The Urantia Book	
Books by Dr. Joe Dispenza:	*Breaking the Habit of Being Yourself*
	You are the Placebo
	Becoming Supernatural
Books by William Buhlman:	*Adventures in the Afterlife*
	Higher Self – Now!
Books by Neale Donald Walsch	*Conversations with God – Books 1,2,3*
	Friendship with God
	Communion with God
	Tomorrow's God
Books by Gary Renard	*The Disappearance of the Universe*
	Your Immortal Reality
	Love Has Forgotten No One
Richard Bach	*Illusions*
Meher Baba	*God Speaks*
	Discourses
AA "Big Book"	*Alcoholics Anonymous*
CoDA "Big Book"	*Codependents Anonymous*
Abraham- Hicks Publications	*Law of Attraction Books*
Ernest Holmes	*The Science of Mind*
Cheri Huber	*There is Nothing Wrong with You*
Ram Dass	*Be Here Now*
Napoleon Hill	*Think and Grow Rich*
Maxwell Matlz	*Psycho-Cybernetics*
Stephen Hawking	*A Brief History of Time*
Pia Mellody	*Facing Codependence*
Melody Beattie	*Codependent No More*
James Redfield	*The Celestine Prophecy*

Made in the USA
Las Vegas, NV
24 December 2020